RESONAI ITY

This collection of papers, published between 1976 and 2003, traces the innovative connections which the eminent group analyst Dennis Brown made between medicine and psychoanalysis. They reveal his important insights into how the principles of group analysis can improve our understanding of philosophy and ethics, and trace the development of transcultural dimensions of group analysis.

Beginning with Dennis's early work in dermatology, the first section of *Resonance and Reciprocity* provides a fascinating overview of the insights gained into psychosomatic conditions through the application of psychoanalysis and group analysis. The second section builds on the tenet of group analysis that therapy should change the therapist as well as the client, addressing the changes that can take place in the therapeutic milieu, both in client and provider. The chapter on drowsiness, a modern classic, provides a significant contribution to our understanding of the emotional and physical changes that the therapist experiences during analysis, and its wider implications for our appreciation of how changes in mental and physical states are affected by a person's emotional world. The final section reveals how Dennis Brown extended his interest and his activities beyond the individual, the small and the large group, and studied groups within and across cultures.

This book provides not only a solid understanding of complex analytical notions but also opens the road for future development. It will appeal to students and professionals in psychoanalysis, psychotherapy and group psychotherapy.

Dennis Brown, psychiatrist, analyst and group analyst was a leading figure in the field of group analysis and for many years worked both in the NHS and at the Group-Analytic Practice. With vast experience in the treatment of psychosomatic as well as psychological/psychiatric conditions, he taught internationally and was read widely. He co-authored *Introduction to Psychotherapy: An Outline of Psychodynamic Principles and Practice*. He was a founder member of the International Library of Group Psychotherapy. He was an important contributor in the development of psychotherapy services in the Health Service.

Jason Maratos is a psychiatrist for children and adolescents and a group analyst based at the Group-Analytic Practice. In his work he integrates the discoveries of medicine, psychiatry (and the findings of developmental psychology), psychoanalysis and group analysis with philosophical trends from Aristotle to the postmodernists. He has published and lectured in the UK, Europe and South America.

RESONANCE AND RECIPROCITY

Selected Papers by Dennis Brown

Edited by Jason Maratos

Routledge
Taylor & Francis Group
LONDON AND NEW YORK

First published 2006 by Routledge
27 Church Road, Hove, East Sussex BN3 2FA

Simultaneously published in the USA and Canada
by Routledge
711 Third Avenue, New York, NY 10017

First issued in paperback 2015

Routledge is an imprint of the Taylor & Francis Group, an informa business

Typeset in Times by
RefineCatch Limited, Bungay, Suffolk

Cover design by
Anú Design

British Library Cataloguing in Publication Data
A catalogue record for this book is available from the British Library

Library of Congress Cataloging in Publication Data
Brown, Dennis.
Resonance and reciprocity : selected papers by Dennis Brown / Jason Maratos.
p. ; cm.
Includes bibliographical references and index.
ISBN 0–415–38077–4
1. Psychoanalysis. 2. Group psychoanalysis. 3. Psychoanalysis– Cross-cultural studies. 4. Medicine, Psychosomatic.
I. Maratos, Jason, 1943– II. Title. [DNLM: 1. Psychotherapy, Group – Collected Works. 2. Cross-Cultural Comparison – Collected Works. 3. Psychoanalytic Therapy – Collected Works. 4. Psychoanalytic Therapy – ethics – Collected Works. 5. Psychophysiologic Disorders – Collected Works. WM 430 B877 2006]
RC501.2.B76 2006
616.89′17 – dc22 2006000242

ISBN13: 978-0-415-75926-7 (pbk)
ISBN13: 978-0-415-38077-5 (hbk)

CONTENTS

EDITOR'S INTRODUCTION

Although I undertook the task of editing this volume out of a wish to 'do it for Dennis', the whole exercise has been a source of pleasure, a fountain of new learning and a stimulus for new thoughts. It has been a privilege to delve deeply into the work of one of the pillars of modern group analysis.

This book is special as it can be read from many angles. Those of us who knew Dennis Brown will be able to understand his contributions through seeing them in the context of his own development. Dennis Brown started with a solid foundation in medicine and almost followed the road of a physician-dermatologist. He built on a sound understanding of the body by understanding the individual psyche through psychoanalysis and explored the interaction between mind and body in his psychosomatic papers.

Through contact with S. H. Foulkes and his colleagues he widened his scope which led to a better understanding of the individual by seeing him or her in their context. We owe a lot to Dennis Brown for our current understanding of the individual as a social being. He was a master at integrating ideas of the nineteenth century with more recent ones such as those of systems, complexity, bi-logic, intersubjectivity and the contributions of younger group analysts such as Nitsun and Dalal.

Dennis Brown extended his interest and activities beyond the individual, the small and the large group and studied groups within and across cultures. He followed a path of creating a new entity by building on differences. He wrote about cultural differences within Europe as well as about differences between the various psychoanalytic movements. Differences which had been a source of conflict became a source of enrichment; this was as true about contact between nations as it was with his efforts to enrich group analysis by combining the works of Foulkes and Bion. His final works contain important insights into philosophy and ethics and how group-analytic ideas improve our understanding of them.

In editing this volume I felt that I travelled this journey (from the individual body to the individual psyche, from there to the group and social psyche, to the individual across cultures and to the metaphysics of existence) with one of the wise men of our time and a great thinker of group analysis. I am sure that a reader with an open mind (and heart) will find this collection an equally stimulating and enriching experience.

Jason Maratos
March 2006

FOREWORD

This remarkable collection may be best described as a biography, but a biography of an unusual kind. It is at once the life of a mind at work over a lifetime of psychiatric practice, and the story of a long and intricate journey of discovery.

At first glance the reader may be startled by the range of topics. How can a compilation of papers starting with the skin and ending with societal and cultural aspects of group psychology form a coherent book? But this is a book in which you are asked to retrace a path already trodden by one of the most creative thinkers in group and individual dynamics, namely Dennis Brown. If you join him in retracing his footsteps you will be amply rewarded. The papers map his intellectual life and demonstrate his persistence and dogged determination to 'find out' and to integrate medical and psychological aspects of illness. As reader you will discover that 'finding out' through resonance and reciprocity is at the core of all therapeutic work and was at the core of Dennis Brown himself.

At a casual level Dennis Brown appears to start on the outside and work his way inwards, and yet his early investigations on skin disease demonstrate his concern for the inner workings of the emotional states of his patients. He emphasises with the use of clinical material the interaction between the emotional mind state and the physical state, the eczema and the person, the doctor and the patient, and the psychological defences and the anxiety. In doing so he underlines the significance of listening to what the patient says and what the skin disease communicates. His view that the mind state and the physical state both give clues to the underlying emotional state of the patient suggest that tackling the eczema via the mind state could be a useful avenue as an adjunct for treatment. Certainly, more recent work on somatic illness and psychological interventions has supported these early conclusions with increasing recognition that many physical disorders are better conceived as psychosomatic disorders with multiple causes and exacerbating factors – physical, psychological and social. The patient's reaction to the illness has an effect on the course of the illness itself.

But Dennis Brown was not simply an embryonic researcher in these early days but also a sensitive clinician. He provides us in every chapter with clinical recommendations to treat patients who present with physical symptoms but few feelings. His proposals have stood the test of time and include containment of anxiety, pain, helplessness and rage, finding meaning in the physical phenomena, naming feelings and asking others to name those feelings. His belief is that these therapeutic endeavours coupled with facilitation of communication at deep levels and therapist ability to 'listen' with the body as well as the ears, including bodily countertransference, will enable the physical to be 'mentalised'. It is to this prophetic suggestion that I would now like to turn because mentalising symptoms as a mechanism of change has become increasingly important in the understanding of mental illness.

Mentalising (Fonagy *et al.* 2002) is the key to psychological resilience, that is the ability of the individual to adapt to adversity, challenges and stress. Promoting resilience through mentalisation enables individuals to cope with vulnerabilities, including genetic vulnerability to psychiatric problems, and reduces somatisation in the face of emotional stress (Allen 2003). Mentalising allows an individual to make meaning out of adversity, to sustain a positive if realistic outlook, to experience a sense of mastery by feeling responsible for one's own behaviour. It gives a sense of purpose, a capacity for open emotional expression and ability for mutual empathy that allows us to see not only our own perspective but that of others also. These characteristics of mentalising are encapsulated in the title of this book – *Resonance and Reciprocity*. In order to develop and to maintain resilience there has to be reciprocity and without experiencing resonance there can be no development of mentalisation and without mentalisation there will be somatisation, impulsivity, loss of meaning and emotional turmoil.

Understanding how we develop mentalisation might clarify how to treat patients better and throughout this book Dennis Brown emphasises the importance of the patient–therapist interaction if reciprocity is to develop. We now know that the single most important factor fostering mentalisation is a secure attachment relationship in which resonance plays a key role (Fonagy *et al.* 2003). The secure attachment relationship allows emotional and cognitive development, acting as a developmental laboratory in which resonance can thrive. The caregiver focuses on the mind of the infant and shows the infant that they have a mind. We might think that developmentally we would become aware of our own mind first and then recognise that others have minds too. But infant research tells us that it is the other way around and our understanding of our own mind comes from outside in – we learn that we have a mind by having our mind represented to us. The clearest example of this is in learning about our emotions. Sensitive caregivers are attuned to the infant's feelings and represent them to them in complex ways. Seeing her infant in distress the mother shows concern and distress on her face, in her voice, in her bodily movements and in her physical responsiveness. If the infant sees and physically experiences this expression, and if the caregiver clearly demonstrates that it is her and not her infant's feeling – a process named 'marking' – the infant 'feels felt'. Two things then happen: first, feeling felt, the infant finds his mother's empathic response to be comforting, resonance has taken place; second, he learns about his own inner state which promotes reciprocity. He knows how he feels in the face of his mother. She has his mind in mind and he discovers himself within her mind. He can then influence her mind further. Thus we learn to mentalise by being mentalised within the context of a secure attachment relationship.

But for many of our patients this capacity is impaired to a greater or lesser degree, most often because of insecure attachments during childhood and an associated fearfulness of exploration. Imagine the person who is fearful of his attachment figure. He will turn away from the mind of the attachment figure, feeling frightened rather than calm. He will not explore the mind of the attachment figure if he only finds disdain and hatred and so the opportunity to discover what is in his own mind is lost and eventually he might close his mind off altogether. Resonance and reciprocity are abandoned. In addition, to control things completely he may have to close down other people's minds simultaneously to ensure that they cannot see what is represented. This pathological state of mind resulting from a failure of resonance is enshrined in the paper on 'Drowsiness in the Countertransference' which has been perhaps one of the most influential papers of those included in this book. Here Dennis Brown introduces the term 'dementalisation' – 'an alternative is *psychosomatic symptom-formation* via regression to a state of resomatisation, or, as I like to think of it, dementalisation'. In this chapter there is a vivid clinical description of a patient who removes things from her mind to control anxieties and withdraws within the transference leaving the therapist identified with a core aspect of a depleted patient. In this way the paper identifies the way in which patients close down their minds and how the therapist can struggle to find meaning in what appears to have become a confused and disorientated state in which their own mind is half closed down. Whilst this work was done within individual therapy, Dennis Brown had already begun to discover that another powerful vehicle was available to promote therapeutic change. His interest in group analysis grew as he recognised what a potent modality it is for stimulating change via rementalisation.

Dialogue, in the sense of intimate reciprocal communication at many levels, is an essential part of group analysis. The multiple viewpoints that are made available in group analysis open up possibilities for reassessing unconscious stereotypes and assumptions about the self and others that are based on the vicissitudes of individual development and on variations of family, social and cultural background. The problem that falls to clinicians is to advise who is and who is not suitable for group analysis, a question which cannot be answered using robust empirical evidence. Nevertheless Dennis Brown, again ahead of his time, offers a structured way of thinking about this topic in the chapter on assessment and selection for groups, outlining a way of thinking about which patient for which group, which group analyst for which patient, and how should a patient be prepared for a group. It is unacceptable to assume that a patient will know that 'a group is good for him and will help him'. There was no 'black box' for Dennis Brown into which patients go at one end and come out at the other having been changed, hopefully for the better, in a mysterious way.

He argues that of particular importance in the assessment for group analysis is a capacity on the part of the patient to engage with another person to begin to understand themselves and their relationships with others at greater depth without the danger of acting out or decomposition. To this I would add an ability to seek to understand the mind of others is also likely to be a positive indicator for group therapy (Bateman and Fonagy 2004). The group forms a vehicle through which individuals can find themselves through the mind of others and in doing so discover who they are in all their multiplicity. Groups allow participants to recognise and to assess a number of different characteristics of themselves as represented in the mind of others and to integrate those representations into a coherent and integrated sense of self. By contrast, individual therapy becomes a milieu in which the patient explores himself inwardly in relation to the mind of the analyst. The subjective matrix of the group is lost.

The strength of the group, as Dennis Brown outlines, is that the individual can become both subject and object, I and me. The patient discovers himself not simply through introspection but through becoming something in the mind of the others in the group. It is here that resonance and reciprocity arise once more. Developmentally we know that the sensitive mother who understands her infant in terms of what is going on in his mind fosters secure attachment. The mind-minded mother stimulates a mind-minded baby. In the same way the group analyst who fosters a sense of mind-mindedness between group members will encourage a more secure group that can explore fruitfully and without excessive anxiety. Reciprocity develops as group members discover each other and discover themselves through others. This is not a passive state but one in which both group analyst and patients have to participate, seeking understanding from others and expressing their own selves to others. Following Langs' ideas, Dennis Brown emphasises the importance of the analyst's contribution to the form that the interpersonal or bipersonal field takes. The group analyst is not a blank slate onto which participants project their anxieties but an important component of the process that develops. To some extent this differentiates group analysis from 'psychoanalysis in the group' and 'analysis of the group'. Group analysis as recommended by Dennis Brown clearly includes reciprocity and involves 'psychotherapy *by* the group, *of* the group, including the conductor'. The conductor is part of the group as well as separate from it, and is inevitably permeated and affected by it. Group analysis aims to increase the capacity of the group-as-a-whole, as well as individuals in it, to act as therapists. At the same time the group analyst is himself changed and one feature that permeates this book is the sense that the author was constantly surprised by what he discovered in others' minds and from that surprise he learned and had more to offer. Just as he himself was changed, so Dennis Brown suggests that the process of change is mediated through 'fuller *discovery* of our inner world, which allows us to *discern* the difference between old internal object relationships and new ones, and in a step towards maturity to *learn* to attune ourselves to *other* people's experience as well as our own'. Thus he emphasises the ability to attune ourselves to others and to understand their processes in relation to our own. This focus on reciprocity in groups was later to receive some empirical confirmation.

Piper and colleagues (Piper *et al.* 1994) made detailed studies of group process of patients in a day hospital setting. They identified a process variable defined as therapeutic 'work'. This was represented by (1) patients' self-rating; (2) others' rating of the patient; (3) therapists' rating of patient; (4) patients' rating of other patients. Each of the 'work' variables was related positively to outcome which makes clinical sense to the extent that those patients who participate more and work harder gain the most benefit. However, the fact that others' rating of your group activity is important underlines the significance of reciprocity. Interestingly there was an interaction between the 'work' variables and psychological mindedness (PM) defined as the capacity of the patients to think about themselves and others in dynamic terms. For patients with high PM the perception of other patients' work had little effect on outcome, but for patients with low PM perception of other patients' work was directly related to favourable outcome. Perceiving others as working may compensate for low PM and such patients may even be more dependent on others' perceptions of them. Piper and colleagues have speculated that other patients in a group may act as an auxiliary ego for patients with low level PM and become their psychological mind which allows them to remain in treatment and perhaps gradually develop their own PM. Further work suggested that the overall perception by the patient of a supportive milieu environment encouraging emotional expression may also be important for change. Again, this has been partially confirmed by a study investigating outcome in a day hospital of a group of personality disordered patients treated in large group psychotherapy with small group expressive therapy. Dazord *et al.* (1997) found that patient commitment to the large group was associated with positive symptom change.

The need for commitment to groups, acceptance of diversity, the understanding of others and struggle to integrate difference is the subject of the last section of this book. It is here that Dennis Brown underscores his respect for and breadth of interest in human and social function. I leave it to you, the reader, to see how the understanding of group process as outlined by Dennis Brown helps us to understand many of the issues that face us today in terms of culture and diversity, philosophy and ethics. Above all, these final papers show how he was an integrationist at heart and how his struggle to understand himself and others was used to positive effect.

There are many who are grateful for his work and his life, and I for one was privileged to work with him on a new edition of *Introduction to Psychotherapy*. He insisted that if we were to understand the mind of the new student eager to learn we had to discard assumptions and return to our own beginnings. In doing so he stimulated a process of reflection, resonance and reciprocity which had been at the heart of his own intricate journey of discovery. It was a journey that has enlightened us all.

Prof Anthony W. Bateman
Halliwick Unit
St Ann's Hospital
St Ann's Road
London N15 3TH

AUTHOR'S INTRODUCTION AND AUTOBIOGRAPHICAL NOTES

These papers, published between 1976 and 2003, trace a theme that is part of my personal development. They are also perhaps, striving unconsciously to adumbrate a philosophical approach to how we influence and are influenced by whom and what is about us, i.e. resonance; and how we create and are created by encounters with others and 'otherness', i.e. reciprocity. One process is passive, the other active.

Part 1: My early interest in psychosomatic medicine was based on identification with the dermatological teachers at medical school, followed by working as a houseman to three outstanding dermatologists in Leeds: John Ingram, Francis Hellier and Stephen Anning. (Like Ingram I started screwing up my eyes and pursing my lips while examining patients' skins.) Skin diseases, especially eczema and contact dermatitis, were the subject of some ten years' study and research, during which I trained as a psychiatrist. Throughout this time I learnt how personalities are reflected in physical responsiveness, and how the interaction of body and mind influenced the onset and course of psychosomatic processes. These resonate with relationships with people around the patient, including medical staff and psychotherapists.

Throughout this time I learnt how personality is reflected in physical responsiveness, and how the interaction of body and mind influences the onset and course of psychosomatic processes. These resonate with relationships with people around the patient, including medical staff and therapists, often seen to be echoing early object relationships in the transference. While at Cornell University, in upstate New York, I came into contact with psychologists, psychoanalysts and ethologists, who helped me understand the subtleties of the differences between those students who had succumbed and those who did not, to contact dermatitis by the locally prevalent poison ivy. Back in England to train as a psychiatrist I extended these studies at an ICI chemical works in Huddersfield and confirmed the area of findings in the dinitration plant where contact with dinitrochlorobenzine necessitated nearly 50 per cent of workers having to be moved elsewhere.

Having trained as a psychiatrist and served as a lecturer at Leeds

University, I was invited by Sir Denis Hill at the Middlesex Hospital, London to set up a research scheme with Dr Rae Bettley, a dermatological colleague. This was to test the hypothesis that psychiatric techniques, added to standard dermatological practice, improved the outcome. In fact it did so if the patients were psychologically minded, were aware that stress factors were active in the months prior to the onset of eczema, and were well motivated to engage in insight and self-responsibility. Many experienced the initial psychiatric interview as intentional treatment. They did particularly well with six months of weekly therapy. In contrast, those without these characteristics did particularly badly.

Part 2: During that time I started personal analysis with Mrs Enid Balint and completed psychoanalytic training. From 1969, both in my NHS work (part-time involving individual and group psychotherapy and teaching) and in my private work (at the Group-Analytic Practice where I became an Associate Member and then a Member of Management), my interest was equally psychoanalytic and group-analytic. Each threw light on the other. 'Drowsiness in the Countertransference', published in 1979, is a paper which has had a big influence. It came to represent an avoidance of contact between individuals, within groups and committees. In recent decades, resonance between therapist and patient(s) has been the focus of the recognition and use of transference and countertransference, in both individual and group analysis. The chapters on 'Drowsiness in the Countertransference' and 'Self Development through Subjective Interaction' (Chapters 5 and 10) illustrate the value of such recognition of resonance between individual patient and analyst or in a group between members.

Group analysis originated in the work of S. H. Foulkes, a German psychoanalyst who came to England in 1933. During World War II he worked in the Northfield Military Neurosis Centre in Birmingham. This was the start of the so-called therapeutic community movement, family therapy and group therapy. Group analysis brought together sociology, psychoanalysis and psychosomatics in the sense that the individual is poised in a state of resonance with others, the world in which he or she, and his or her body, interacts with others. Without taking this trimodality into account, the abstraction of the individual is never fully recognised and understood.

Alongside the development of group analysis, Foulkes and his colleagues working at St Bartholomew's Hospital after the war and then for many years at the Maudsley Hospital and Institute of Psychiatry, set up in 1952 the Group-Analytic Society. Among these pioneers were the distinguished German sociologist Norbert Elias and the psychiatrist Pat de Maré, notable for his pioneer work on large groups and latterly median groups of 15 to 30 people. In contrast, Wilfred Bion, who with John Rickman had preceded Foulkes at Northfield (Harrison 2000), developed his own theory of groups founded around the central concepts of the 'basic assumptions', and has in some ways been seen in competition with group analysis. Bion's theory had more to say about group and individual functioning. Foulkes's theory illuminates more the interaction between individuals and the groups from which they originate and participate in.

In 1972, the Group-Analytic Society set up the Institute of Group Analysis in London which has become the principal training organisation for those centred in London and the South East of England. Over the years, branches have developed in Manchester, Glasgow, the Midlands (at Turvey), the South East (Brighton) and the South West (Bristol). These centres have linked with European centres to form the European Group Analytic Training Network (EGATIN) to consolidate standards and develop educational links with emerging centres in eastern Europe and the former Soviet block.

About this time in the development of the group-analytic movement I was preoccupied with integrating ideas from psychoanalysis and group analysis and with promoting the theoretical understanding by linking these notions with ideas of the transpersonal and of the individual as part of group(s) within their society and across societies. The papers referring to context, dialogue, confrontation and interaction aim to advance our understanding of psychological development and of the process of therapy.

Part 3: In the 1980s, during which for five years I was President of the Group-Analytic Society which was becoming increasingly international, several European group analysts and psychoanalysts, following Foulkes's death in 1976, founded the European Association for Transcultural Group Analysis (EATGA). This was at a time when political changes in Europe were creating tensions between different cultures in the moves towards integration, and the consequences of historical traumas during the political crises and wars earlier in the century. At one point I was Vice-President of EATGA and deeply involved in its work, partly through participating in the workshops. These were residential events in which about 100 members met in various cities in Western and Central Europe for some five days. Facing up to trauma, guilt and paranoia, forgiveness and reciprocity were often important learning experiences with ethical complications.

The development of the European Union was mirrored in the group-analytic movement. The group of chapters contained in this section was inspired by participation and contribution to the events held in the transcultural context of EATGA. In these conferences we lived the experience of being with the other, we experienced how our own histories influenced our understanding and our misunderstanding of each other. The same experiences informed us of our need for power and our anxieties about how contact with other cultures may influence our own personal and cultural self. The ethical implications of such interaction are explored in a separate chapter.

The concluding chapter, the text of the annual Foulkes Lecture delivered on the hundredth anniversary of his birth, demonstrates how group analysis has moved on from the days of its founder. The idealism of the first days has been tempered with the exposition of its limitations, and even dangers, and has been enriched by connections with newer theories of systems, complexity, bi-logic and others. Group analysis has extended its field of application from simply therapy to understanding organisations and the development of ethics.

ACKNOWLEDGEMENTS

I would like to thank the following publishers for permission to reprint each of the chapters in this book.

Chapter 1 Listening to eczema: deductions and predictions. Originally published in *Integrated Medicine* (ed. H. Maxwell) Bristol: Wright 1976. Out of print. Every effort has been made to contact the copyright holder for this chapter.

Chapter 2 The psychosoma and the group. Originally published in *Group Analysis*, 1985, Vol. 18, pp.93–101. Reprinted by permission of Sage Publications Ltd. Copyright © Group-Analytic Society (London) 1985.

Chapter 3 The Royal Road to the Mysterious Leap: the psychosoma and the analytic process. Originally published in *Australian Journal of Psychotherapy*, 1997, Vol. 16, pp.11–26. Reprinted with permission.

Chapter 4 Drowsiness in the countertransference. Originally published in *International Review of Psycho-analysis*, 1977, Vol. 4, pp.481–492. Reprinted with permission. © Institute of Psychoanalysis, London, UK.

Chapter 5 Assessment and selection for groups. Originally published in *In The Practice of Group Analysis* (eds. J. Roberts and M. Pines) London: Tavistock/Routledge 1991. Reprinted with permission.

Chapter 6 Text, context and texture: free speech in the service of health and healing. Originally published in *Group Analysis*, 1982, Vol. 15, pp.207–218. Reprinted by permission of Sage Publications Ltd. Copyright © Group-Analytic Society (London) 1982.

Chapter 7 Dialogue for change. Originally published in *Group Analysis*, 1986, Vol. 19, pp.25–39. Reprinted by permission of Sage Publications Ltd. Copyright © Group-Analytic Society (London) 1986.

Chapter 8 Confrontation in the group-analytic matrix: towards a classification. Originally published in *Group*, 1988, Vol. 12, pp.191–197. With kind permission of Springer Science and Business Media.

Chapter 9 Change in the group-analytic setting. Originally published in *Psychoanalytic Psychotherapy*, 1987, Vol. 3, pp.53–60. Reprinted with permission. http://www.tandf.co.uk

Chapter 10 Self development through subjective interaction: a fresh look at 'ego training in action'. Originally published as chapter 6 in *The Psyche and the Social World: Developments in Group Analytic Theory* (Eds. Dennis Brown and Louis Zinkin) Routledge, 1994 (now Jessica Kingsley, 2000). Reproduced by permission of Jessica Kingsley Publishers.

Chapter 11 Fair shares and mutual concern: the role of sibling relationships. Originally published in *Group Analysis*, 1998, Vol 31, pp.315–326. Reprinted by permission of Sage Publications Ltd. Copyright © Group-Analytic Society (London) 1998.

Chapter 12 Context, content and process: interrelationships between small and large groups in a transcultural workshop. Originally published in *Group Analysis*, 1987, Vol. 20, pp.237–248.

Chapter 13 Views of Maastricht and Heidelberg: some questions arising from two transcultural workshops seen by observers with different roles. Originally published in *Group Analysis*, 1992, Vol. 25, pp.87–96. Reprinted by permission of Sage Publications Ltd. Copyright © Group-Analytic Society (London) 1992.

Chapter 14 Use and abuse of cultural differences: analysis and ethics in transcultural workshop settings. Originally published in *Group Analysis*, 1992, Vol. 25, pp.97–105. Reprinted by permission of Sage Publications Ltd. Copyright © Group-Analytic Society (London) 1992.

Chapter 15 Group analysis, transculturality and ethics. Originally published in *British Journal of Psychotherapy*, 1992, Vol 12, pp.170–177. Reprinted with permission.

Chapter 16 Foulkes's Basic Law of Group Dynamics 50 Years on: abnormality, injustice and the renewal of ethics. Originally published in *Group Analysis* 1998, Vol. 31, pp.391–419. Reprinted by permission of Sage Publications Ltd. Copyright © Group-Analytic Society (London) 1998.

Chapter 17 Pairing Bion and Foulkes: towards a metapsychosociology? Originally published as chapter 6 in *Building on Bion: Roots, Origins and Context of Bion's Contributions to Theory and Practice* (Eds. Robert M. Lipgar and Malcolm Pines) Part I. London: Jessica Kingsley, 2003. Reproduced by permission of Jessica Kingsley Publishers.

Chapter 18 Bion and Foulkes: basic assumptions and beyond. Originally published as chapter 10 in *Bion and Group Psychotherapy* (Ed. Malcolm Pines). Routledge & Kegan Paul, 1985 (now Jessica Kingsley, 2000). Reproduced by permission of Jessica Kingsley Publishers.

I would also like to personally thank Dorothy Brown who has given her full support throughout this project.

Part 1

PSYCHOSOMATICS

Introductory comments

1

LISTENING TO ECZEMA

Deductions and predictions

Introduction

Eczema, like any illness, occurs in people who are in a state of dynamic adaptation to their environment. This environment is really a complex interaction between objective and subjective worlds, outer and inner, present and past. One may argue that we are all in such a state of constant adaptation. Recently we have had hard evidence that illnesses are more likely to develop in times of change, when challenges to the adaptational resources of the individual are increased (Holmes and Rahe 1967; Rahe 1968; Brown 1972). This is true whether the illnesses are psychiatric, physical, or those so-called psychosomatic disorders in which psychological factors are widely held to play a prominent part in the onset and course, such as hypertension, ulcerative colitis, asthma and eczema. Understanding the illness and its role in the adaptational struggles of the patient necessitates an awareness of the patient in these interacting environments, and of why the illness is thus in a sense appropriate, if not 'ideal'.

The new environment provided by the doctor and his treatment can then be seen as intervening in a way that colludes with the adaptation that incorporates the illness, or – if a psychotherapeutic approach in its broadest sense is intended – strives to modify it (Balint 1957; Balint and Balint 1961). If psychotherapeutic endeavour is to succeed, it is necessary to discern what troubles the patients are attempting to cope with. It requires us to listen to what they are telling us. They might do this directly in words, or else indirectly through mood, posture and gesture, or even merely through the physical disorder itself. Important clues might come from the way we feel in their presence, or after they have gone.

Eczema and its causes

Eczema is a specific inflammatory reaction of the skin, which can be acute, subacute or chronic. It is the commonest such reaction and accounts for over 50 per cent of dermatological practice (Pillsbury *et al.* 1956). It is probably responsible for the greatest number of rashes presented in general practice, which still account for one in six, or thereabouts, of attendances in such practice, despite the introduction in recent years of powerful steroid ointments and creams (Fry 1972). It is likely that very many cases occur in the general population which are either self-treated or clear spontaneously. In seeking to explain why some cases become chronic or seek the help of general practitioners, and why some are then referred on to dermatologists in a hospital, we need to take into account the various aetiological factors, prominent amongst which are psychological factors.

Eczema is readily recognised by the itching it causes, and by its fairly constant sequence of erythema, vesiculation, weeping and/or scaling; when chronic, lichenification often occurs. Histologically it is characterised by epidermal vesiculation and spongiosis. Clinically, however, it takes many forms, has many causes, and classifications have been based on a mixture of morphology and aetiology. Generally recognised types are: contact dermatitis, atopic eczema (disseminated neurodermatitis, the only form with an important hereditary factor, with coexisting predisposition to asthma, hay fever, and vasomotor rhinitis), seborrhoeic eczema, nummular eczema, lichen simplex (circumscribed neuro-dermatitis), infantile eczema, stasic dermatitis (secondary to peripheral venous disease), and chronic eczematous dermatitis (in which the original cause and pattern have been lost sight of, and various secondary factors play a predominant role). Among the causative factors which have been incriminated in eczema are:

1 External irritants, allergies, trauma, infection and gravitation stasis (as described in all dermatological texts).
2 Constitution – heredity, type of skin, neurophysiological constitution (e.g. Brocq and Jacquet 1891; Becker 1931; Ingram 1933; Schwartz *et al.* 1947).
3 Childhood experiences – especially in the mother–child relationship in infantile eczema (e.g. Spitz 1951; Williams 1951; Rosenthal 1953; Woodhead 1955; Selesnick and Sperber 1965).
4 Personality vulnerability (e.g. Vidal 1886; Walsh and Kierland 1947; Wittkower and MacKenna 1947; Allerhand *et al.* 1950; Kepecs and Robin 1950; Wittkower and Edgell 1951; Obermayer *et al.* 1952; Seitz *et al.* 1953; Fiske and Obermayer 1954; Cleveland and Fisher 1956; Sainsbury 1960; Brown and Young 1965a, 1965b).
5 Stress in the current life situation (e.g. Klauder 1925; O'Donovan 1927; Blaisdell 1932; Stokes 1932; Brunstig 1936; Finesinger and Greenhill 1942; Lynch *et al.* 1945; Robertson 1947; Brown 1959a, 1972).
6 Psychiatric illness (e.g. Wilson 1842; Lovett Doust 1952; Fonseca 1963; Herron 1965).

Obviously one or more causes may coexist. As in any problem in medicine, we are dealing with multiple causes, and while it is unlikely that psychological factors can be viewed as sufficient or even necessary for the development of eczema in many cases, it is proposed here that their recognition is of practical as well as of theoretical importance. Psychologically eczema presents a far from uniform picture, though in my experience emotional factors are almost invariably operative in all forms.

Clinical presentation

Eczema patients vary greatly in the overtness of the affective disturbance of which the rash is usually a part or a sole presenting feature. Some are so obviously distressed or disturbed that they are instantly recognisable by the family doctor or dermatologist to whom they are referred. Such cases are often treated by these physicians with tranquillisers or antidepressants, and if they fail to respond are often referred to a psychiatrist. In a previous study (Brown 1967) of 82 cases of eczema referred to the skin department of a London teaching hospital, the author interviewed 73 patients aged 18 to 65 who had had their rash for between six weeks and three years. Particular inquiries were made regarding the presence of new psychological symptoms; i.e. symptoms which were emerging for the first time along with the eczema or during a period preceding it. This was to distinguish between patients with 'lifelong' tendencies to experience psychological or psychophysiological symptoms, usually in response to minor stresses, and those with more definite episodes of emotional disturbance; and in order to distinguish between neurotic personality disorders and psychiatric illnesses or relatively clear-cut stress reactions. To do this, criteria were laid down to avoid the risk of wrongly interpreting such symptoms as evidence of an emotional disturbance that was significantly linked with the onset of eczema, rather than a 'coincidental' chronic emotional instability. Symptoms were to be counted as signifying neurotic personalities unless they appeared clearly worse from the history, plus either (a) they were complained of spontaneously, or (b) there was definite evidence of affective disturbance at interview. That is, a clear history of emotional disturbance had to be confirmed by the patient's spontaneous behaviour at interview, whether verbal or non-verbal. In distinguishing between psychological and psychophysiological symptoms, irritability and insomnia were counted as psychological unless plausibly attributable to the rash, fatigue was counted as physical. Clearly this was somewhat arbitrary, but seemed to accord with the view of the patients and the popular interpretation of the symptoms. On this basis two-thirds admitted to new psychological symptoms as shown in Table 1.1.

Those complaining spontaneously or admitting to new psychological symptoms on direct inquiry scored significantly high on the Neuroticism scale of the Eysenck Personality Inventory (Eysenck and Eysenck 1964), and were termed Unstable. In contrast the third who denied such symptoms

Table 1.1 Incidence of new psychological symptoms in 73 cases of eczema

	Percentage	
Complained of spontaneously	37	67
Admitted on direct enquiry only	30	
Denied, with signs of emotional disturbance	10	33
Denied, no signs of emotional disturbance	15	
Denied, no signs, but had them earlier in course of eczema	8	

Table 1.2 Time relation of new psychological/psychophysiological symptoms to onset of eczema

	Percentage	
Symptoms preceded eczema by one year or more	36	61*
Symptoms preceded eczema by up to one year	25	
Simultaneous	1	39
Eczema first	16	
Not clear	18	
Not applicable (no new symptoms)	4	

* 76% of those with new psychological symptoms.
25% of those with new psychophysiological symptoms.

scored significantly low, and were termed Superstable. They preferentially reported psychophysiological symptoms. Table 1.2 shows that, in both groups, psychological or psychophysiological symptoms preceded the onset of eczema in the vast majority. This, and the fact that the mean duration of the eczema in the Unstable and Superstable groups was identical, 11 months, points to the emotional disturbance as a cause or concomitant of the rash, not a result of it as some suggest (including some proponents of psychosomatic ideas, e.g. Leigh 1968).

The commonest symptoms were a mixture of anxiety and depression, and precipitating stresses tended to activate conflicts about aggression and dependence (Brown 1972). Further experience has confirmed this.

Description of a case

Mrs A, aged 40, falls into category 2. She presented herself as physically ill when seen at the outpatient department. She had had a rash on her hands and forearms for four months, spreading in the last month on to her face and neck. She had been subject to abdominal pain for four years, to migraine from her school days, and for six years in her twenties she had asthma. She gave a zero score on Sections M-R of the Cornell Medical Index dealing with psychological symptoms (Brodman *et al.* 1949) but scored 12 on a health questionnaire devised to detect the physical concomitants of emotional disturbance (Brown 1970).

Mrs A was a strikingly handsome and intelligent woman, self-driving and given to good works. After talking readily about her physical complaints, direct inquiry led to admission that she was having difficulty falling asleep because of worrying, that she had been more irritable over the last two years, had found it difficult to relax for about a year, and in recent months had felt suddenly tired in the evenings. Finally she admitted to worrying about her health since her mother-in-law developed abdominal cancer and died four years ago, after which her husband developed epilepsy. She realised how important it was for her to remain well, but worried, when her abdominal pains started, lest she had cancer too. This abated after a 'talking-to' by the family doctor, but was replaced by a fear of something happening to her husband. When asked how her spirits were she denied depression, insisting how much she enjoyed her many activities. However, if she sees her husband overworking she gets tense and 'sort of angry with him for not being more cautious'. But at times her husband had commented on her appearance and said 'What's the matter?' She would reply 'Oh, nothing!' She thus showed a good deal of suppression, repression and denial of anxiety, anger and guilt.

Knowledge of her background throws a lot of light on her anxieties and defences. She did not remember herself as a nervous child, but at three and a half years of age she was in hospital for three weeks for a broken arm, and parental discord marred her early years, culminating in a divorce when she was 13. An older brother was awarded to mother, whilst she and a younger brother went with father, but were passed on to be cared for by different aunts. Mrs A seems to have felt particularly responsible for her parents' discord, and still plays the role of pacifier between them. Apart from migraine, a tendency to worry, and a special sensitivity to disappointments, she had been fairly well adjusted, but from the age of 21, for six years, she had a possibly asthmatic condition following the loss of her younger brother on a wartime flying mission (the brother would have been about 18 months old at the time when she was away with a broken arm). She did very well at school and work, and reports herself as having been very happily married for 20 years. However, their one child was conceived after ten years of trying, and a Caesarean delivery was necessary, which was followed by a puerperal depressive illness.

Listening in more detail to her account of the last four years we find that she developed abdominal pain about a month before her mother-in-law died of cancer. Mrs A, who had looked after her for a while, feared she had cancer too. The pain has continued on and off since. X-ray showed no organic lesion. After her mother-in-law's death Mrs A became depressed and weepy, in contrast to her husband, who she said 'took it inwardly'. Four months later he developed epilepsy. Naturally Mrs A was extremely worried about him, and this increased her depression. She felt increasingly unable to cope, and went to see her doctor. Finally, in an attempt to help her, he told her 'rather severely' as she says, to pull herself together. With an effort she was able to do this for the sake of her husband and daughter, but continued to be apprehensive about her husband's potential fits. Her abdominal pain and dyspepsia continued intermittently. Mr A's epilepsy led to a rearrangement of their lives. He continued with his professional work, travelling into London from the Home Counties by train, but Mrs A, who had formerly regarded him as a 'tower of strength', took on more responsibility and became, among other things, the family chauffeur. Mr A stopped having sexual relations, ostensibly because of the danger of conception, and this caused Mrs A a good deal of sexual frustration at first.

After we had been talking for about half an hour, she suddenly remembered, with a cry of surprise, that something had happened a week or so before the rash had started on her hands and arms four months before. One evening she had not collected her husband as usual from the railway station. He finally arrived several hours late, with broken teeth and a cut head. He had fallen off the bus (not in an epileptic fit as it turned out) and had been taken to the local hospital. It was as though her negligence had realised her greatest fear. Mrs A was diagnosed as having a neurotic personality of anxious obsessional type – sensitive, prone to anxiety and depression, self-driving with mild obsessional traits of perfectionism and checking. It seemed likely that the origin of these traits lay in her early separation and consequent insecurity, and the fear of her own aggressive impulses, and perhaps death wishes towards, for example, her younger brother. It also seems likely that unconscious hostility towards her husband played a big part in the current emotional disturbance.

Dermatological diagnosis was contact dermatitis due to primula plants which she had kept in the house for the last several months. However, she had previously handled these with impunity until the recent acute emotional stress. This seems to have upset the balance of her adaptation by bringing her fears, and presumably the unconscious sources, associations and elaborations of these, threateningly near to realisation. How this created the physiological state mediating the emergence of a state of allergic hypersensitivity, remains an area for research based on an adequate psychobiological theoretical framework such as that described by Engel (1962).

Listening to what the patient says

It will be apparent from Table 1.2 that like all of us, eczema patients vary widely in the extent to which they are aware of their emotions, and experience distress in the face of difficulties. We must bear this in mind when interviewing them and, as it were, listen between the lines. We have to provide the right atmosphere in which patients can feel secure enough to unburden themselves and join in, without feeling threatened, with an inquiry into the possibility that feelings about themselves and others close to them are having an effect on their skin. Most patients feel anxiety and sometimes awe in the face of doctors, and this is particularly so with psychiatrists. If he can give himself time, it is the general practitioner or the dermatologist who can often most easily prepare the way, if not do the job completely himself.

Once the skin has been examined, we can ask how the patients feel 'in themselves', explaining that this can often affect the onset of the rash or delay its cure. Once they have begun to talk about feelings of irritability, tension or anxiety, or depression, these feelings can then be related to their life situation. Feelings of frustration are very common in eczema patients (Graham and Wolf 1953), and inquiry about them can often help the patient talk about stresses and conflicts in his life. The categories of symptom-reporting behaviour described in Table 1.2 probably represent a continuum which is influenced by several factors:

(a) *Practicability*. Many patients in situations of chronic frustration and conflict, particularly those who do not have relationships with people in which they can unburden themselves, get used to keeping things to themselves, or 'making the best of it'. Some, like the young widow left with several small children, put on a brave face 'so that the children won't suffer'. Given an opportunity, in a relaxed and non-threatening, non-judgemental atmosphere, such patients will very readily talk and unburden themselves.

(b) *Defensiveness*. Some people feel it is a sign of weakness to admit to emotional disturbance to anyone, whilst some are particularly defensive when confronted with a doctor or psychiatrist for fear they be considered mad. Such people require sensitive handling and explanation, and might need to be seen a time or two before they can feel safe in talking about themselves. To a large extent defensiveness is socially determined, and is more likely amongst social classes 4 and 5 (at any rate when interviewed by a class 1 doctor), and amongst young men who have learnt not to weep or show fear.

(c) The '*repressor personality*'. This approximates to what I have called 'Superstable' personalities and Leary (1956) termed 'hypernormal' personalities. Such people tend to use primitive mechanisms of repression, denial, splitting and projection to defend against awareness of emotional disturbance. They often deal with guilt by blaming others. They sometimes present an almost schizoid detachment from feeling of any sort. This may produce a mask-like face which seems to be rigidly controlling all emotion. Quite often depression will be dealt with by denial, resulting in a hypomanic cheerfulness and overactivity. Where patients are unwilling or unready to talk about themselves and their feelings, we have to be especially alert to such signs as the shaking hand or the moistening eye, and such negative signs as avoidance of certain topics or feelings.

Sometimes in constructing the histories of such patients it becomes clear that rigid control of feelings develops as a way of coping with new adaptational challenges – traumatic or developmental crises – in people who were previously emotionally hyper-reactive (e.g. Miss B, see below). Others seem to have always been out of touch with feelings and fantasies. It is as though they have never developed the ability to form mental representations of affects or fantasies. These patients have been beautifully described by Nemiah and Sifneos (1970) as 'alexithymics'. They are unable to express feelings in words, and show an absence of drive-directed and affect-directed fantasy. Thought content reflects and is directed by the surroundings. I have recently described such a patient (Brown 1972) and Mrs D (see below) is another example.

Listening to what the eczema says

As a response to stress, eczema can represent a 'substitute reaction' (Groen 1957), an alternative to 'neuropathic' or 'sociopathic' reactions. The underlying psychopathology may be neurotic or near-psychotic.

Miss B, aged 42, denied any new psychological symptoms when seen in the outpatient department. Four months before her first attack of eczema she was again sensitised to loss by the death next door of the mother of a lifelong friend. She was 'shocked, but otherwise unaffected', but kept 'expecting' her over the garden wall for several weeks. A couple of months later her favourite boss in her responsible Civil Service job left the country and was replaced by a man who one day 'put her on the mat' and deliberately and repeatedly humiliated her. She became so furious and tearful that she retired to the lavatory for an hour to cool off, lest she should hit him. She remained extremely tense for three days, after which eczema broke out on her legs, spreading to other parts of her body. She thought at the time 'Fancy him giving me a rash!' and began to allow herself to be more assertive with him, with the consequent resolution of her state of tension. Following a lengthy holiday away from him, the rash gradually resolved. The dermatological diagnosis was chronic eczema of obscure origin. She had controlled her wish to strike her new boss, and she may have been afraid of becoming depressed in view of her history.

The background to this incident supports the idea that the suppression of disappointment and rage were in some way causally related to the eruption of eczema. All the details cannot be given here, but she had marked temper tantrums as a child and has remained more sensitive and emotional than she appears outwardly, though expressing this mainly through physical anxiety symptoms. An early hostile relationship with her brother gave way to a close one, and following his death in action she volunteered for the VAD, where she forced herself, against repugnance, to nurse on skin wards. She did not marry, cared for her aged parents, and found great consolation in nursing her father in a long illness. Following his death she began a relationship with a man ten years her senior, which ended after only a year. This blow was succeeded by influenza and haemorrhoidectomy, and finally a severe depressive breakdown, which cleared after five months of drugs and psychotherapy. About five years later, at the age of 39 – her mother's age when she was born, perhaps a further sign that her sexual and reproductive life was passing – she developed hay fever for the first time in her life. She is now tied to her mother by bonds of considerable ambivalence, sexually unfulfilled, and sublimating a lot of her longings into her work and relationship with her boss. In this light the hostile rejection by the new boss can be seen as a very profound blow. In fact although the eczema cleared up in a couple of months, after six months she was slipping into another severe depressive illness which took over a year to clear with treatment by another psychiatrist.

One might well ask why some patients 'speak with eczema'. The question of specificity in psychosomatic medicine is a complex one, but obviously influenced by the multifactorial causation of such conditions. In the large series quoted above, only 15 per cent of cases had a family history of eczema, and local factors (irritation, sensitisation, infection, stasis) were clearly playing a part in only 21 per cent of cases. Psychological factors were thought to be operative in all of them. Table 1.3 shows that, compared with a control population of dental outpatients, eczema patients are more prone to both psychiatric illness and skin disorders other than eczema. They seem to be predisposed to reacting through the skin.

Sometimes this type of reaction can plausibly be traced back to facilitating experiences in childhood, which invest the skin with highly charged personal significance.

Mr C aged 38, had a miserable childhood marked by gross parental neglect.

Table 1.3 Incidence of previous illnesses in eczema and dental patients

	Percentage		
	Eczema (n 82)	*Dental (n 123)*	*Difference**
Psychiatric illness	23	8	$p<0.01$
Other skin disorders	46	5	$P<0.001$
Other psychosomatic disorders	34	39	N.S.

* x^2 test, 2-tail.

His earliest memories were of falling into a bed of nettles and stepping into a wasps' nest. After both accidents his mother revealed her nursing training by rubbing him all over with vinegar – the nearest thing he got to efficient maternal care. His eczema came out when his wife was in hospital, his children away, and he was trying to adapt himself, uncertainly, to a new job; his own family showed no concern at all. His current feelings of rejection and neglect reminded him of the times when the only maternal attention he had was to his intensely stinging skin.

The meaning of the skin to the individual is usually more subtle than this. Physiological reactivity in the skin has been related to the body image and its firmness of delineation – the extent to which it is experienced as a barrier between inner and outer worlds (Fisher and Cleveland 1958; Brown and Young 1965b). The development of personality and a sense of basic security involve the skin through its role in the mediation of the mother–child relationship (Harlow and Zimmerman 1958; Bowlby 1969). With its protective functions it is also the organ through which we experience pain and punishment. And it is through our skin and that of others that our eroticism is experienced and transmitted. All these functions of the skin can enter into its meaning for the individual. The search for body contact, aggressive, erotic, sadomasochistic and exhibitionistic impulses can all be discharged into the skin by autonomic pathways and by scratching. Sometimes it is possible, in the course of a long-term contact with patients, to see the skin reflecting feelings and aspects of relationships which they are unwilling to admit to.

Mrs D, aged 59, was a jolly little domestic cleaner who had always presented a very brave face to a hard life. Her eldest child, her only daughter, died at the age of four and this was a great blow to Mrs D and her husband. However, they had four sons to follow. One by one, they left home to marry. Mrs D developed eczema on her hands and arms within a year of her last and youngest son leaving home. She was now alone with her husband who by this time was having repeated trouble with his back, which interfered with his working capacity, leaving her to carry on as a cleaner. When seen, having failed to respond to dermatological treatment for two years, Mrs D was reluctant to admit to feelings of resentment or depression. In the course of about a dozen sessions of largely supportive psychotherapy she at times came near to doing so, but soon forgot it. Nevertheless, to her great surprise, the eczema eventually cleared. However, on three occasions in a row, after I had suggested to her that we make the next session the last one, she came to the 'final' session announcing that her skin had flared up the night before whilst quietly watching the television, and demonstrated to me an acute eruption on the outer sides of her upper arms. We discussed this in terms of her feelings of resentment and loss, her frustrated longings to hold and be securely held, and ultimately we were able to have a truly final session. However, she knows that she can always come to see me again if necessary. It is this knowledge, I think, which obviates the need for a relapse. Such development would be a natural part of a doctor–patient relationship in general practice.

Treatment

In a large part, the psychological treatment of eczema consists of listening to the patient and helping him to translate what the eczema says. The feeling of being listened to and understood is beneficial in itself. In a recent controlled trial of psychiatric treatment in eczema (Brown and Bettley 1971) we found that some patients who were supposed to be having dermatological treatment alone had construed the initial psychiatric interview as treatment, and had attributed their improvement to this. We therefore changed the form of the study in the latter end, so that we had a group of nine control patients who had had no psychiatric interview at all. These patients did notably worse than the control patients who had had such an interview. In that study, in which psychiatric treatment was limited to four months and consisted of psychotherapy and, where depression and anxiety were marked, of tranquillisers or antidepressants, we found that the overtness of emotional disturbance and the motivation of the patient were critical factors. Where these were present, the proportion of patients whose eczema was cleared by 18 months was doubled; where they were absent, psychiatric treatment seemed to make no difference, or in the short term actually worsen it. It is necessary to curb one's therapeutic zeal and to keep in touch with both the unconscious and conscious parts of the patient which seem germane to the symptoms. Those patients who feel too threatened by their underlying anxieties or impulses, or who feel they are in a life situation which would become even more difficult were they to face the 'true' nature of their feelings and relationships, will resist insight and often merely stop coming for treatment. It is wise not to push them too hard, though in my experience they are in a minority. The motivation to change of many defensive patients, or even 'repressor personalities' of not too severe a degree, can be mobilised in a therapeutic alliance. Allowing patients to express their feelings and predicaments can often help them to an awareness of what needs to be done to alter frustrating situations, to learn more assertive reactions where possible, and to accept the few things which are inevitable. Having someone listen to them who does not judge them can help them to accept themselves more tolerantly, especially when that person can allow the patient to express towards himself the patient's feelings of disappointment, resentment or hostility. Such measures are clearly within the capacity of the interested general practitioner or dermatologist. Not many patients, I think, require specialised psychotherapy.

Thymoleptic drugs are often used in treating the emotional disturbance when overt. My inclination is to avoid their use if possible on the basis that emotions are best recognised and worked through if a psychotherapeutic approach is being made. After the effect of two or three interviews has been assessed, drugs might be indicated if it seems that the underlying affective disturbance is very great, and beyond the capacity of the patient to deal with even with the extra resources provided by the doctor–patient relationship. If they are prescribed and have a beneficial effect on the rash or the way the patient feels, this change can be used to foster the relationship and the patient's understanding of the way the rash reflects or expresses disturbed feelings.

When eczema is part of a total adaptation to a stressful life situation or personality problem, in which changes are impossible or resisted by the patient, who consequently does not want the 'real' nature of his problems to be 'heard', then the prognosis is likely to be poor, unless skilled psychotherapeutic help can uncover possibilities for change. This is particularly so if there is an infantile type of personality integration, precariously held together, and threatened by psychotic anxieties. Otherwise, if the patients can join the doctor in understanding stress reactions, translating into words what the eczema is saying, and working out new solutions by mobilising the resources of themselves and others, including the relationship with the doctor, then the need for eczema will often evaporate. Many who have transient episodes know this. It also applies to those who have a more chronic and organised disease, so long as the organic component (as in some cases of atopic eczema) is not predominant and uninfluenceable; but even such cases can often be helped if not cured.

Summary and conclusions

Deductions

We can deduce the role of the eczema in the personal economy of the patients (the balance of affects and defences) and their motivation for treatment and change, by listening to what they say and what the eczema seems to be expressing. They may talk spontaneously or with a little encouragement. Or the eczema itself may reveal significant facts about them which they cannot express verbally because of anxiety and defensiveness in the interview situation, or because of a personality structure which defends against awareness of unpleasant and conflicting feelings.

Predictions

If emotional disturbance is relatively overt, and/or precipitating problems can be talked about and explored with the doctor, and the wish for change can be mobilised, then the outlook for a favourable response of eczema to the psychotherapeutic endeavours of the doctor is good. What one needs to do is to provide a setting and relationship in which communication with the patient can develop. A prime requirement is the opportunity and ability to listen.

2

THE PSYCHOSOMA AND THE GROUP

It might seem a truism to say that group analysis takes into account the bio-psycho-social nature of human beings. However, group analysis is rooted in Foulkes's integration of medicine and neurology in Germany, with psychiatry and psychoanalysis in Vienna and then finally with the influence of the sociologists in Frankfurt – i.e. he moved from the body to the mind to the social context, and integrated them. Further, Foulkes's *professional* development reflects the development of the *individual*. The baby's *physical* experiences, from which its *mental* functions emerge, are deeply influenced not only by mother's relationship with the baby, but also by father, family and the *social culture* in which it is embedded. Mother, father, family and social culture all *precede* the birth of the baby, and their expectations, hopes and fears inevitably influence its body and its development and emergence as an individual self. We engage from a network or in Foulkes's term a matrix – bodily, psychological and social.

This emergence, and the complex web of relationships and communications are illustrated by Foulkes's diagrams of levels of communication and levels of group functioning. Foulkes gave priority in his theory to communication at many levels, non-verbal as well as verbal. He saw this as extending upwards from 'mimicry, direct emotional expression, conversional manifestations, organ language and organic affections' (Foulkes and Anthony 1957: 245–8; Figure 2.1).

Foulkes also conceived of four levels of functioning in a group, which coexist (Foulkes 1964: 114–15; see Figure 2.2) Analysis involves going deeper, as deep as is necessary to contact and resolve the problems of the group and its members. The bodily level is seen to be a deep level, both for individual functioning and group functioning. As group therapists we need to keep all our senses alert to what is going on in the bodies of individuals, the group and of *ourselves*.

Here I shall give the first of two examples from group-analytic groups illustrating the psychosocial basis of somatisation. Richard was a 40-year-old computer executive who had come to therapy because of his inability to present himself verbally before groups of colleagues at work, and a severe degree

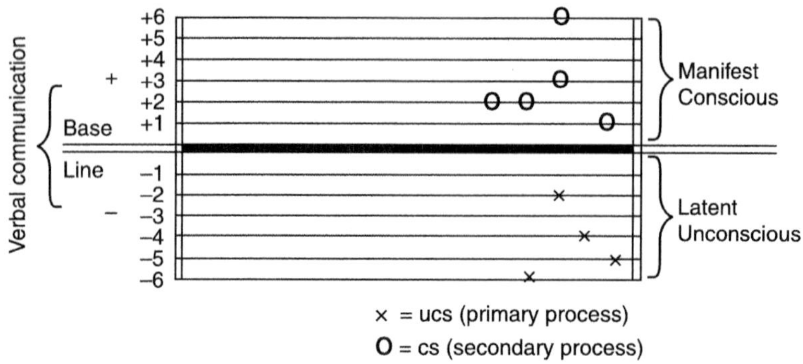

Figure 2.1 Foulkes's levels of communication.

Levels

1 Everyday level of current relationships.
2 Transference level.
3 Levels of projected and shared feelings and fantasies, often preverbal and bodily ('intrapsychic' shared in matrix).
4 Primordial level (collective unconscious).

Figure 2.2 Levels of communication.

of emotional blocking which made his marriage sterile for his wife in a way that he himself could not understand. However, he could contrast his feelings for her with his intense emotional attachment and concern for his young son. From joining, his involvement in the twice-weekly group was precarious and puzzling. He constantly felt unable to understand what 'people were going on about'. However, after a while it became clear that he longed for attention, but waited for it, and when it didn't come he would rage inwardly.

After one such occasion he didn't return. In a letter he said he despaired of being able to use the group. I offered him an individual session in which we explored his feeling of being forgotten and defeated in the group. Though formerly denying early memories he had gradually uncovered some in the group, and this time he talked of being put aside by his mother when his sister was born (at two and a half) and when father returned from the army when he was three; also of mother's suppression of his feelings, saying 'boys don't feel', while the sister was allowed her tantrums. In the session he acknowledged with pleasure my telling him of the projected tearfulness I felt. After recognising that the group was experienced as a family in which he could not find a place and afford to be spontaneous (transference to the group one might say), he decided to return to it.

When he did so, he spoke of realising he needed the group every day and feared he would fall flat if not picked up. One could thus see that an important part of his character defence was against dependence and abandonment. At the next session he reported fury with me for not 'bringing him out' despite my declared knowledge of his need, but this only happened after someone else had talked about leaving and wishing to be special. Richard had been sitting impassively, but flicked a speck off his tie once and glanced quickly at his watch. I had withheld indicating that I had observed these signs, and the man who had been talking asked him how he was. Richard replied, 'Furious, there is no point. I nearly walked out.' He could not 'understand' what was being talked about (even though it was obviously very relevant to him). He saw no point in coming if I was aware of his needs and did nothing about them. Another member expressed his anger at Richard, but explained that he also *identified* with him, realising that he covered his own needs by *talking* rather than by *silence*.

Again, this time in the group, I pointed out my own tears, recognising them as well as the anger, as his and that of others in the group. At this he was deeply and dramatically moved, and felt intense pain in the neck and shoulders 'as though being choked'. I made the apparently banal comment that he was choking his own *feelings*, which instantly released his tears. One member passed him the tissues and another put her hand on his shoulder, but he could not talk about it until the intensity had worn off. He was afraid he would be embarrassed but was reassured by the others.

At last, asked how it related to feelings in the family, he could clearly see it was, especially being ignored and overlooked. He said he had only once got furious with his mother (who, from when he was eight or so, had become emotionally disturbed, constantly raging, until she developed a paranoid breakdown). On this occasion she nagged him so long that he told her to 'close her fucking mouth' and walked out. Later father remonstrated with him and sent him to his bedroom where he wept and sobbed alone.

After this opening up, and the discovery that his rage and tears could be accepted and understood, for the rest of the session he was able to keep up very much with the ebb and flow of conversation and understanding in the group.

In a later session, Richard revealed to us how his distress is experienced somatically in any situation linked with that with his parents. For example, he told us how one evening, after talking to his wife in one of his periodic attempts to get through to her, he went to bed hoping for physical closeness. However, she turned her back on him, and he, speechless but with intense pain in his stomach, went downstairs to walk about on his own.

Emergence and separation

Freud (1923: 26) spoke of the ego as 'first and foremost a body ego'. Mental functions gradually emerge from bodily functions in the first year or two of life, as does a sense of self from the original infant–mother unit – though never completely. Indeed Foulkes used to quote the idea of Gunther Ammon that psychosomatic symptoms represent *holes* in the ego. Development thus involves a process of desomatisation, as described by Freud's physician Max Schur (1955). This of course is what Bion (1970) implies in his concept of a protomental state, prior to the development of the capacity for thought and imagery, before primitive bodily impulses and sensations, what he called beta functions, are replaced or joined by alpha functions, the prototypes of imagery and symbol formation.

Joyce McDougall (1974) holds that the process of differentiation of mind and body can be interfered with by the principal attachment and caring figures being either too consistently close and impinging, or too distant, and that either can predispose to both psychosis and psychosomatic disorder. Later (1982) she linked the paucity of dreams and imaginative life to attacks on affective links and perceptual consciousness, and to the ejection from the mind of both affect and of representations with a 'somatic outburst!' (as with Richard's dramatic choking sensation in the group, and his attack of stomach pain in bed with his wife). While I agree with McDougall that such phenomena point to psychosomatic disorders representing profound difficulties and disturbances at an archaic level of relationship, it is a generalisation that requires unpicking.

Causes and types of psychosomatic disorder

Firstly we need to recognise that psychosomatic disorders often have multiple causes – physical, psychological and social. We also need to differentiate between (1) 'true' psychosomatic disorders – major life-threatening or crippling conditions like asthma, hypertension, peptic ulcer, ulcerative colitis, thyrotoxicosis, eczema, rheumatoid arthritis – with clear histopathological changes, visible under the microscope; (2) lesser, more functional disorders in which abnormalities in the autonomic control of bodily functions create symptoms (e.g. irritable colon and migraine); (3) those conversion symptoms which are disguised but decodeable expressions of conflicted impulses and fantasies, and represent ego defences against them.

A young woman developed a weakness in her right arm on leaving a group session and sought help in the hospital casualty department. The sensible casualty officer examined and reassured her and told her to bring it up in the group next week. When she did it became clear that she was in conflict over her wish to hit the therapist, sitting next to her, when he had announced that he was leaving the hospital in a few months' time and would be passing the group to another therapist. The significance becomes clearer when we know the patient was adopted when young by an elderly couple who couldn't tolerate her liveliness. Expression of negative feelings would be met by threats to send her back to the orphanage from which she had been adopted.

Conversion symptoms are more like communications. 'True' psychosomatic disorders are more like somatising regressions to more primitive preverbal states (protomental in Bion's terminology). Between the two, the consequences of undischarged affects and drives might be like what Freud (1894) called 'actual neuroses' in contradistinction to 'psycho-neuroses' the consequence of undischarged drives.

It seems likely that *families* which do not provide psychological containment nor allow the expression and reception of affects actually perpetuate somatisation by not talking about feelings and by giving support and attention only when children are physically distressed or ill. It is well known that many emotionally and psychiatrically disturbed patients present with physical symptoms – indeed in general practice in Britain it is the commonest presentation. This was made clear in a recent *British Medical Journal* leader, 'Somatisation: Embodying the Problem' (Murphy 1989). The doctor, clinical interviewer or therapist can collude or try to change this (Wolff 1977). In other words, predisposition to psychosomatic disorders and symptoms, as well as genetic and environmental factors, can reflect failures at the level of mother–infant interaction, family communication, and sociocultural attitudes. The latter include medical attitudes. To be effective, group-analytic psychotherapy needs to mitigate these failures.

The concept of alexithymia

The idea of each psychosomatic disorder being predisposed to by a specific personality and focal conflict has been largely superseded by the concept of alexithymia, perhaps too much so, as I hinted in a recent lecture to the Freud Conference. I quoted some of my own early non-analytic work on personality factors predisposing to the development of contact dermatitis, that in retrospect makes more sense from our understanding of the crucial role the skin plays in containing the early infant, and communicating both good and bad emotional experiences between infant and mother (Bick 1968; Pines 1980; Anzieu 1990).

The term alexithymia was originally coined in the USA by Nemiah and Sifneos (1970) to describe the inability or difficulty in finding words for feelings. The idea of poverty of verbal expression of feeling, fantasy and drive had been adumbrated earlier by the French analysts Marty and de M'Uzan (1963) in their concept of pensée-operatoire, or concrete thinking associated with underdeveloped subjective and fantasy life. You will recognise such people, acquaintances as well as patients, whose accounts of events and experiences are matter-of-fact, often detailed, but without a sense of the personal, emotional and imaginative. Richard, who I described earlier, was a good example. Apart from Joyce McDougall, mentioned earlier, workers in the field have attested to the value of this concept. Graeme Taylor (1987) has reviewed much of their work in his masterly book *Psychosomatic Medicine and Contemporary Psychoanalysis*.

Among the research Taylor quotes is work that I did with Ross Kalucy (now at Flinders University in South Australia) in the sleep laboratory at St. George's Hospital. We investigated a group of alexithymic eczema patients who scratched their skin throughout the night. Our initial hypothesis was based on the hope that waking them during REM periods on the EEG would give us access to emotional and fantasy life unavailable in psychotherapeutic interviews. In fact we were disappointed. But instead we discovered that these patients had greatly reduced slow-wave sleep and reported few or no dreams on being woken. Some when woken even denied they had been asleep. The few who reported dreams showed a significant lack of involvement in their dreams – they were always passive onlookers. It was as though the tension and associated scratching either prevented or was an alternative to the mental activity manifested in dreaming (Brown and Kalucy 1975; Tantam *et al.* 1982).

It is sometimes assumed that the alexithymic personality is based on a developmental arrest. However it can also be a defensive reaction to trauma and to intolerable conflict and pain, i.e. it can be secondary rather than primary. This results e.g. in a high incidence of psychosomatic disorder in numbed survivors of disasters such as the Holocaust. Alexithymia we now know is also common in addictive states and perversions, which can also be alternatives to intolerable emotional states.

One of the subjects of our sleep laboratory study was a middle-aged woman whose father had died when she was eight. At 21 she married a man 20 years older who represented for her, as she put it, a tower of strength. Twenty years later he had a catastrophically disabling stroke which left her as his carer. She shouldered this burden gladly, but started scratching her skin so severely and deeply that she was diagnosed by the referring dermatologist as having prurigo of unknown origin. What quickly became clear was that she was in acute conflict between her wish to care for her crippled husband cheerfully and willingly, and her grief, disappointment and rage. She opened up, at first, with considerable relief, both emotionally and dermatologically, but broke off a planned series of psychotherapeutic sessions because the emergence of her negative feelings threatened her capacity to stay in the situation. She chose, barely consciously, to suffer rather than disrupt the fragile status quo.

Earlier research

Some years ago, I studied 82 adult cases of eczema – a 'true' psychosomatic disorder. They had been referred to a dermatological outpatient clinic, where I saw them as a colleague of the dermatologist (Brown and Bettley 1971; Brown 1972, 1976a). I found that two-thirds complained spontaneously or on direct inquiry (accompanied by definite evidence of emotional disturbance at interview) to new psychological symptoms. One-third denied them, but sometimes with non-verbal evidence of emotional disturbance currently or earlier in the course of the eczema. In over 60 per cent of those *with* new symptoms, they clearly *preceded* the onset of eczema. But it was the one-third who *denied* new psychological symptoms and whom I labelled *Superstable*, who were most like the primary alexithymics. They tended to use primitive mechanisms of denial, splitting and projection to defend against awareness of emotional disturbance. They often dealt with guilt by blaming others. They sometimes presented an almost schizoid detachment from feeling of any sort. This often produced a mask-like face which seemed to be rigidly controlling all emotion. Quite often they dealt with depression by adopting a hypomanic cheerfulness and overactivity. I learnt that with patients unwilling or unready to talk about themselves or their feelings, we have to be especially alert to such signs as the scratching hand or the moistening eye – to the level of body language Foulkes alerted us to – as well as such negative signs as avoidance of certain topics or feelings.

Paradoxically physical signs and symptoms can be communications *and* blocks to communication. It depends on how much and what patients are prepared to know and share, but also how much we are prepared to participate – to hear, see, inquire and imaginatively and empathically tune in. Indeed, in a controlled trial of psychiatric treatment in eczema (Brown and Bettley 1971), we found that those patients who were aware of their eczema developing in a situation of emotional disturbance did particularly well in terms of their skin when offered psychotherapy – even one psychodynamically orientated consultation – and particularly badly when denied it (see Table 1.1). In contrast, the third who were not so aware tended, in the short-term, to be made worse by psychiatric procedures (see Table 1.1). Indeed because some patients construed the psychodynamic assessment as *treatment*, we had to change the method of entry into the controlled trial.

Psychotherapy with psychosomatic disorders

Such willingness to participate on the part of both patient and therapist is essential if the psychotherapy of psychosomatic patients of all types is to begin. The *meaning* of physical symptoms and expressions needs to be discovered, and at the most primitive ('true' psychosomatic, or protomental) level *created*, for mentalisation to bypass, reverse, or better still, grow out of somatisation. As I sometimes say to patients, we need to grow *down* as well as up. This calls for trust *on both sides*, that anxiety, pain, helplessness and rage can be tolerated. Whether in group or individual therapy, we must be able to facilitate communication at deeper, primitive levels, and ultimately translate them into words. We have to dare to go to levels where it is hot, as Foulkes put it. However, at this level, which Joyce McDougall reminded us is also the level of psychosis, there is a danger of making people worse, even precipitating psychosis (Hill 1977); for some, the best psychological treatment is *physical treatment and support*.

I'd like to add a personal note of warning to the danger of creating *false* meaning for physical symptoms. In 1976 Foulkes died of a sudden heart attack while conducting a group of which I was a member. In the corner of my eye I saw him slump back in the chair to my left. The image stuck with me, and when I developed a flickering in the same quadrant of my field of vision the day after his funeral, I associated it with a malicious thought I had had when I saw him die (we were due to finish the two-year group experience the following week). I felt guilty and ashamed about it, but mentioned it to a colleague who urged me to see an ophthalmologist. I was whisked into hospital for a detached retina!

Another warning is not to underestimate the amount of help patients need to cope with the depth and intensity of the emotional disturbance underlying psychosomatic disorders. I treated one of the 82 eczema patients, a young man in his twenties, by once-weekly analytical psychotherapy. By the terms of the controlled trial we were conducting (Brown and Bettley 1971), we limited psychiatric intervention where possible to four months. When he became paranoid and semi-psychotic, I had to change tack to become less analytic and more supportive with clear benefit to his emotional state, and indirectly to his skin.

Thus we have to provide a setting that is safe and containing enough to hold and make sense of deeply disturbed and disturbing affects. If we cannot provide it in individual or group therapy, we should not start, though the level and degree of disturbance might not be obvious at first. In the case of the young man with eczema once a week on the couch induced regression, both pathologically and in the transference, that was not sufficiently containable in the setting. Individual work, if intense enough, can be sufficiently supportive and containing to allow a sense of being attended to at a primitive dyadic level. But with alexithymic individuals, not psychologically minded, both patient and therapist can quickly become either bored or flooded by primitive material 'out of nowhere' (as in the example I give after talking about some of the principles of treating psychosomatic problems in group settings).

Group psychotherapy

One of the advantages of groups is that psychological mindedness can develop gradually, whether in the group as a whole in specialised psychosomatic groups, or in one or several psychosomatic patients or somatisers in a mixed group – commoner in group-analytic practice.

Homogeneous groups of psychosomatic patients often get stuck in passive-dependent states, with both aggression and longing for *and* intolerance of closeness shown only negatively, with little mutual concern and interaction.

However, when one or two do begin to move from somatic preoccupation and symptoms, insisting that their physical condition is their only problem, this can be especially effective to others, providing a living lesson and inspiration to try the move themselves. Such groups are particularly likely to take place in medical settings, including psychiatry departments in general hospitals. This is where my experience with such groups was gained.

In Germany the system of psychosomatic hospitals and clinics allows a range of different treatments – individual and group psychotherapies, creative and body-based therapies – all supported by state insurance. It is possible there to provide a level of therapy tailored to a patient's ego strength (Knauss 1985): (1) For those with the weakest egos, e.g. severely borderline patients, *individual analytic psychotherapy* is started as inpatients but continued as outpatients, supplemented by the therapeutic milieu and non-verbal methods such as movement therapy. This allows the re-enactment of primitive defences and a gradual discovery of meaning along with the development of verbalisation. (2) For intermediate patients, a *combination of individual and group analytic psychotherapy* for three months as inpatients is followed by similar outpatient treatment. (3) For patients with relatively well-functioning egos, *daily inpatient group analysis* is augmented by non-verbal group methods for three months, followed by *weekly outpatient group analysis* for two to three years.

Such flexible and readily available facilities are clearly enviable to those of us working in countries where analytical psychotherapy is not supported by state insurance schemes to that extent. My own experience in Britain is that milder forms of psychosomatic disorder and reaction can be very successfully treated in mixed groups, along with people with neurotic or personality problems of a general sort.

I find that the more severe forms of psychosomatic illness, associated with weak ego and often borderline personality, are better treated in either special psychosomatic groups, or in *twice weekly* mixed groups where they can if necessary have individual sessions.

Special psychosomatic groups usually need a hospital outpatient setting, where sufficient numbers of such patients can be found. Here their special needs and vulnerabilities can be concentrated on, and physical supervision and intervention are readily available. Here too the group's experience in supporting and confronting and in dealing with the danger of dropouts, can develop at a rate appropriate for the psychosomatic patients. This is often slower than is optimal for non-psychosomatic, non-alexithymic individuals. However, as I have stated elsewhere about such patients (Brown 1985):

> Although many patients discern what they are capable of and drop out of group therapy at an early stage, adequate individual preparation can minimise unnecessary treatment failures. Patients who do persist, despite early discouragement, helped by patients who have

> already trodden the same path, sooner or later give up their dependence on somatic forms of communication and blocking and on their way to making real progress become more like 'ordinary neurotics'. This double process makes such cases particularly satisfying to treat. When the group proves a more successful container than the early mother and family, frustration no longer inevitably activates the primitive psycho-soma (Bion's protomental system). Experience in the group matrix permits the capacity to think about feelings and relationships which were previously so threatening as to be unthinkable in the early maternal, family and social matrix.
>
> (Brown 1985: 93–101)

The second clinical example is of a middle-aged woman treated in a twice weekly group. She was deeply split between feeling a terrorised infant and being seen as a highly intelligent woman of considerable academic and personal achievement. Rona had been referred by a distinguished psychotherapist who had treated her individually for ten years, but already had had a history of decades of a range of physical symptoms extensively investigated. He described her as 'undoubtedly one of the most difficult patients I have treated and I remain unsatisfied with the therapy . . . The first effect was to change a smiling efficient automaton into an increasingly helpless person with both physical and emotional pain and marked incapacity for thought; she had to give up driving, could not read and described a state of despair'. The therapist described the sessions as often leaving him bored and exhausted as there was no access to direct emotion; but it became clear that the level of symptoms reflected failure to express anger and emotional 'overload' when exposed to others. After several years he found himself locked into an idealising transference, and eventually had to terminate therapy.

Rona had been adopted at six weeks by a working-class couple of very limited means and her adoptive mother was clearly educationally subnormal and immature. She couldn't tolerate her baby crying and frequently hit her. When Rona was two and a half mother had a breakdown and for a few weeks the child was cared for by a relative in the country, which was like an oasis of sanity and kindness. Her adoptive father worked so hard she rarely saw him, and she was sexually abused by a lodger who 'seduced her' with books. Clearly much brighter than her adoptive parents, she used her academic progress through scholarships, not understood by them, as a refuge and way out of the nightmare of home. Interestingly when young she had a recurrent dream of lions trying to get into the house, but later no dreams at all. In keeping with our ideas about alexithymia, following a partial opening up of her imaginative life at 13, when she began reading poetry, she started with constant headaches. During therapy she resumed dreaming but about babies dying or crying.

Rona joined a twice-weekly group with me about two years ago. I thought it likely that a group would be less likely to lock her into a split idealising transference, and provide experience of a more normal family, and a wider range of identifications through which to develop and integrate. She took to it quite readily, talking in the first session about her somatic and psychic pain, how her whole body swells up, and she cannot 'see' to read or drive. The issue of the group being too soft emerged, as though we needed to recognise the element of sharpness and suffering in relationships as well as caring for each other. I shared with the group an image of Auschwitz. Within three sessions Rona described leaving last time with a headache, the result of being stirred up by themes of caring and sadistic rage yet shut off from her own feelings. She saw me as bored and brittle, like mother when she was not sadistic and violent, and revealed she had dreamt about mother being alive. In the next session she reported feeling disturbed by the group, its closeness challenging her mistrust of longed-for empathy. She wept when a male patient shed tears at feeling touched by experiencing me as a warm father who had affection for and faith in him.

An increasingly positive transference to me was balanced for a time by a violently negative transference interaction with another woman group member who also had a disastrous early relationship with her mother. It was the sort of mutual projection that we call 'malignant mirroring' (Zinkin 1983) and which had to be worked on repeatedly to allow its resolution. Moreover Rona's combination of infantile neediness, self-absorption and inarticulacy, contrasting with her adult capacity to understand and show interest in others, created a confusion and conflict in group members which made them feel a sadistic intolerance which could only eventually be talked about openly. Until then Rona oscillated very much in her response to sessions. In one session in which we explored her experience and provocation of sadism in others while she sought holding and comforting, we actually witnessed her tears becoming converted into severe back pain.

After about a year she became more integrated into the group and struggled more successfully towards becoming, as she puts it, 'psychosomatically whole'. In one session she reported feeling more together since the previous session, but hearing a male group member talking and wanting to 'put herself into him' (a physical metaphor for empathy) caused an exacerbation of pain and her skin became flushed. In the subsequent session, she linked this with the recognition that the lodger had abused her from the age of six to ten, feeding her mind but causing her body to shrink with penetrative kisses and genital fondling. Soon after she discovered she could read again.

The translation of physical symptoms into feelings became at times an important feature of this group, doubtless aided by the issue being highlighted by Rona. For example, one woman came with a headache to a session after conducting a creative therapy session in a psychiatric hospital. She was able to link this with having to contain disturbing projections. As she talked she began to feel hunger and thirst at the back of her throat, which she linked with her mother's milk drying up when she was three months old. (She had till then been bringing a beaker of water into the sessions.) In another session a man reported again developing a mysterious toothache since feeling angry with me for unfairly complaining about his lateness the previous session. (I had forgotten that he had accompanied his pregnant wife for a scan.) This put him in touch with the important role played by recurrent pains in his childhood.

Let us think back to Joyce McDougall's idea that psychosomatic (and psychotic) problems originate from very early experiences in which the primary objects are too consistently distant or impinging at the point of emergence of self from infant–mother symbiosis and of mind from the undifferentiated psychosoma. This makes sense of both Richard's and Rona's symptom formation. The rebuff of Richard's attempts to get close to his wife triggered off voiceless rage and stomach pain. Rona's provocation of sadism in members of the group when she sought closeness led to tears quickly turning into severe back pain; the wish for closeness led to the experience of punishment. Richard kept himself at a protective distance from a too-distant object. Rona could not negotiate the space between her need and an impingingly hostile mother. In the early stage of her life in the group, other members' eyes were frequently seen as hateful, and their hands as about to strike her. Later this gave way to greater trust, as she learnt to trust the power of her own resentment – i.e. she withdrew her projection.

One can thus see that an analytic group provides a containing transitional space where split transferences can be experienced and integrated, where the move from isolation to empathic attunement can take place at the pace each member can manage, and where bodily levels, as well as transference and projective levels of functioning can be explored. I have deliberately chosen examples of the most difficult alexithymic or psychosomatic patients. Less severe pathology can be resolved on the same principles often with greater ease. But in treating psychosomatic problems in group we have to bear in mind several important points.

Concluding maxims

Therefore I'll finish with six maxims as a guide to therapy with such people, and as a starting point for discussion:

1 Profound disturbance necessitates support and preparedness to intervene (beware of dropouts).
2 We need to contain anxiety, pain, helplessness and rage.
3 The meanings of physical phenomena have to be discovered (or created) for soma to be mentalised.
4 The therapist/others need to name feelings.
5 We need to facilitate communication at deep levels.

6 Therapists need to 'listen' with their body as well as their ears, including bodily countertransference (Yassky 1973; Brown 1977; Taylor 1977; McDougall 1978; Janssen and Wienen 1995).

A recent paper 'Group Analysis with Ulcerative Colitis and Regional Ileitis: the Discovery of the Scream' (Janssen and Wienen 1995) describes how the scream was first detected in the countertransference of the group conductor.

If we think back to the two clinical vignettes we can see these maxims illustrated. For example: (1) my need to offer Richard an individual session in order to hold him in the group; (2–6) my need to tolerate anxiety about whether the group situation could contain the underlying pain and rage of both Richard and Rona; my sharing the image of Auschwitz for Rona's group; and the need to experience tears – Richard's tears – and put them into words. All these need to be tolerated, shared and understood by the group for alexithymia to be modified – in the alexithymic patient and the alexithymic part of all the group members, including the conductor.

3

THE ROYAL ROAD TO THE MYSTERIOUS LEAP

The psychosoma and the analytic process

Introduction

This chapter attempts to bridge two of Freud's major early insights. The first is his reference to dreams as the Royal Road to the Unconscious (Jones 1956: 38), the second his discovery that physical hysterical symptoms are psychogenic. The latter left us on the brink of what was sometimes called the Mysterious Leap from mental to physical. What I am proposing is that the analytic treatment of psychosomatic processes enables us to bridge the gap between these two ideas, but in ways that Freud had not envisaged – in short, that the analytic treatment of people with psychosomatic problems and little capacity to dream is the Royal Road to the Mysterious Leap.

Freud discovered that the symbolic meaning of symptoms of hysterical conversion could first be uncovered by the catharsis of dammed up emotions arising from early trauma and later by free association. Treatment involved physical symptoms being *converted back* into their previously unbearable psychological form. What he did not foresee is the later psychoanalytic understanding that many psychosomatic difficulties arise in preverbal, presymbolic experiences. They may never have *had* a psychological form, and they may be based more in psychotic parts of the personality than in neurotic mechanisms. Their treatment may involve the *creation* of meaning and symbolisation by individuals who for one reason or another remain restricted to the somatisation of distress, as in early infancy. The modern concept of *alexithymia* – not having words for feelings – refers exactly to this restriction (Taylor 1987), and I shall return to it shortly.

Emergence and separation

You will recall that Freud (1923: 26) spoke of the ego as 'first and foremost a body ego'. Mental functions gradually emerge from bodily functions in the first year or two of life, as does a sense of self from the original infant–mother unit. Development thus involves a process of desomatisation, as described by Freud's physician Max Schur (1972). This of course is what

Bion (1970) implies in his concept of a protomental state, prior to the development of the capacity for thought and imagery, before primitive body impulses and sensations – what he called *beta* functions – are replaced or joined by *alpha* functions.

Joyce McDougall (1974) holds that the process of differentiation of mind and body can be interfered with by the principal attachment and caring figures being either too distant or too consistently close and impinging, and that *either* can predispose to both psychosis and psychosomatic disorder. I shall return to these alternatives in considering the results of some earlier non-analytic research I was involved with in the 1950s and 1960s.

In addition to the mother–infant dyad it seems likely that *families* which do not provide psychological containment nor allow the expression and reception of affects, also perpetuate somatisation by not talking about feelings, and by giving support and attention only when children are physically distressed or ill. It is well known that many emotionally and psychiatrically disturbed patients present with physical symptoms – indeed in general practice in Britain it is the commonest presentation (Murphy 1989).

In a controlled trial of psychiatric treatment in over 80 cases of eczema (Brown and Bettley 1971; Brown 1972, 1976b), two-thirds complained spontaneously or on direct enquiry of new psychological symptoms, which in the majority of cases clearly *preceded* the onset of eczema. However, one-third denied them, though sometimes with non-verbal evidence of emotional disturbance currently, or earlier in the course of the eczema. It was the one-third who denied new psychological symptoms – and whom I labelled Superstable – who were most like the primary alexithymics. They tended to use primitive mechanisms of denial, splitting and projection to defend against awareness of emotional disturbance. They often dealt with guilt by blaming others. They sometimes presented an almost schizoid detachment from feeling of any sort. This often produced a mask-like face which seemed to be rigidly controlling all emotion. Quite often they dealt with depression by adopting a hypomanic cheerfulness and overactivity. From these findings I learnt that with patients unwilling or unready to talk about themselves or their feelings, we have to be especially alert to such signs as the shaking hand or the moistening eye – that is to the level of *body language* – as well as such negative signs as avoidance of certain topics or feelings.

Paradoxically, physical signs and symptoms can be both communications and blocks to communications. It depends on how much and what patients are prepared to know and share, but also how much we are prepared to hear and see, how much we are able to enquire and tune into their experience (Wolff 1977).

Motivation is essential if the psychotherapy of psychosomatic patients of all types is to begin. As I mentioned earlier, the *meaning* of physical symptoms and expressions needs to be discovered, and at the most primitive level *created* for mentalisation to bypass, reverse, or better still, grow out of somatisation. This calls for trust *on both sides*, that anxiety, pain helplessness and rage can be tolerated.

Earlier studies and the question of organ choice

We now recognise alexithymia as being an important element in predisposing people to psychosomatic disorders in general, but also to be a characteristic of many addictions and perversions, and of post-traumatic stress states, such as that of the woman I have just described (p. 20). Why people develop one form of psychosomatic disorder rather than another is now often explained in terms of genetic predisposition or environmental factors rather than specific personality types or focal conflicts, common subjects of research in the 1940s, 1950s and 1960s.

In my early studies I attempted to elicit personality factors predisposing people to develop contact dermatitis to commonly occurring allergy-producing substances – poison ivy among students in New York State (Brown 1959a), and dinitrochlorobenzine in a large chemical works in Yorkshire (Brown and Young 1965a, 1965b). Such a predisposition tended to be associated on the Rorschach Inkblot test with an experience of the body image as firmly bounded, in keeping with research (Fisher and Cleveland 1958) that indicated high 'Barrier Scores' in people suffering from body boundary disorders (e.g. skin and musculo-skeletal systems) compared with those suffering from internal disorders (e.g. gastrointestinal ones). Other traits such as lower ego strength, lower threshold of anxiety, and a greater degree of erotic frustration and affect or touch hunger depended on their being what we called *pseudo-introverts*, i.e. social introverts prone to impulsiveness or thinking extraversion (Guilford 1940). If they were *pseudo-extraverts*, i.e. social extraverts tending to rumination or thinking introversion, they were more constricted and rigid in personality.

For the purpose of this paper the complex statistics of personality traits dependent on the introversion–extraversion dimensions are less important than the overall picture of a discrepancy between orientation inwards or outwards. *Clinically* it is not so much a *general* orientation as an 'encapsulated' urge involving conflict and defensive somatisation.

With psychoanalytic hindsight one could now ask whether the divergence between introversion and extraversion could be explained by the role the skin plays as a psychic envelope, as the psychoanalysts Esther Bick (1968), Dinora Pines (1980) and Didier Anzieu (1989) suggest. Could the envelope be too thin or too rigid?

Bick (1968) proposed that the mother is experienced concretely as a skin, a containing object. Her capacity to contain the infant's anxiety is introjected by the infant, giving rise to the notion of internal and external space. Failure to accept the containment of self and object in separate skins gives rise to pseudo-independence and to 'adhesive identification' and inability to recognise the separate existence of self and object. Pines (1980) drawing on her experience as a dermatologist and her analysis of a woman with a history of infantile eczema, pointed to the key role of the skin after birth in re-establishing the mother's intimate feelings for her baby, as when the mother's skin contained them both. Later it has a key role in establishing the boundary of the self and non-self. It is, Pines writes:

> one of their most primitive channels for preverbal communication, where non-verbalised affects may be somatically experienced. Through her handling of the child the mother's skin may convey the full range of emotions from tenderness and warmth and love to disgust and hate. . . . The infant may react through its skin to the mother's positive feelings by a sense of well-being, and to her negative feelings by a skin disorder, which can take varying forms. The child's non-verbalised affects may find expression through the skin. The skin may itch, the skin may weep and the skin may rage. It will be dealt with by the mother according to her capacity to accept and soothe her blemished child.
>
> (Pines 1980: 315–23)

To return to my non-analytic research findings one could ask if the introvert–extravert divergence is based on a longing for contact in pseudo-introverts and avoidance of contact in pseudo-extraverts. We might postulate that in the introverts the skin holds the anxious person together and expresses their wish for contact with others. In the extroverts it reflects their rigidity and their wish for a barrier to withdraw behind. With further analytic hindsight one could wonder whether such divergences reflect a fundamental orientation springing not only from Jung's typology of introvert and extravert, but at a 'deeper' level from the infant's earliest experience in differentiation from a primitive symbiosis with a mother who is *either too distant or too impinging*. You will recall Joyce McDougall's (1974) claim that either can predispose to both psychosomatic disorders and psychosis. Perhaps our findings point to why this should be so.

Clearly we are into the realm of speculation. While surveys using controlled trials can point to trends, clinical engagement with individuals is necessary for more focused study involving emotional interplay.

Clinical studies

One of the series of eczema patients included in the controlled trial of psychiatric treatment in eczema (Brown and Bettley 1971) was in his twenties. He had had infantile eczema and was subject to attacks of asthma. I mistakenly attempted short-term analytical psychotherapy on the couch. He quickly became paranoid and semi-psychotic, necessitating my moving him from couch to chair, and adopting a less analytic and more supportive role with rapid improvement in both his psychological and physical states.

I should have known better, even though I had not yet started analytic training, but at least I learnt that in treating psychosomatic disorders we have to provide a setting that is safe and containing enough to hold and make sense of deeply disturbed and disturbing affects. If we cannot provide it in individual or group therapy we shouldn't start, though the level and degree of disturbance might not be obvious at first.

One of the advantages of groups is that psychological mindedness can develop gradually, whether in the group as a whole in specialised psychosomatic groups, or in one or several psychosomatic patients or somatisers in a mixed group – commoner in group analytic practice.

An individual case, Miss Y, allows us to see that it is less the treatment modality that matters than the capacity of the setting, the patient and the therapist to contain and make sense of disturbance at the deepest level of neediness, anxiety, pain and rage. (Incidentally this reminds me of the title of a recent article entitled 'Group Analysis with Ulcerative Colitis and Regional Ileitis: subtitled The Discovery of the Scream', Janssen and Wienen 1995. Interestingly in the paper the authors describe the wish to scream arising first in the countertransference of the therapist.) Miss Y originally came to me over 20 years ago as a trainee in one of the helping professions. She was a skilled professional who had made a lot of her life despite a disastrous beginning. She was the fifth child and only daughter of an overburdened and depressed mother, and a sexually abusing father whose contempt for her was echoed to varying degrees by her four brothers. She had survived but at great cost. In childhood she had sought solace in masturbation, in her inner fantasy world and in a solitary relationship with landscape. Burdened with low self-esteem and guilt Miss Y's adolescence and young adulthood were handicapped by severe agoraphobia and separation anxiety.

Paraphrasing Kohut, I had thought of referring to 'The Two Analyses of Miss Y'. Her first analysis with me was part of her professional training as a psychotherapist and lasted about six years. It was good enough for her to qualify, despite the fact that I felt, and frequently interpreted, that she was avoiding letting herself be dependent upon me. We learned a great deal about her early experiences and object relationships, but something was missing in the transference and countertransference. One might say that my own feeling of 'missing out' was a countertransference response to being mistrusted.

Six years after completing the first analysis Miss Y suddenly developed acute rheumatoid arthritis. By this time both her parents were dead and although her work was going well, she was in a relationship dominated by conflict with a married man, and the youngest of her brothers was developing a severe and eventually fatal depression. He was the one with whom she had been the closest, and the least involved in aping father's denigration of her. The rheumatoid arthritis threatened her livelihood which involved a good deal of travelling, her great joy of playing a musical instrument, and the appearance of her hands which she maintained were her best physical feature.

Miss Y clearly needed skilled physical treatment, but it also seemed that the breakdown of her physical health represented the breakdown of the precarious structure of self-sufficiency with which she had defended herself in the first analysis. She half recognised this, and quite readily agreed to explore a new second phase in her analysis. She realised that she was burdened by the needs of others and needed to find a way of safely putting her own needs into my hands. However she was still not ready to re-enter analysis. We had monthly sessions for a year or so, and in this time the acute phase of the rheumatoid arthritis settled with treatment by gold and steroids.

Eventually we agreed to start meeting four times a week. Quickly the issue arose of her need to control the closeness of the relationship. She needed to be alone but also feared both abandonment and intrusion. In terms of Joyce McDougall's threats of her primary objects being too distant or too impinging, she had both, respectively maternal and paternal. Both types of relationship have been experienced strikingly in the transference.

When the second analysis was approaching its end Miss Y's rheumatoid arthritis was no longer a major issue. What had been central throughout this second analysis were her deepest needs for containment, holding and empathic attunement. The sense of falling into a black hole, and dreams about buildings collapsing have, we discovered, been reflections of an unbridgeable gulf between us – as between her and mother in early infancy and throughout childhood – and of having to create her own 'false self' structure. Miss Y has had a sequence of truly catastrophic responses to what I had regarded as minor failures, e.g. of understanding, memory or bad time-keeping. Initially the consequences of these would last many sessions, latterly they could be coped with within a session. I believe this change is connected with what Kohut (1977: 87) described as 'failures of the self-object leading, under normal circumstances, to structure building via transmuting internalisation'.

It might be instructive to refer back to Fisher and Cleveland's work on body image and both physiological reactivity and the site of psychosomatic pathology (Fisher and Cleveland 1958). I have not submitted Miss Y to a Rorschach test. But her need to keep herself intact by overactive attention to the needs of others would accord with their finding that arthritis patients have high Barrier Scores and low Penetration Scores. Miss Y's frequent dreams of collapsing buildings and of falling I believe sprang from the collapse of her former adjustment and her anxious transition to *really* risking dependence on me – unlike in the first analysis. Interestingly, as her arthritis and self-sufficiency became less central concerns, so did gastrointestinal disturbance become more prominent. I believe this reflected a greater need for me to contain and hold her needy baby self, which made her both more touchy and sensitive, and more in danger of impingement. Amongst other things, this involved a fear of my intruding on her, as did her sexually abusive father.

Conclusion

I hope this personal account of my encounter with psychosomatics has not been too diffuse. To me the thread has been about the struggle to *integrate* bodily and mental experiences, and orientation towards the self and others. This involves engaging the *understanding* of the healer, and preferably also the sufferer, at a deep, primitive and unconscious level. The concept of *alexithymia* is of great use in understanding the clinical encounter, and in considering predisposition to psychosomatic symptoms and disorders. The integration of bodily functions, and their interface with mental functions and relationships can be related to the body image, or body schema. We could think of the body schema as forming the physical subjective experiential frame corresponding to the ego and body ego in classical Freudian theory. The body, like the ego, can be conceived of as providing protection from and as a launching pad towards others.

Psychosomatic symptoms and disorders in our days, like hysterical conversion in Freud's, embody the Mysterious Leap between mind and body. Their treatment, like the analysis of dreams, can provide another Royal Road to the Unconscious, revealing disavowed and split-off aspects of the person within his or her matrix of relationships, even from a time – in Enid Balint's words – 'Before I was I' (Balint 1993), before body and mind were differentiated. Their treatment is the Royal Road to the Mysterious Leap.

Part 2

PSYCHOANALYSIS AND GROUP ANALYSIS

4

DROWSINESS IN THE COUNTERTRANSFERENCE

Following Freud, we have aimed to maintain during analysis an attitude to our patients which he called 'evenly suspended attention' (Freud 1912). We try to avoid excessive and exclusive interest in details of what our patients say and do lest selection hinder perception of the subtler clues and patternings which may be the only derivatives of the unconscious elements we seek to discover. Too specific or intense interest and involvement suggest to us that we are colluding with our patients' impulses, fantasies or defences, or using them to buttress our preconceptions or for our own needs, e.g. for gratification or to establish contact with aspects of ourselves. Likewise, lack of interest and inattention indicate a possible block in the analytic process, something to be reckoned with in patient, analyst or both.

Enid Balint (1968), writing of the continuing importance of this analytic stance in her discussion of Freud's metaphors about the analyst functioning as 'mirror' and 'receiver', states that this is even more important with less severely disturbed neurotic patients, as the disturbances of those patients nearer to the psychotic end of the spectrum are more powerful and thus less likely to be distorted by the analyst's interference. The patients with whom I had the experience which led to this paper, though very different, both showed pathology at a primitive level of development, and it is reasonable to suppose that the great impact of the experience of drowsiness in the analyst is related to this as well as to the *force* of the provoking processes in the patient. Also they both evinced a marked potential for regression, which tends to foster countertransference complications, as Kernberg (1965) has pointed out. These opinions supported my impression that the origin of the experiences lay at least as much in my patients as in me.

Countertransference, in the restricted sense recommended by Sandler *et al.* (1973: 61), and adopted here, refers to the *specific emotional responses aroused in the analyst by the specific qualities of his patient*. It is transmitted through such processes as preconscious empathic contact, adaptive use of the primary process (Schafer 1959), and projective identification. The analyst in a state of 'evenly suspended attention' scanning the surface of his own consciousness as well as the surface of the patient's manifest communications, is prepared to be surprised by glimpses, as it were, of 'fish among the weeds under the water'. Inexplicable feelings, fantasies, even dreams can be projected on to this screen. A recent case, in analysis for three years, provoked in me what could be seen as the negative of these – drowsiness. This was felt as an overwhelming paralysis of thought and feeling, accompanied by a wish to withdraw and sleep, which the patient would seemingly be aware of only occasionally.

The drowsiness threatened my function as an analyst, and would have prevented the registration and recall of some sessions. It required an effort of will to decide to take an interest in the phenomenon, and try at least to recall something of the way drowsiness related to other material in the sessions. There always seemed to be a danger of clinging to understanding as to a straw, though ultimately an emerging trust in the understandability of what was happening reduced my anxiety and let me go along with it. Thus I stopped interfering with it by fighting it. In other words, priority was given to Freud's recommendation to aim at 'evenly suspended attention' over his injunction not to make a determined effort to register and recall (Freud 1912). At times the aim became to remain capable of attention by attending to what seemed to prevent it. The validity of the experience appeared to be confirmed in this analysis by the regular emergence of certain psychopathological associations and the uses to which these could be put. These form the main clinical basis of the present paper. But it also seemed to be confirmed by experience with a patient who started analysis during the latter part of the first analysis, and by recollections of rare but clear countertransference reactions of drowsiness during many years in psychotherapeutic and analytic practice. In the past these were treated as a nuisance. A review of the literature reveals that my observations are not new, but it is hoped that by drawing attention to the findings of others and presenting some of my own, others will be reminded of similar experiences and the value of recognising them as meaningful. The paucity of detailed descriptions of this phenomenon in the literature is likely to stem from our reluctance to admit to these occurrences, to the difficulty of remembering the details, and to the neglect of its possible significance rather than to its rarity in clinical practice. It is proposed to start by singling out some relevant papers which might have contributed to my being alerted earlier in the course of the analysis.

Review of literature

Sandler *et al.* (1973) have skilfully traced the historical changes in analysts' views of countertransference since Freud (1910) first used the term. They point out the residual confusions and disagreements arising particularly from too wide and general definitions, and recommend that we restrict the term as mentioned above. A notable trend through the years has been the recognition of the inevitability of countertransference, and its harnessing for therapeutic ends, much as transference changed in earlier years from being a nuisance to being one of our most valued tools.

Nearly 40 years ago Alice and Michael Balint (1939) wrote about the impossibility of controlling all countertransference phenomena. They asserted that our individual techniques must incorporate ways of satisfying our own needs, and that we need to be conscious of these as well as the impact on us of our patient's transferences, in order to distinguish them. Winnicott, although he has described countertransference as based on those neurotic features of the analyst which spoil his professional attitude and performance (Winnicott 1960), elsewhere describes the value of recognising powerful countertransference feelings, particularly in the analysis of severely disturbed and psychotic personalities (Winnicott 1949). He drew attention to the fact that hate and fear as well as love are felt by people professionally involved with such patients. Recognition of this can liberate us from unnecessary guilt and anxiety. Perhaps the same can be said about drowsiness.

But it was Paula Heimann (1950) who gave the most coherent and persuasive impetus to our changing attitudes. She described how the analyst notices feelings which it is his task to sustain and use, rather than discharge them as the patient does. These feelings which develop through rapport with the patient cannot be understood in terms of the patient's immediate associations, but point to a role which the patient is forcing on the analyst. About the same time Annie Reich (1951) warned of the difference between 'healthy' and 'pathological' countertransference interest during analysis in terms of the former being desexualised and sublimated in character. Racker (1957) has particularly emphasised the role of object relationships in countertransference. In the light of present-day understanding it stands to reason that feelings arise within object relations (even though these might be essentially narcissistic) but, if we are trying to decide whether our countertransference feelings are 'healthy' or 'pathological', and stem primarily from the patients or ourselves, we need to think about who is feeling what about whom, and who is making whom feel what about whom; which part of whom, representing whomever, whose wishes or prohibitions; the presence of whom, the absence of whom, etc., as well as what feelings are being expressed, repressed or split off. Indeed the object may be more crucial than the feeling in understanding countertransference phenomena; so too may the Self (Jacobson 1964; Lichtenberg 1975).

M. Blake Cohen (1952) in a valuable review article includes drowsiness, sleepiness and difficulty in attention as one of a provisional list of 16 responses through which the analyst can recognise that he is involved anxiously or defensively with the patient. She comments:

> Sleepiness in the analyst is very frequently an unconscious expression of resentment at the emotional barrenness of the patient's communication, perhaps springing from a feeling of helplessness on the

> part of the analyst. When the analyst recognises that he is sleepy as a retaliation for his patient's uncommunicativeness, and that he is making this response because, up to now, he has been unable to find a more effective way of handling it, the precipitating factor – the uncommunicativeness – can be investigated as a problem.
>
> (Blake Cohen 1952: 231–43)

Menninger (1958: 88) also includes persistent drowsiness of the analyst in the analytic hour among no fewer than 22 signs of countertransference.

There are, however, very few detailed clinical descriptions of these phenomena in the literature. Dean (1957) describes two analyses in which he felt intense drowsiness in response to tenacious, defiant and challenging resistance which produced feelings of powerlessness and discouragement that made him drowsy until he recognised it, and told the patients what he thought their attitudes to be. These could be seen as examples of transference resistance, as can the phenomenon described in this paper, though for different reasons.

Dickes (1965) describes a hypnoid state (usually termed fatigue, drowsiness or sleepiness) occurring in patients and analyst as well as in such everyday situations as the theatre. In his view it represents an ego defence against unacceptable sexual and aggressive impulses related to repressed memories. He presents instances from his own practice, as well as from the literature, starting with Ferenczi (1914) writing about hypnoidal states in patients. Dickes's severest cases were exposed to *major trauma in childhood during which the hypnoid state was used defensively*. This is certainly true of the principal patient here.

Miller (1972) describes how his falling asleep in an analytic hour came to be understood, through his patient's reaction to this and the analyst's analysis of a preceding dream of his own. It was related to the patient's childhood Oedipal wishes towards her father who used to fall asleep after she had woken him at night and gone downstairs with him feeling sexually excited. The understanding of this in the transference led to a resumption of analytic empathy and to the patient giving up the monotonous stream of trivialities that had characterised the previous two weeks of analysis. Pearl King (personal communication 1974) tells of a case in which her own countertransference drowsiness came to be understood as related to her patient's experience in childhood of his father withdrawn behind his newspaper. This links with Racker's emphasis on the role of object relationships in countertransference phenomena, and the themes of regression, withdrawal and absence which are prominent in the cases presented in this paper.

McLaughlin (1975) makes a very valuable examination of the phenomenon using, as illustrative material, both an episode in psychotherapy he had conducted and episodes in analyses conducted by two candidates he had supervised. He points out how our receptivity in a state of free-floating attentiveness makes us susceptible to the regressive pull of the patient's dynamic concerns and our inner reverberation to these. We have to be able to succumb to many inner experiences, among them *sympathetic identification* (feeling feelings like the patient) and *reciprocal identification* (feeling feelings that would be appropriate for the transference object in the patient's past and its counterpart in our own inner world). Sustaining the analytic atmosphere in a state of reduced motility and heightened sensory responsiveness, allowing himself to regress 'in the service of the patient' and restricting his discharges to 'high-level synthetic functions of the ego in assessing and communicating with the patient', balancing between activity and passivity and between sleep and wakefulness, involves a strain in the analyst which inevitably leads to disturbances in the balance at times. True countertransference responses, McLaughlin believes, are less frequent than those arising in the analyst from physical and emotional depletion, by which he means periods of fatigue and reduced interest in the outside world which can be attributed to illness or the drain of external demands, but often turn out to be 'depressive, masochistic and psychasthenic reflections of heightened internal conflict and narcissism'. Sleepiness as a recurring phenomenon is particularly likely to develop in 'devoted physicians' in whom fatigue and overcommitment are reactive attempts to expiate for competitive, destructive and erotic strivings. Regression into sleep is an escape from both a neurotic need to be overburdened, and the revived hunger and narcissistic rage which this expiation increases.

McLaughlin describes three types of patients with whom the phenomenon is likely to occur. The commonest is what he calls *passive-obsessional and narcissistic character disorders*, who use isolation, inactive rumination, concealment and displacement of affects, to control and dull into passivity the patient himself as well as others. The analyst often reacts with *boredom* to the patients' efforts to keep him soothed and at a comfortable distance. The next category is *borderline and chronic psychotic* patients, whose negation of the therapeutic alliance and the basic rule seem to destroy the analyst's identity and reduce him to *rage and despair, from which he retreats* to sleep as a defence and narcissistic solution. Thirdly, there are patients whose '*character defences and areas of specific conflict are too similar to those of the analyst or of important transference objects from the analyst's past*' [all italics mine]. This group provides the most striking and revealing instances of the phenomenon, as the episodes are more isolated and dystonic, surprise the analyst and prompt further self-analysis.

It is difficult for me to fit my patients into exclusive categories along these lines. Both could be seen as fitting (along with me) into the third category, but Jane in some small but crucial respects belongs to the first, and Margaret belongs to both the first and second category. But the material will speak for itself, I hope, and support the idea that the countertransference drowsiness reflects a characteristic defence of the patients which involves withholding an aspect of themselves in order to preserve it *and* the relationship with which they believe it to be incompatible. McLaughlin concentrates on the factors within the analyst which lead to his sleepiness. Here attention is confined to those factors in the patient to which the analyst responds with sleepiness. It is proposed that this experience of drowsiness casts light upon important details of history and psychopathology.

Clinical material

Patient A

The analysis which first aroused my interest in this topic was of a highly gifted and organised professional woman who showed a remarkable facility to regress from an early stage. From infancy she had been prone to attacks of vomiting, frequently associated with states of drowsiness. As in Dickes's cases, analysis showed these drowsy states to be defensive, but also expressive and used to assert control in relation to a possessive narcissistic foster-mother whose need for the child was played upon *and in whom states of drowsiness were induced as a way of controlling and getting revenge*. Inevitably I questioned how much my accesses of drowsiness, often intense and sudden, represented my own ego-defences – my patient is an attractive woman who happened to be my own age, and thus of a twin sister. But gradually they became an orientating focus, especially in the first two years of a three-year analysis. They ceased to be threatening, felt as an obstacle and something to be anxiously combated. When they appeared I was on the lookout for repressed or split-off instinctual material, naturally in myself, but increasingly in the patient, particularly in relation to the transference. When they receded I often sensed that the analysis had resolved something for the time being; indeed they were frequently followed by successful regression and progress in integration.

> Jane was illegitimate. Father was a successful artist who visited her occasionally in her first nine years. Mother, a resident housekeeper, went back to work immediately after her birth, leaving her in the institution where she was born until she was fostered at the age of four months. She visited Jane fairly regularly; and later indulged her with cream cakes and ice cream to the point of nausea, but deprived her of a feeling of real caring, whilst holding out a fantasy of setting up a happy home with her which was never realised. This was finally extinguished when Jane was 12 years old, by her mother's marriage to a very rich man in whose Rolls Royce she now visited her.
>
> When taken into foster-care by an elderly working-class couple, the four-months-old baby's survival was in doubt, so puny was she and so wracked with vomiting and retching. Her foster-mother,

> however, rose to the challenge. She was a professional, seemingly needing to care for young dependent children (she adopted two in addition to her own children, and took in several foster-children), and resenting their developing independence. Jane remembered frequent rows over payments; her moralistic foster-mother often threatened to tell mother of her misdemeanours and have her sent to an orphanage, and yet systematically denigrated both her parents. The foster-father was a remote, mysteriously rough and masculine figure with whom she had an exciting relationship of mutual provocation and respect. Her own father's succumbing to her foster parents' denigration and discouragement by going away, not to return, when he tried to visit her for the last time, was felt as a great betrayal and loss.
>
> Jane continued, throughout childhood, to have frequent attacks of 'stomach trouble', for which she was often kept off school. Then she was shown motherly concern by her foster-mother. Somehow she managed to survive and thrive, despite great feelings of rejection and shame about her abandonment and lack of secure status. She frequently felt that she had no room for herself – as though she was just a series of adjustments to others. Perhaps she managed by maintaining her secrets – her loyalty to the validity of her own feelings and fantasies – through her capacity to withdraw. She got married early to a man who promised to be a father-figure, but quite soon revealed his deep addictive personality problems. He came to use her as a strong container and colluded with her false-self organisation. (Of course, in some sense this suited her – all her weakness, self-indulgence and disorganisation was in him.) She could not be weak with him and had to be the responsible one for both of them and their two children. It was his death by suicide which plunged her into a state that was more an acute crisis of identity than a simple bereavement reaction, and which brought her into analysis.

The *first year* of analysis was marked by the recognition of the phenomenon of countertransference drowsiness and its relation to Jane's conflicts over regression and merging, her fear of closeness, dependence, destructiveness and loss, and to primitive techniques of splitting and projective identification with which she would control her objects as mentioned above; when she became more in touch with them, abdominal pain and vomiting developed, e.g. during breaks in treatment. In the *second year* the phenomenon was more clearly linked with conflicts over her libidinal feelings, particularly towards her father; and as she came to own these more, they gave rise to psychosomatic symptoms of intense chest pains and recurrent back pain linked with fantasies of incorporating his penis (e.g. when sliding down between his knees as a toddler.) Finally, in the *third year* countertransference drowsiness steadily disappeared as dreams, fantasies and affects became increasingly available and Jane seemed more truly and completely present in the sessions, more integrated and yet more able to tolerate confusion and be disorganised. The phenomenon did re-emerge briefly in the final weeks of analysis in response to her rage at abandonment, but its transience now seemed to be a function of her readiness to acknowledge and express her feelings and fantasies. The countertransference drowsiness (CTD) came to be seen to reflect:

(a) Self-sufficiency as a defence against total regression to a longed-for but dreaded dependence and merging, and thus both abandonment and loss of self. (At times I felt her to be analysing herself regardless of my presence.)
(b) Control of an object who threatened possession *and* rejection, and whose need of Jane was provoked by withdrawal and mystification (foster-mother), but who also represented the needy part of herself; and of another object (foster-father) who threatened intrusion and flooding with excitement, and again, represents the intrusive curious part of herself.
(c) Defence against acknowledgement and expression of primitive affects of violent rage and longing, for fear of punishment and loss.
(d) A state of absenting herself in order to find herself at the moment of separation from fusion with a longed-for absent parent, to be herself, and to be true to her own potentiality (Khan 1960; Green 1974, 1975).

The following clinical details are presented in the hope of giving a flavour of the experiences which led to these hypotheses. It is difficult to know which instances will be most convincing and helpful. After all, it was the intensity and frequency of the experience, and the variety of its apparent determinants, which provoked my interest. However, a selection will have to suffice, the first few and then one from each year of the analysis.

1. The first experience of CTD in session 13 followed Jane being able to use the couch (session 4) and acknowledge both her vulnerability and her aggressive assertiveness. She had expressed guilt over her 'ruthlessness' in separating herself from her husband, saying 'enough' to him, feeling she had thus killed him by ceasing to tolerate his passivity and inability to take responsibility, which also represented a feared part of herself. She began to experience pleasure at giving up the organising and adult part of herself, but became anxious about her 'real' nature. She began to want to tolerate her confusion and contradictions, despite experiencing pain and grief, ostensibly in relation to a man with whom she felt she could establish a permanent relationship but who had decided to leave her. On the day that he left her (session 11) she recounted a story he had told about an injured cat that looked at him after his car had struck it, as though to say: 'Leave me alone, *and* don't leave me!' She was tremendously moved by this sign that he knew how she felt. She described the fragmented loyalties of her childhood and accepted my interpretation of her wish for someone to contain all of her – the hurt child, her love and her hostility – her wish for me to do this but her fear lest in so doing she would lose control of herself. In the next session she was aghast that she might be putting herself at the mercy of the needs of another (ostensibly the man friend, who had now expressed a wish to return for a few days but, in the context of the session, the analyst) so that there would be no room for herself in the outside world, as in her childhood. She asserted that she preferred the pain of the past week to resuming such compromises. In the thirteenth session she recounted how she had told the man to leave, but then went on to describe progress and recognition in her work in what seemed to be a defensively complacent and chattering way. As she went on CTD overwhelmed me. She stopped, and then talked about her foster-mother's funeral when she was 15 years old, when her mother appeared with a sheaf of flowers and left immediately. She accepted as true an interpretation of her fear, near the start of analysis, of being abandoned at the end – but now I see it as something more to do with long-existing anxieties about remaining intact and continuously herself despite the comings and goings of others who come to matter to her. In the next session CTD soon reappeared, and it emerged that she was afraid of her resentful destructive feelings challenging her ability to conjure up good experiences, as in childhood. Then she used to imagine killing everyone; e.g. when foster-mother asked what they should do when no money came in for her, she secretly imagined sticking a knife into her, which was what she felt was being done to her.

In the next session Jane felt much softer and less anxious. She could tolerate being alone in the house, as though I were there. She talked in the next few sessions about being miserable over the weekend, guilty about her destructiveness, and about her children having 'hate pains' in their stomachs when young – clearly a reference to herself – but she seemed much more real and present, and CTD was absent from two subsequent sessions. It then reappeared in two sessions, in the second of which she talked about her dreaminess and withdrawal as a child, which was tolerated by her foster-mother, but which incensed her mother. Then, following a weekend, she reported a disturbing regressive feeling in bed that morning in which her face and body swelled as into the shape of a rugby ball; she felt as though floating out of her depth, unable to put her feet on the ground and aware only of her mouth and eyes which had to be kept shut. This seemed to relate to a fear of dependency and regression which she had always fought off in the past. CTD cleared in the next session as her talk of the uselessness of protesting at her mother's comings and goings was accepted as belonging to the transference, and was then absent for a week.

Before the first (Christmas) break she became very anxious about abandonment, her dreams and associations contained a lot of references to food and eating, but also to the feeling in childhood that her stomach was controlled and owned by her foster-mother, and to the idea that she had something hard and stone-like created by herself inside. In one session she said she felt I was dreamy. This was correct and I admitted it and said I wondered what she was doing – perhaps shutting me out, making me feel shut out and useless, like a reflection of *her* dreamy withdrawal. She described how she did this with her foster-mother. She now recognised that her foster-mother's toleration of her going to her room contrasted with her provocation by subtler withdrawal, which Jane used to make her foster-mother anxious, when she felt threatened by her foster-mother's withdrawal – like mine over Christmas. Three sessions before the break, CTD resolved as her dreams and associations led to her fear of protesting lest she be thought unreasonable and so rejected. In the next session she said the exhaustion she felt yesterday was due to the effort to suppress anger, and indicated that she had reproached me instead by withdrawing.

Survival of this first break led to a considerable reduction of defensiveness, and CTD was rare except in relation to impending primitive rage and sexual excitement in the transference, especially at a level of narcissistic fusion and part-object relating, as seen in the next two examples.

2. After four months she told how as a child she felt she had nothing of her own, not even her body. I felt CTD for a short while as she went on to talk of closeness and affection being felt as a threatening intrusion. It cleared as she revealed a fantasy baby she had in her stomach as a child, self-created, which belonged to her completely in a way her own body did not, and *was kept a secret* from all. Having told me this, she became anxious that if she gave up the self-created baby she might not be able to rely on me to care for her *and* let her grow to independence; that is, she feared that without the secret she would not have the space in which to be herself and grow. My understanding of this leans heavily on the insights of Winnicott (1971) and Khan (1977). About this time I had to tell her that I would have to miss a midweek session in about a month but could see her on the Saturday. In the next session she spoke of her impotent rage when her soft cuddly toys were given away by her foster-mother without consulting her. It was only the imaginative things that were safe. I again experienced CTD intermittently as Jane talked about the giving away of a particularly important soft doll, a Dutch boy, e.g. at the points when she said:

- The doll was like a person who shared her bed, and suddenly it was not there.
- She had to kill the doll off, insisting it was just a doll without feelings.
- She subsequently turned 'nasty' with her foster-mother and felt for the first time in her life that she had power, albeit of a vicious vengeful sort.

Feeling extreme CTD I managed to comment that I felt something very heavy, and was it something she was doing with the strength of the rage she felt towards me? She said she felt fury at having something taken away and given to someone else, then grief at having to kill it in order to bear its loss. Finally she could link this with the missed session. In the following session she brought *a dream* that was clearly related to it, in which *there was a war and people were looting a shopping area. As a tank shot flames into a window, she grabbed a watch – not the most expensive one, but one worth a sum which was her sessional fee*. In the next session she talked about her inability to protest except in dreams, and how this started very early in her life. She would go off to cry and kick something on her own. She did this lest people discover her vulnerability and then feel they could do absolutely anything to her.

Two sessions later I again felt drowsy early on, and she described vividly the conflict which led to drowsiness in herself and her foster-mother when a child, and was alive in the session. She started by saying she does not know whether she is a child or an adult, but wants to be safe. She asked whether this meant she wants to push away a lot of threatening things. She wanted a coffee and cigarette before she came in to remain adult, and is now trying to stop herself from crying. She finds clinging so hard because she wants to curse at the same time, but like a child, she feels I would want to put her down and push her away. As a child she would be sent to her own room to simmer down if she showed any spirit. Feeling CTD I said to her that I felt that there was a drowsiness between us. She then recalled that when in this predicament as a child, she would sometimes feel sick, sometimes drowsy.

> I feel when I'm angry I'll be cut off somewhere – then I both feel drowsy myself, protectively, but also try to lull the other into it, so we can then both cuddle each other like a toy, then we can avoid the shouting, anger and vomiting. Then I'd feel safe again . . . If I really said 'I hate you' they'd put me away. The only way out was this withdrawn drowsiness. As a child I often drifted off. Sometimes I even fainted, usually when I vomited.

When asked whether she was feeling drowsy now, she said, less so, but her arms ached. She agreed with my linking this with her yearning to hold and be held by me and her anxiety about it.

It would seem therefore that Jane had to preserve a secret space, an analogue of a transitional object (Winnicott 1953) in which to be herself and grow, and to express longings and indignant rage which were denied expression in 'real life'. Because of her fear of ultimate abandonment she was unable to say 'go away'.

3. After about a year of analysis a major theme emerged, that of letting go and merging herself with the analyst. Initially the wish to lose herself in a 'harmonious and interpenetrating mix-up' (M. Balint 1968, Part 2: 35ff) encountered great anxiety lest it were satisfied and then stopped because of the intensity of her feelings. During this period CTD occurred when the rage of frustration or secret bodily excitements were near to expression, but usually disappeared as they were acknowledged and safely expressed. Before the first summer break she described a powerful image of herself as a tick which had been pulled away from its parasitised host leaving behind its arms and legs and thereby reduced to helplessness. After surviving the break and completing a year of analysis it was possible to regress into a state in which tension seemed to trickle down from her throat into her stomach, and then experience what I can best call an unanxious confusion as to whether she was outside or inside my abdomen as she imagined herself stroking it, and not knowing whether stomach noises were coming from her or me. This, like other episodes of regression, was followed by a process of integration, a greater tolerance of contradicting feelings and aspects of herself.

The libidinal material was related to excitement about her foster-father, but increasingly about the father who had ultimately deserted her. It was the emergence of this in the transference which seemed to determine a striking hysterical collapse with intense chest pain whilst driving to a session in the middle of the second year of analysis. This was so dramatic and convincing that I referred her urgently to a physician and was very relieved to find that she had not had a coronary infarction. (It is hoped to report the psychosomatic material in more detail elsewhere.) A few sessions later, in a session in which CTD gradually lifted, she brought material related to childhood masturbation and its prohibition, to fantasies from childhood of babies, not only self-created but also given by father, and to memories of hearing him say: 'You are *my* little girl!' Next session she reported drawing the chest pain, and discovering it looked like a vagina. After this CTD was absent for about 30 sessions.

Though ostensibly sexual, this material seems to be important in the context of this paper mainly because of its relevance to the emergence of Jane's self from a state of primary narcissism or, as I prefer to see it, of 'a harmonious and interpenetrating mix-up'. It is as though she needed to revisit the scene of 'criminal' interference with her development of flexible boundaries, so that she could be at one with and yet separate from someone whom she could love and hate with passionate intensity. CTD seems to reflect her anxious guarding of an inner space in which to build up internal objects.

4. Near the end of the second year, Jane returned from a weekend feeling empty and bereft, as though in a desert. She felt as though she was aware of something that she had been experiencing without knowing about it. She did not want to make any effort and could have been sick from the effort to talk. She felt limp and parched, and wanted to be completely looked after and understood without having to do or give anything. It was frightening because in the past she would have feared that this would result in her abandonment. She mused in a regressed way, as though a baby in a pram, about her sadness at her lack of ability to look at a branch or the sky and relate to it in a peaceful sharing. She associated this with seeing the external approach of a mother who meant a lot to her inside. It was as though she had always had to grab at things – a branch or sky – to get something to relieve the awful emptiness. In her words: 'So much of my frantic grabbing was like putting my teeth on a bit of bone. All the satisfaction was to have *something*, better than nothing. Perhaps this dazed feeling is to avoid getting into that "having briefly then losing completely" panic.'

The separation anxiety was very painful, and related to her drive to establish a good internal object which was threatened by her rage at the coming and going which bore no relation to the rhythm of her needs. *A dream* reported in this session was about *being in Ireland, and having to run the gauntlet of a trail of booby-traps which might at any time explode and prevent her reaching home.*

In the following session CTD was felt for the first time for a long while after she had begun by saying she felt depressed and miserable as she used to when bilious as a child. But she wanted to hold on to the misery and not give it up by organising. It was part of *her*. She was scared it might go on but now thought she trusted me enough not to let it. 'You will see if my eyes are closed (as they were most of last session) and know what it means – whether I'm asleep or dead or thinking.' She said she would kill whoever walked away, thinking about mother visiting her as an infant in the home, and then going away.

CTD developed strongly and, feeling she was doing something to me, I managed to say that I wondered if she was feeling that if I betrayed her she would withdraw and kill off her memory of a good analyst, a good mother. She replied, as the CTD lifted: 'That's why I don't want food – I don't want a bad horrible mother.' I said I thought she was saying that to me now, at the end of the session. At this she replied with a strong voice: 'I want to spit you out!' As she left, she looked at me with gentle closeness and a feeling of mutual intimacy. CTD was again absent for a considerable time.

It seems that in a state of regression to a very early phase of struggling for object constancy, the CTD reflected a split in her personality in which her deepest good and bad feelings were kept apart. Reduction of the split was paralleled in the analysis by disappearance of CTD.

5. The last experience of CTD was two weeks from the final session of the analysis, and the associated material seemed to condense much of the psychopathology already worked over. Much work was done towards the end of the analysis on her anxiety, grief, resentment and gratitude, integrating some of the deepest levels of her development with the processes of separation and internalisation. I had had to take a long-planned week off early in the final month, and CTD was marked in the first session following this premonitory break. Jane started the session by talking about how close she had felt to me during the week, but brought a *dream* in which she was *coming to the session in a taxi, which near my consulting room crashed into a man crossing the road and threw him on the bonnet*. CTD remained despite her coming to see how much her welcome concealed murderous rage at my 'stealing' a week from her. It was only in the subsequent session, in which CTD was absent, that she talked of trusting me not to retaliate and desert her if she told me how much she hated as well as loved me, and went on to reveal the full intensity of primitive rage. Her murderous fury was felt like hungry biting and gulping, leading to a fear of destroying what she wanted. Discovering I was still here, she said she had had to imagine me without arms and legs which could push her and walk away. [Her earlier images of herself as a rugby ball (section 1, above) and as a tick whose legs were left embedded in the host (section 3, above) came to my mind.] Wanting to say 'Come here, I love you!' but also, 'Come here I hate you!' she described choking and spluttering with rage, and wanting to pour out her feelings, not just down her front, but also over my back, so covering us and binding us together. She agreed that this was like her vomiting with hatred *not* confirming her isolation, but establishing the possibility of being both safely together and safely separate. As she left, she smiled and proudly announced that her only grandchild was now walking. It seemed clear to me that she was telling me this about herself.

Patient B

About this time another patient, Margaret, started analysis, a severely schizoid girl with borderline features, also very intelligent, with whom I experienced similar CTD, though much more rarely. She both longed for closeness and feared the helplessness and loss of herself in merging.

A vivid example of the way drowsiness in the analyst reflects an anxious withholding of herself by the patient occurred as follows. After about six months Margaret began to allow transference feelings to develop. In one session she started by saying she felt much nearer to me on the couch, as though she were much further up the couch than usual. She associated this to an experience in her teens which she had told me about some weeks before, in which she had secretly buried her face in one of her brother's suits hanging in the wardrobe. In the next session she said she must not talk about herself, and went on to speak about helping a distressed friend over the weekend, *before* the session previously described. During this time I felt intense CTD but said nothing about it. The next day Margaret came in and announced that *she had not been here the day before*.

A striking feature of Margaret's early relationship with her depressed and preoccupied mother was her feeling that mother's attention could never be relied on to match her own needs.

Discussion

In both analyses the CTD came to be understood as a response to the patient not being present in some important sense. This can be a transference resistance, an expression of hostile withholding and defiance (as in Dean's 1957 case) or a defensive denial of powerful aggressive or libidinal feelings. It can have a manipulative element in it in the sense of attempting to control a frustrating or intrusive object. But I feel that with both of my patients, most fundamentally, it represents a primitive splitting in which a whole part of the self is dissociated. By a process of projective identification, the analyst feels depleted or half alive, and thus disorientated and out of touch with the basis of what is most alive, or would be most alive at that time if the patient were truly there.

Another way of describing it might be that the analyst's mental ego is eclipsed by the patient's body ego, seeking but avoiding a state of merging. We might be helped here by the concept of ego defect postulated by Ammon (1974: 9) to be the core of psychosomatic disorders, which he sees as filling the 'hole in the ego' and which originate in a disturbance of the emergence of the ego out of the primary symbiosis with the mother. In our cases it might be seen as a functional ego defect which casts its shadow on the perceptual functions of the analyst's ego. Some of the material described in the first case (sections 2 and 3 above) can be seen as supporting this psychosomatic hypothesis, the defect being a rigidity or block in the boundary between mental and body egos. This can be seen as guarding against irruption and awareness of the primitive bodily matrix of urges and fantasies which, when they emerge, tend to do so using the un-neutralized primary processes characterised by Schur (1955) as typical of somatic reactions. Reduction of the functional block in states of regression led to emergence of the primitive material often along with somatic reactions, but this in turn permitted its processing at a 'secondary process' level, and hence its integration.

Khan (1960) describes very vividly a phase in an analysis in which his patient passed from a manic state into a regression felt by her as a 'state of being nothing'. This followed a breakdown into physical ill-health, with a severe cold and something described as mild asthma. She felt that until then she had been living neither in her body nor her mind, and had been unable to surrender to the transference relationship. During the regression the analyst relied very much on countertransference experiences. For example, he used his body, or body-ego, to perceive the intensity of this patient's pain. Through this she was able to regress to a 'true anaclitic dependence'. Khan saw his role as being there, alive but not impinging with any personal need 'to translate her affective experiences into their mental correlates'. In particular, his patient was intensely sensitive to any reduction in *body-attention*. (In a later paranoid stage it was his ego-attention that she needed and demanded.) It seems likely that CTD developed in Jane's analysis when her anxieties prevented maintenance of contact between us, perhaps particularly between our body-egos. As in Khan's case, integration was achieved through toleration of regression, for Jane, to a state of confusion of boundaries.

In his paper 'Hate in the Countertransference', Winnicott (1949) describes the anxiety provoked in therapists of psychotic and borderline patients by contact with a patient with seemingly no body; because of the patients' fears that emotional contact produces in the therapist 'the same crude and dangerous state of coincident love–hate which they are frightened of in themselves'. This certainly resonates with a consistent strand in Jane's analysis, which shows in the material presented here. That is not to say that she is a psychotic or borderline person, but that there has been such a core in which the traumatic first few months of her life were embedded. It might now be possible to propose that, in Jane's case, CTD developed out of a chain reaction, as follows:

1 *A powerful longing to merge* into the 'harmonious mix-up' of primary narcissism or primary love (Balint 1965: 14) *provoked intense fears* of attack, annihilation and abandonment based upon the paranoid-schizoid stage of her early development. These fears, and genetically superimposed fears of disapproval and punishment for libidinal and aggressive impulses which reactivated her earlier fears, led to
2 *transference resistance* and
3 *attempts to control her anxieties by controlling the objects* who are seen as dangerous but manipulable and also represented unacknowledged parts of herself, by
4 *withdrawal within the transference*, perhaps particularly from a primitive psychosomatic contact. This could be seen as absenting herself, or part of herself, or her body, via a process of (this might be the part most specific for Jane and others who are separated from important love objects)
5 *identification with absent parents* who are simultaneous but separate targets of excited longing and destructive rage, and the people she maintains a life-asserting contact with by reflecting their absence within herself. Their/her absence then becomes the secret core of her real self. (The image of a door into a secret garden often occurred to me when experiencing CTD.)
6 An alternative to (3), (4) and (5) is *psychosomatic symptom-formation* via regression to a state of re-somatisation (Schur 1955), or, as I like to think of it, dementalisation. (It seemed to me that through her psychosomatic crises we were better able to get at and integrate highly conflictual material, because through psychosomatic symptoms she was able to speak a richer language than she did by simply 'slamming the door' as she slipped back defiantly or anxiously into her 'secret garden'.)

When the speculation is finished, my experiences of drowsiness with Jane leave me with a question. Was the key paradox expressed by the twin claims: 'Leave me alone' and 'Don't leave me'? In other words: 'Give me space in which to be myself!'[1] When this seemed to be threatened by what was happening in the transference, she slipped back into the secret space she had always reserved for herself, her most prized objects and most dangerous and endangered drives and fantasies. As the pressures and anxieties lessened with analysis, she resorted to this less and less – as though the analytic space was tried and found to suffice.

It may be argued that the understanding reached for in this paper is insufficient to explain the occurrence of drowsiness in the countertransference. It might be that parallel exploration of the analyst's psychopathology should have been presented to build up a complete picture of what is by definition an interactional process. Whilst this is probably true, it might not be much more true than saying that we cannot analyse individuals without at the same time analysing all the relatives who are represented in their internal worlds, or even all those involved in their intimate social networks. What is more important is that this particular analyst was able to use countertransference drowsiness to monitor significant events in the analysis of these particular patients. Perhaps others can do so with their patients.

Summary

Drowsiness in the countertransference, in the sense of a specific emotional response aroused in the analyst by specific qualities of the patient, has been described but rarely illustrated in the literature. Clinical material is presented, chiefly from the analysis of one patient in which striking accesses of drowsiness in the analyst aided the understanding of certain basic needs, coping mechanisms and defences of the patient, such as the longing for and fear of fusion; the need to create a space in which to be herself and get in touch with absent objects; withdrawal as a way of controlling and mystifying; and splitting and projective identification. The phenomenon throws light on a possible disturbance of ego boundaries which is relevant to the emergence from primitive symbiosis and to somatisation reactions.

Acknowledgement

The author wishes to thank Dr Jonathan Pedder for reading the manuscript and making several helpful criticisms and suggestions.

1 Since writing this, a performance of Samuel Beckett's *Waiting for Godot* revealed to me that Estragon said virtually the same thing near the beginning of Act II: 'Don't touch me, don't question me, don't talk to me. Don't leave me!'

5

ASSESSMENT AND SELECTION FOR GROUPS

The initial consultation is a crucial meeting. It usually decides a person's suitability for group-analytic psychotherapy. Both patient and consultant assess the nature and significance of the presenting problems and their background. Both need to agree on the appropriateness of group analysis in the Practice as a way through them. This is a complex process and I shall therefore describe it in eight more or less consecutive stages:

1 Preparation for the consultation.
2 The nature of the assessment.
3 Selection of the most appropriate form of therapy.
4 Preparing the patient for a group.
5 Procedure for matching new members and the groups they join.
6 Management of the waiting list.
7 Limits of group analysis.
8 Several important issues, such as contact with referrers, cover over holiday breaks, private health insurance, claims and illness of the conductor.

Preparation for the consultation

All medically qualified members of the Management Committee,[1] currently six out of seven, see an average of one to three new referrals each week for consultation.[2] Patients are referred to these consultants personally or to the

1 The author refers to the work at the Group-Analytic Practice of which he was a member from 1975 to his retirement in July 2000.

2 Like other members of the Management Committee, the non-medically qualified person is well known within the referral network and beyond, is a qualified analyst as well as a group analyst, and has worked in the National Health Service as well as conducting training courses overseas. She gets patients referred to her for consultations, and because of the need for medical cover, one of the medically qualified members of the Management Committee will then see the patient in order to assess them for medical cover. We believe this provides an important safeguard, medical and psychiatric as well as legal.

Group-Analytic Practice as a whole through the Clinical Secretary or Administrator. Probably because the Practice is seen to function as a team, personal requests are often made to 'you or a colleague'.

Patients are usually seen within two to three weeks of the referral, sometimes sooner if spaces become available – for example, through cancellation. We regard anything longer than this as unsatisfactory, and if too much of a waiting period develops, we make arrangements for more consultation spaces. When the appointments are sent to patients they are requested to confirm that they will keep the appointment and a letter is sent to the referrers informing them. This enables the referrer to arrange to see the patient again before the appointment, should this be necessary, and to know when to expect to hear the outcome of the assessment.

Patients rarely fail to keep their appointments if, as requested, they confirm them. Such a failure is less likely if the waiting period for the consultation is not so great that they seek alternative help, or feel themselves to have improved spontaneously. Anxiety and misunderstanding about the referral, or poor motivation for self-exploration and radical change, are probably the main factors in failed attendances. It is perhaps not surprising that a failure to keep initial consultation appointments seems to be much rarer among self-referrals, particularly those resulting from the recommendation of an ex-patient or somebody currently in a group.

People referring themselves as well as new professional referrers are informed, when they phone, about the procedure, fees for consultations and therapy and, if appropriate, the nature of the Practice. (Sometimes enquiries are made by people in the belief that the practice is part of the National Health Service.) All patients are sent notes for guidance (see Figure 5.1) along with their appointment.

Nature of the assessment

At this point I shall be drawing on my own methods and experience, which I believe are basically the same as those of my colleagues. What happens in the consulting room when an individual assessment is made is inevitably private. Having introduced myself to the patient in the waiting room, greeting him or her with a customary handshake, we go to my consulting room where we sit in identical chairs to emphasise the joint nature of the evaluation. This is the room in which I conduct both individual and group analysis, so it gives the patient an opportunity to assess me in the atmosphere in which I work, while I assess both the patient and his or her problems, and our interaction.

I explain that we have an hour or so in which to talk in order to gain a better understanding of the problems that led the patient to seek help; and that at the end of this time we should be able to decide on the best way of arranging it. Indicating that I would like to hear about the problems and also the patient's background and development, I leave it to them to tell the story

Patients have occasionally attended for an initial consultation under the misapprehension that the diagnostic and treatment services available from the Group-Analytic Practice or its members are part of the National Health Service. This note is therefore enclosed to ensure that patients referred are aware that the initial consultation for diagnostic assessment, and any treatment which may subsequently be recommended, are on a private fee-paying basis.

The purpose of the first consultation is to examine and clarify the nature of the problem, to give an opinion whether or not it can be helped by any of the forms of individual, group, marital or family therapy available within the Group-Analytic Practice and, if it does appear treatable, to discuss the various possibilities so that the patient can reach a decision either during the interview or at a later date after further consideration.

The cost of the different forms of treatment is of course fully explained at the initial consultation, but if you do require more information in advance, the Secretary will be pleased to provide it for you if you telephone. However, you may like to know that the normal fee for the initial consultation is £ (or £ in the case of a married couple seen together and £ for a family). This is payable whether or not further treatment is in fact advised or arranged, and it is also chargeable if the interview is cancelled too late for the time to be offered to another patient. PLEASE GIVE US AS MUCH NOTICE AS POSSIBLE IF YOU CANNOT COME.

Figure 5.1 Notes for the guidance of patients referred for diagnostic assessment or treatment.

in their own way and order. Few of us write any notes during the assessment interview, but we all use the same 'assessment form' (see Figure 5.2) in the writing-up of the assessment afterwards.

This form provides an underlying structure to our collection of information in the consultation that facilitates efficient formulation by the consultant, and communication of this to the referrer, to colleagues at our weekly clinical intake meeting and to the therapist who eventually takes the patient on for treatment. It also frees us to attend to the details of the patient's story and also to how they tell it, to what they do not tell us spontaneously, to body signs and language, and to the interplay of communications between us. This includes transference and countertransference as they develop in the interview. It is important to discern whether and how the patient brings his or her problems into the consulting room through their relationship with the consultation procedure and ourselves.

However, direct questioning in some detail may be necessary in assessing the patient's response to any previous therapy, but particularly when there is a possibility that there is an underlying psychotic or organic condition. It might then be helpful to know about genetic loading, suicidal risk and so on. In such instances it is important to make a psychiatric diagnosis to facilitate communication with referrers, sometimes to ensure that the patient has psychiatric treatment in addition to or instead of psychotherapy.

For all types of psychotherapy my experience is that psychiatric diagnosis

PATIENT No.:

NAME____________________GROUP WITH_______DAY________TIME________

(Mr, Mrs, Miss, Ms, Dr)

ADDRESS____Tel: Home________

Work ________

AGE D.O.B. OCCUPATION____________________

MARITAL STATUS: Single/Married/Separated/Divorced/Widowed/Cohabiting

RELIGION______________________

INTELLIGENCE: Sup/Above Average/Average/Below Average

NATIONALITY___________________

SOCIAL BACKGROUND: Upper Mid/Middle/Lower Middle/Working

EDUCATION: University/Tech College/Public School/Grammar/Secondary/Comp/Primary

CAN ATTEND:

Morning: Monday/Tuesday/Wednesday/Thursday/Friday/Saturday Not before

Lunch: Monday/Tuesday/Wednesday/Thursday/Friday/Saturday Between

Evening: Monday/Tuesday/Wednesday/Thursday/Friday/Saturday Not before

REFERRED BY__________________ON________________LETTER___________

INITIAL INTERVIEW WITH__________ON________________LETTER___________

PRESENTING SYMPTOMS

PERSONALITY AND INITIAL CONTACT

DYNAMIC FORMULATION

(Continued)

PREVIOUS TREATMENT

Motivation: Strong/Moderate/Fair/Poor

Capacity for Insight: Strong/Moderate/Fair/Poor

Personality Resources: Strong/Moderate/Fair/Poor

Agreed Fee________________Once/Twice Weekly________________Leaflet Yes/No

FAMILY HISTORY

RELEVANT INFORMATION

Next of Kin______________________________ G.P.____________________

Address_________________________________ Address_________________

____ ______________________

____ ______________________

____ ______________________

Began Group Treatment________________________________

Ended Group Treatment________________________________

Result: Recovered/Relieved/Not Improved/Deteriorated

Reason for Leaving____

Letter to Referrer____

Figure 5.2 Assessment form.

is less important than the patient's balance of strengths and weaknesses. The former include their motivation for insight and change, and their creativity. Of particular importance is their capacity to engage with another person to begin to understand themselves and their relationships with others at greater depth without the danger of acting out or decomposition. The rule-of-thumb criteria I use for analytic as opposed to supportive or behavioural therapies are: (1) the patient's problems are understandable in psychological terms; (2) he has adequate motivation for insight and change; (3) has sufficient ego-strength; and (4) the capacity to form and sustain relationships (Brown and Pedder 1979). The history of even one good relationship can make a big difference in helping a person towards sufficient trust and toleration of frustration, especially in the short term.

A less tangible factor that can swing the balance towards long-term analytic therapy in doubtful cases is what (as a Yorkshireman) I can best call an element of 'grittiness' in the patient's personality. However chaotic or desperate he or she is, one senses a core of strength and determination in them that is very different from stubbornness. It is similar to what Rayner and Hahn (1964) called 'positive persistence', which (along with the capacity for self-appraisal and self-responsibility) they describe as a necessary characteristic for brief analytic psychotherapy. But what I am describing can be more covert, and may require much of the interviewer's intuition and countertransference to pick up. In cases of doubt I prefer to base the decision on how best to treat someone on the psychodynamic formulation (see below) rather than on impersonal psychiatric classification. However, commonly accepted generalisations are useful as a warning against over-optimistic therapeutic zeal when dealing with particularly vulnerable patients – such as those with a strong personal or family history of psychotic illness, or evidence of a serious personality problem, be it borderline, narcissistic, hysterical or obsessional.

The well-known generalisation that phobic states are best treated by behavioural therapy has probably more to do with the patient's predominant defences in such states (for instance, externalisation) and their generally poor motivation for self-responsibility and insight. There are exceptions to this general rule, which lead to some patients doing well with analytical psychotherapy, group or individual. Likewise, the fact that schizophrenics tend to do better with support and family intervention in the acute stages of the condition has, I believe, more to do with their ego-weakness, and if this can be restored with appropriate treatment, including medication and hospital care, some can later benefit from a more analytical and insight-orientated approach, especially in a group, albeit a gentle and supportive one.

The psychodynamic formulation is of greater importance to the patient than a psychiatric diagnosis; it is more meaningful and useful in furthering their self-understanding and less static and stigmatising in its implications. It is also more useful to the therapist who takes on the patient for treatment. It should reflect the developments and relationship problems that the patient has had in his or her family of origin and/or current networks, taking into account the effect of trauma, developmental deficit and unconscious conflict. It should give us some idea of the degree and developmental level of the psychopathology, and the possible hazards of treatment as well as mitigating factors. These latter will include any good early experiences and relationships, any areas of achievement in which a sense of self-worth could be developed, and satisfying current relationships, creative work and hobbies.

Of special interest when assessing indications for group psychotherapy is an appraisal of the social birth of the person. Did it allow the person to feel safely at home in himself or herself and with others, without excessive reliance on defences that are too primitive or too prominent? Or was it so traumatic and conflict-laden that it led to severe distortions and restrictions of character, and thus failure to achieve and attain life's rewards? This appraisal includes an assessment of difficulties in relation not only to parents but also to siblings, including those who have died or never been conceived. These can often help us to understand problems in establishing peer groups and a sense of belonging that require a therapeutic group to resolve.

In assessing ego-strength and motivation for insight and change, we have to consider both the patient's hold on external reality and their contact with their own inner selves. How they deal with stress, anxiety, frustration and loss are very important – including their experience in and finishing any previous therapy. How much can they bear without recourse to denial and splitting, dangerous loss of impulse control or self-destructive tendencies? Repeated risk-taking, resorting to addictive behaviour or serious somatisation into major psychodynamic diseases can indicate the overrunning of their limits. A history of repeated dropping out of relationships and failing to complete ventures can be a bad augury for sticking at therapy.

The degree and extent of childhood amnesia is a valuable indicator of repression and restriction of personality, and soon becomes apparent when one enquires about childhood memories. I usually ask patients to tell me their very earliest memories, as these are often significant, and like recurrent early dreams and nightmares can be used in dynamic interviewing and formulation. The readiness to make contact with unconscious aspects of themselves can also be gauged by asking whether they remember their dreams now. Sometimes a dream the night before the consultation can bring to life the patient's concerns and anxieties about meeting the consultant or entering therapy.

The interview should provide a taste of the psychotherapeutic approach, which includes an aliveness and readiness to discuss what goes on between patient and therapist. Patients have a right to learn something about themselves and their relationships from the interview. I always make of point of feeding back to patients the essence of my psychodynamic formulation of their problem, and the way in which psychotherapy might help if group therapy seems specifically indicated, and point out what particular advantages it would have. Their responses can prove crucial.

An important part of the assessment interview is the discussion of treatment options, including what is practicable and the patient's capabilities, preferences, wishes and fears. This might well include discussing the patient's feelings about being referred on for treatment by someone other than the consultant.

Selection of the most appropriate form of therapy

S. H. Foulkes (1975: 65) held that group psychotherapy is indicated whenever psychotherapy is appropriate and that its range is broader than individual psychotherapy. This statement needs qualifying. If we consider the range of group methods, including activity groups and homogeneous groups, almost anyone can benefit from a group approach. But if we are thinking of group analysis – that is, long-term analytical group psychotherapy – we have to consider for each patient (1) their motivation; (2) the practicality of intense prolonged psychotherapy in a group; and (3) the indications for and against an analytical uncovering approach, as discussed earlier. It is not a cure-all. In acknowledgement of this, Robin Skynner and I wrote a clinical paper (Skynner and Brown 1981) that was designed to guide general practitioners, psychiatrists and other referrers in making a decision about what form of psychotherapy is likely to be helpful, and proposed a framework in which to consider this. We decided to reverse the historical and 'common-sense' order of individual, group and finally family therapy, in which the modalities of treatment have developed in the course of this century. (Skynner came to group analysis from a background of child psychiatry, working with children and their families, while I came from a background first in adult psychiatry and then in psychoanalysis.) We decided to put the family modality first to emphasise the value of taking a systems approach to emotional disturbance. We suggested that each approach – family, group and individual – had its own advantages.

Family therapy has the broadest spectrum of applicability and the greatest economy in time. It enables us to influence others in the system than the presenting patient, who might not be either the sickest member of the family or the most treatable. As S. H. Foulkes (1975: 11) put it, we should consider the patient's intimate plexus in which disturbances arise, not just internalised childhood experiences, and treatment of this (family) plexus should, if possible, have priority over individual or group psychotherapy.

Group therapy has also a very broad spectrum and great economy in terms of therapists' time. It has a particular advantage for those with initially low self-understanding and psychological mindedness, dependent people and those with uncertain identity and social difficulties. Foulkes (1975) also believed it not helpful to select patients in terms of diagnostic labels except in considering the contra-indications – for example the very paranoid, acutely psychotic, severely depressed, suicidal or antisocial. Individual therapy has the particular advantage of flexibility. It allows the level and rate of therapy to be 'titrated' for each individual's need – for instance, short-term counselling for those in a crisis – and also provides the undivided attention that those people with very severe early deprivation might require even to begin to trust and contact their 'true selves'. It is also useful for those needing prolonged preparation for either individual or group therapy. And of course it is essential for those who wish to work as psychoanalysts, as is group analysis for those who wish to work as group analysts.

Because we provide a special facility and expertise in group methods, most of our referrers will already have done some of the selection by referring to us patients for whom a group approach is particularly appropriate. However, there are a large number of patients who are referred for a general psychodynamic and psychotherapeutic assessment. Dr Skynner in particular gets a large number of referrals of couples and families because of his particular experience and renown. Others of us are more often referred individual patients for whom a series of consultations or individual analytical psychotherapy might be provided within the practice, but more often through our wide-ranging network of therapists in London and elsewhere.

In the late 1970s Clarkin and Frances reviewed, on the basis of research and clinical consensus, the selection criteria for family evaluation and therapies, group therapies, brief psychotherapies, and finally no treatment. They give a good account of the indications for group psychotherapy gleaned from the research literature (Clarkin and Frances 1982). As this accords well with our own clinical experience I will summarise these indications here:

1 Problems in interpersonal relationships.
2 Patients willing to share and be open with others.
3 The showing of excessive intellectualisation.
4 A danger of regressive transference.
5 Intolerance of dyadic intimacy and the likelihood of producing harmful countertransference in individual therapists.

Likewise they give a list of contra-indications that also accords with our clinical sense and experience. These are:

1 Acute psychiatric emergencies;
2 Patients who are likely to respond to brief therapy.
3 Patients who are likely to refuse group therapy.
4 Patients who would be destructive to the group process or be made worse by it. For example, they are too ill, too demanding, too dishonest, manipulative or explosive; to which I would add, they are too likely to be isolated and unpopular in a group.

It is usually possible to make a reliable judgement in one consultation lasting between an hour and an hour-and-a-half, but in a proportion of cases, particularly when motivation is uncertain and the degree and nature of the disturbance are problematic, a second consultation is called for within the next week or two, and there are even some cases where a decision can be postponed over a period of a few months, during which time the patient might be seen a few times to assess his or her progress and use of the dynamic consultations. Currently, only about one in three consultations leads to patients joining an analytic group – more when the referral was of an individual than of a couple or family. Recently there seems to have been an increase in highly disturbed or doubtfully motivated patients for whom a quick move into a group is not indicated without lengthy assessment, consideration of other options and gathering of information from previous professional carers, psychiatrists or psychotherapists. To quote from a recent annual report to referrers:

> In 1988 there were 437 consultations with individuals and families of whom 157 were taken on for ongoing group-analytic psychotherapy, once- or twice-weekly. Most joined as individuals, but a proportion joined couples' groups with their partners. Of those who did not join groups, some were taken on for individual analysis or psychotherapy within the Practice or, more frequently, placed with colleagues outside the Practice for this; some only wanted or needed a few further consultations, either individually or as a couple or family. Occasionally we recommended counselling, behavioural psychotherapy, relaxation techniques (e.g. Autogenic Training) or bodywork (e.g. Yoga, Alexander Technique) as an alternative or adjunct to a more exploratory analytic approach.[3]
>
> At the time of writing we had 52 groups running, 29 once-weekly (five are couples' groups) and 23 twice-weekly. Most of the once-weekly groups are held in the evening or late afternoon, but we have one on Saturday morning. We recommend that patients join for at least a year, and most stay for two or three years, and aim for a general maturation of personality and improvement in relationships.
>
> Most groups have a fairly wide age range, but we aim always to have at least one group specially catering for young people (usually 18 to mid-twenties), and at least one for older people (usually fifties and sixties). We are hoping to start a group shortly for people with psychosomatic problems and difficulties in expressing their feelings, and we are considering short-term groups (say, for one year) both for men and women who would like a single-sex group perhaps as a prelude to joining a mixed group.
>
> If there are particular types of groups which you feel we could usefully provide, we shall be very interested to hear from you.

3 Counselling or behaviour therapy are especially indicated where the need and motivation for an analytic approach are absent, or if such an approach is likely to be too disturbing. Relaxation techniques are helpful when tension is a major problem; and bodywork can be indicated when a person is out of touch with or not at home with their body.

Prominent among those for whom group analysis is specially indicated are people who have had long periods of individual analytic treatment in the past. Even those who have gained much from intensive psychoanalysis can remain stuck in their development towards maturity in relation to others. The relationships in a group are closer than the psychoanalytic dyad to those in everyday life. Confrontation with the experiences, reactions and needs of others inevitably throws light on one's own. It develops our altruism and capacity to share, both to give and receive.

Preparing the patient for a group

Preparation for a group can usually be done within the first consultation meeting, though it may require several consultations or even a period of individual therapy. During the initial consultation we give people a brief information sheet about the nature of group analysis (see Figure 5.3). Here the nature of the commitment and issues of confidentiality and fees are

Group-analytic psychotherapy

Joining a group for psychotherapy is in many ways a new experience and will involve your making certain arrangements. These notes are offered for your guidance.

Group sessions last one and a half hours. It is important for your own progress and for that of the group that you attend regularly. Holidays should be arranged with this in mind.

The relationships in a psychotherapeutic group are exceptionally close and confidential and it has been found that meetings between members outside the session tend to retard progress. If you do chance to meet other members outside, it is best not to discuss Group matters and to mention it later in the Group.

Termination of treatment should be by agreement. You are asked to give one month's notice of termination.

If you have to be absent from the Group for any reason, it is helpful if you can inform the therapist in advance. If you have to be absent at short notice, you can telephone the secretary.

The standard fee of £   per annum is payable at the rate of £   per month in advance. This fee is calculated to cover 40 sessions of treatment in any calendar year. If fewer sessions are provided the fee will be adjusted pro rata. For twice-weekly groups the fee would be £   per annum. (Fees are reviewed and may be adjusted from the start of each calendar year in the light of changes in the economic situation.)

Accounts will not normally be rendered for Group sessions but if you wish to have one you should ask your therapist.

Figure 5.3 The nature of group-analytic psychotherapy: notes given to new group patients.

described. We also point out at this time that fees need to be adjusted each January in line with increased costs, more or less following the rate of inflation. We point out that at least a year's attendance in a group will be required and that most people will stay for two or three years.

Patients usually leave by agreement when they feel they have got what they want from the group, or progress has come to a 'plateau'. Although this is usually by mutual agreement, patients are free to leave when they wish but are asked to give at least a month's notice. This is very useful in the early stages when some people have difficulty in settling into the group, and might be tempted to make an impulsive and later-regretted withdrawal. It provides the patients and the group with a breathing space in which to question the nature of their anxiety and to rally their motivation.

It is often helpful for patients for whom we expect that entry into a group might be difficult to discuss with them some of the dynamic issues that can reasonably be anticipated in joining a group. For the group itself there might be feelings about the replacement of a departed member, which might include relief as well as a sincere sense of loss, the resentment of which might be related to the revival of early experiences about new siblings arriving in a family. For the patient there will be inevitable anxieties, particularly for those who have difficulties joining and trusting groups, perhaps related to a disrupted childhood: so that entering the therapy group might stir up feelings originally experienced on starting at a new school: feelings of exclusion and exposure, loss of previous relationships and anxiety about establishing new ones. We explain that they will be joining an already existing group, from which someone has recently left – a so-called 'slow-open' group. This may stir up feelings about replacing a sibling in early life. If more than one new member is due to join at the same time, it is usual to inform them. They often develop a special twin-like alliance, a mixture of mutual protection and rivalry.

We also bear in mind the danger of newcomers saying too much too quickly with consequent anxiety and withdrawal, though this can usually be left to the conductor in the group once the patient has joined.

Matching individuals and group

Ultimately we are talking about patients' characteristics and their capacity to be contained within and to promote, or at least not to destroy, the therapeutic processes in a group. Therefore, ultimately the most important question is whether this patient is going to fit in to this particular group. This accords with the earlier statement of Foulkes (1964) that contra-indications are few 'and show themselves individually if each case is considered on its own merits'. He noted that while strong paranoid features are unfavourable and psychotics should not be in the majority (except in groups of psychotics) 'individual psychotics inside a group of psychoneurotics did particularly well and influenced the group as a whole favourably' (p. 35). We believe the same is true of reasonably contained borderline personalities.

Of course we also need to think about the therapeutic potential of the group as a whole, and therefore to consider the need for a good balance of personalities and problems – for example, not more than one or two borderline personalities, nor a predominance of severely depressed people, or extremely stuck 'alexithymic' personalities. If we have a choice of groups, then we also need to know which groups are dynamic, fast moving, sophisticated, confronting rather than supportive – or the reverse. In the Group-Analytic Practice we have a weekly clinical meeting which reviews all the patients assessed in the previous week. Here we discuss their selection for group analysis, and their suitability for particular groups or for a period on the waiting list until an appropriate vacancy arises. Therapists are able to say what sort of patients they would like to fill a vacancy (see Figure 5.4), and we are able to consider the particular interests and skills of therapists in dealing with particular sorts of patient.

The range of patients who can be helped is very wide, both in age and personality, and quite severely disturbed patients can be contained and helped in well-functioning, well-selected groups, differentiating between, for example, faster and slower moving groups (see Figure 5.5). These include borderline personalities, alexithymic personalities, people with past histories of manic-depressive and schizophrenic illness, those recovering from severe eating disorders, and sexual problems and other psychosomatic disorders.

At any time we have about 50 groups meeting once or twice weekly at a wide variety of times, early morning, lunchtime, afternoon and evening during weekdays and on Saturday mornings. During the initial interview patients will have been asked about their availabilities at these various times,

Conductors having a vacancy:

Group number (if more than one):

Group time(s):

Ideal new member for optimal balance of group:

Sex __________

Age-range __________

Marital status __________

Other characteristics__________

Wish to avoid:

Figure 5.4 Vacancies in groups: a form for therapists to specify vacancies.

As at January 1990
(0–4) – absent to high

Dear ____________

It would be helpful, in matching potential recruits to your groups, to have a picture of current composition and characteristics. (We plan to repeat this enquiry every six months).

1 Group time(s)	
2 Approximate age range	
3 Analytic (0–4)	
4 Supportive (0–4)	
5 Regressive potential (0–4)	
6 Inhibited (0–4)	
7 Confrontational (0–4)	
8 Speed (0–4)	
9 Nature of any recent crisis: e.g. drop-outs, problem patients	
10 Special features of group:	

Figure 5.5 Matching patients in groups: a form for therapist's group.

and told that the more flexible they can be, the shorter is the time that they are likely to have to wait for a suitable vacancy. As most people leave groups at the Christmas, Easter and summer breaks, newcomers are most often taken in after these breaks.

At present all group are 'slow-open' (as defined above) with equal numbers of men and women, and with mixed background and psychopathology. One of the difficulties of starting specialised groups is to get eight people who would benefit from it to meet at one time. We can always maintain some groups for late adolescents and for people in later life, but a new group for psychosomatic and alexithymic patients recently failed in that form because of the problem of recruiting enough patients at the available time; it was finally merged into a more heterogeneous group. Whether we can succeed in setting up time-limited, single-sex groups will depend on recruitment. If we cannot, with our large number of referrals and therapists, one wonders whether this could be achieved in a very specialised setting such as the Women's Therapy Centre.

The presence of colleagues in the team with expertise with couples and families enables us to run not only couples' groups, but to have them available for consultations with the spouses or partners of those patients who are having difficulties in an ongoing relationship for which both partners need to take responsibility. Sometimes this results in both of them joining either a couples' group or separate stranger groups. It would seem that any group practice should have at least a close working relationship with a colleague skilled at working with families and couples; ideally, a colleague who combines these skills with being a group analyst.

Management of the waiting list

Management of the waiting list is important in order to ensure that patients do not wait unduly long. Each consultation is given a sequential number which enables us to assess how long they have been waiting if they are not taken into a group straightaway. It has been very useful having a word processor and computer to reduce the work needed to keep the list constantly updated for the weekly meetings of the Management Committee, and to keep a check on the times that the new patient will be available for a group so this can be matched with the vacancies as they arise.

This facilitates regular supervision of the waiting list and communication with all 16 therapists to ensure that we have accurate information about current and expected vacancies in their groups. It is the principal responsibility of the Clinical Secretary, and on the whole works quite sensitively. Not only has the patient been assessed in depth, but we know a lot about the therapists and the type of group that the patient will be joining. However, before a patient joins a new group, the group conductor arranges what we term a 'preliminary interview'. This is a meeting of variable length, for which no charge is made, in which patient and therapist can get to know each other, make a final commitment and arrange practical details such as when the patient will join. Some conductors like a longer preliminary interview than others, more of a second assessment, feeling that it increases their understanding of the patient and increases the motivation of both of them. Indeed we all feel this need with some new patients. Very occasionally a conductor will choose to see a new patient a few times individually to further this end before the patient actually joins the group, and it might be specifically recommended at the initial consultation.

Occasionally there are problems with a patient settling into a group. Because of the structure of the Practice it is possible for the group conductor to discuss the difficulties with the initial consultant. This might lead to an offer to the patient of an opportunity to discuss the difficulties individually with either, especially if there seems to be a risk that the patient might drop out. Then, very occasionally it may be though worth considering a change of group and therapist, or the addition of some initial sessions with the same therapist or another.

The limits of group analysis

As discussed earlier, despite the existence of clear-cut contra-indications to group analysis as a long-term analytic therapy, it has a very wide spectrum of indications and applicability. Nevertheless there are patients who get to a certain point in their group analysis, but cannot progress without moving into a period of individual therapy, sometimes concurrently, but sometimes leaving a group altogether to continue their 'voyage' in individual therapy. More often than not, in my experience, these are people who have been very damaged within the dyadic relationship, sometimes experienced as a tremendous narcissistic vulnerability, for whom mirroring at a very infantile level is necessary for healing and the emergence of a 'true self'. Sometimes the period of time they need in individual therapy seems very short – much shorter than if they had been in individual treatment from the beginning. Such deep borderline or narcissistic damage cannot always be predicted in the most skilled assessment interview, and the treatment has to be started in order to deepen and complete the assessment. My impression is that these people need a degree of 'benign regression' within a relationship that can be tested over a sufficient period of time, in order to allow a 'new beginning' (Balint 1968). Sometimes a particular group cannot provide this, and a patient may need to move into concurrent individual therapy or, less often, move entirely from group to individual analytic psychotherapy. Thus the fact that groups promote maturity can, for a few very damaged personalities, be a disadvantage. They may finally benefit from a group after they have had experience of themselves in a facilitating dyadic relationship. But as Rutan and Alonso (1982) have said: 'It is possible to overcome resistance, in each modality, by sometimes adding the other concurrently, but in that case, as usual, the group is the central treatment.' In other words, the advisability of adding individual to group psychotherapy for a group member should not be taken by the group and its conductor as indicating any lessening of the value and centrality of their work with that patient.

Other important issues

It is very important to keep in touch with referrers. This is done by writing to them, and perhaps phoning, after the initial consultation, and letting them know when patients start in groups and finish, and informing them of the outcome. We also keep in touch with them at a more personal level by inviting them to an annual Christmas party, and sending them an annual report about the work of the practice.

If we are concerned about a patient during the 12 weeks in the year when the groups do not meet, we inform his of her general practitioner or, if they were referred by one, their psychiatrist. Moreover, we let the patient know that there is always medical psychotherapeutic cover available through the Practice office.

When the group conductor is not medically qualified, medical responsibility is carried either by the medical qualified member of the practice who carried out the initial assessment, or sometimes, when more appropriate, by the patient's general practitioner or psychiatrist. This extends to providing medical backing for private health insurance to cover the cost of the initial consultation and therapy itself.

One further advantage of working in a group practice, beyond the advantages of pooling patients, experience and mutual support, is that when a member of the practice falls ill (or even dies) other members can help out. A group can often continue well for a few sessions without a conductor, depending on its stage of development. But should the conductor have a protracted illness, we can make arrangements for a colleague (usually from within the Practice) to take over the group until that conductor returns.

Conclusion

In assessing and selecting someone for group analysis we need to ask whether this patient is likely to benefit from and benefit a group of fellow patients committed to long-term exploration of themselves and interpersonal relationships through processes of insight and change; or is the patient too disturbed or poorly motivated to tolerate exploration and insight, or too deprived and damaged to tolerate sharing in a group, or as yet too unprepared? In that case would psychiatric management or individual therapy – supportive, brief or analytic – be more appropriate? Or, if the family as a whole is clearly involved, would a conjoint approach be more effective?

For a whole range of patients and problems, a long-term analytic group can be an effective therapy and an experience that promotes growth and maturity (Brown 1987). But we need to evaluate the group; how much support and holding (Winnicott 1960) can it give, how much containing (Bion 1962; James 1984), how much confrontation (Brown 1988), how much intimacy, how much benign regression, what range of subjects is it equipped to explore; also in what phase of the group; and with which therapist? Only then are we able to complete the assessment of the indications and contraindications for psychotherapy of this patient in this group and select each appropriately. The procedures we have developed, and described above, from referral to consultation, and finally to the preliminary interview with the would-be therapist, aim to answer most of these questions. We believe that the methods of working together over the last few decades at the Group-Analytic Practice have enabled us to refine these procedures in a way that may provide a useful model to others.

6

TEXT, CONTEXT AND TEXTURE

Free speech in the service of health and healing

The idea of free speech assumes the value of people being truthful with themselves and with others, and that they listen as well as speak. Free speech is not superficial laissez-faire. It is not sufficient for people to say meaningless or deliberately trivial things, or to spout their prejudices at Speakers' Corner for health and healing to follow. The blocks to health and healing are inside each of us and at the same time between us. A therapeutic group provides a setting par excellence in which these blocks can be discovered and conquered. This is true whether they are rooted in the Scylla of schizoid autism and secrecy, or in the Charybdis of false-self compliance and a spurious and superficial adjustment. The task of therapy, especially in a group, is to be truly and securely yourself with others; *with* in a way that allows them to be truly *themselves*, respectful of differences as well as similarities.

The group analyst fosters a climate of safety and honesty, in which things said and unsaid are heard, where the meanings of silence can be discerned as well as those of positive communications. He has to be alert to the text, context and texture of communications in the group. *Text* refers to what people say, explicitly and implicitly, verbally and non-verbally, and therefore also what they do not say; i.e. their words spoken and unspoken. *Context* refers to what they say in terms of what they or others have said before or say afterwards, and also the setting in which these things are said that gives them special meanings not always immediately apparent. *Texture* refers to the richness or poverty, the range and quality of interaction and speech in a particular setting, the contrasts and similarities between different people's contributions to particular themes, to the warp and woof of communication. The interplay between these three elements of a group – text, context and texture – can be looked at in many ways. One way is to see them respectively as figure, ground, and the moment-to-moment atmosphere and culture created within the lifespan of the group matrix.

Putting things into words is a very human characteristic; words represent some of the pinnacles of civilisation, and their importance for health and healing have long been known. In *Macbeth*, Shakespeare made Malcolm say to the grieving Macduff:

Give sorrow words;
the grief that does not speak,
whispers the o'erfraught heart
and bids it break.

Freud highlighted the importance in therapy of putting unspeakable things, and eventually unthinkable things, into words. Psychoanalysis – 'the talking cure' as Anne O called it – has always been interested in words, their meanings and functions. They are an essential part of expressing 'primary process', unconscious material in a form that is available to rational conscious thought in 'secondary process' terms, and thereby more readily understandable and shareable with others. Pat de Maré has pointed out that *conscious* originally meant knowable with others (*con-scio*). Foulkes's emphasis on deepening and clarifying communication also implies the importance of putting things into words. Dynamic change is fostered by these processes, though not entirely dependent on them; and some communications are 'better' than others. We will come back to this issue later, but first I would like to examine the origin of the words text, context and texture, and also – because of its importance in group analysis – the term matrix.

All three words – text, context and texture – are derived from the Latin *texere*, to weave. Context comes from *contexere*, to weave together. Text and texture also come from the Latin *textus*, a tissue, or style of literary work. Foulkes's idea of the matrix as a web of communication and relationships as well as the background in which and from which they develop clearly has a bearing on the text, context and texture of what happens in any sort of group. We can only speculate that he may have unconsciously chosen the word matrix because it resonates in sound and meaning with the idea of mother substance and with these three words. But it is an appealing thought. The widening and deepening of communication within clarifying and growing relationships is the main thrust of the group-analytic process. In group-analytic psychotherapy 'the individual is being treated in the context of the group with the active participation of the group' (Foulkes and Anthony 1973). Given an opportunity to 'lose' himself in the group, the individual has a chance to redraw his own boundaries, discover what was repressed or projected, and so to individuate at the same time as recognising others more clearly.

The word context has apparently only recently taken on the meaning of 'setting'. Indeed according to the recent 1975 edition of the two-volume *Shorter Oxford English Dictionary*, the word has four meanings: (1) The construction of speech. (2) A continuous text or composition. (3) The connection of the parts of a composition. (4) The parts which immediately precede or follow any particular passage or text and determine its meaning. (Even the 1972 supplement to the full OED has no hint of the newer meaning.) The last textual meaning has a particular relevance to what Foulkes called 'free group association', in that in the tolerant flexible culture of the analytic group, discussion between members takes on an associational quality that is influenced by unconscious themes and connections. The meaning of what is said is determined by what precedes and follows it from moment to moment in the dynamic exchange, as well as by the longer term structure of the group and its relationship as a system to the internal and external systems which each individual represents (intrapersonal, and interpersonal in their networks outside the group). Finally, of course, the relationship of the group as a system to the larger systems (suprasystems) which it is a part of, especially in institutional settings, might also determine the meaning of communications within the group. It is interesting that the meaning of 'setting' does occur in the American *Webster's Dictionary* (1961): 'The interrelated conditions in which something exists or occurs', and the Scottish *Chambers Dictionary* (1972): 'associated surroundings, setting'. Could it be that the American and Scottish scenes provide an environment in which narrow bookishness is more readily objectified and put in its place? Are the English – perhaps because of the wide acceptance of static class compartmentalisation – less context conscious, less conscious of open systems and social relativity?

Whilst we are considering etymology, it might be worth noting how rich are the meanings of the word *matrix* that Foulkes chose to depict the area in which group processes occur. They provide the missing elements which the word context in its OED meaning still lacks. Again according to the *Shorter OED*, the word matrix comes from the Latin word for 'a female used for breeding', which I suppose is a distancing and contemptuous way of referring to mother! Its five meanings can each be related to therapeutic processes. (1) '*A womb*' represents the containing and supporting function of the groups as well as illustrating symbolisation, metaphor and transference. (2) '*A place or medium in which something is bred, produced or developed*'. (3) '*A place or point of origin and growth*' reflects the initiation, discovery and growth that need a favourable place to occur in and which the group provides. (4) '*The substance situated between animal or vegetable cells*' can be likened to the space between individuals in a group which offers contact and opportunities for renegotiation of individual boundaries. (5) '*A piece of metal by means of which typeface is cast, or the letter stamped on it in intaglio with a punch*' expresses the dynamic interaction between figure and ground akin to that between individual and group and between events and their context.

What has all this etymology got to do with health and healing, and in particular with the practical contributions to them of group analysis? In what way do ideas about text, context and texture contribute to prophylaxis and treatment of human suffering and the restriction of the potential for growth in individuals, families, and institutions? What light do they throw on what Foulkes saw as the therapeutic effects of the communications processes we seek to promote in the group matrix?

I shall illustrate some group-analytic answers to these questions by giving examples from the fields of (a) personal development, (b) clinical practice with groups of people with neurotic and personality problems, (c) institutional dynamics, and (d) politics. Finally, I shall ask whether putting things into words is sufficient or even necessary for health and healing; and whether 'free speech' is an end in itself or a means to an end that can be reached in other ways. Some of the ideas of Jacques Lacan about speech, and of Robert Langs about interactional fields, will be invoked in trying to answer these questions. However, before turning to Foulkes, let me quote from the Gnostic Gospel of St Thomas: Jesus said, 'If you bring forth what is within you, what you bring forth will save you. If you do not bring forth what is within you, what you do not bring forth will destroy you' (Pagels 1974). Psychotherapy is about overcoming the difficulties of doing what He said.

Personal development

In his first book, *Introduction to Group Analytic Psychotherapy* (Foulkes 1948), written in 1945, Foulkes clearly stated his view that the essence of Man is social, and that the idea of the individual is an abstraction as each of us is basically determined by the world, the community and the group we live in – primarily the family as the setting for the first dyadic relationship into which we are born. In Winnicott's later and famous words: 'There is no such thing as a baby; only a nursing couple' (Winnicott 1975). The individual, in Foulkes's words, is a nodal point in a network – both externally and internally. Neurosis is individualistic and group destructive because it originates in a supposed incompatibility between the individual's view of himself and his safety in his or her original family group. Neurotic symptoms represent autistic expressions of those aspects of the individual – impulses, feelings, fantasies or memories – which seem dangerous and are therefore blocked from direct expression or memory. If they originate at a preverbal stage of development, the words have never been there and have to be found. If words were originally present, the words themselves can be charged with anxiety. In either case, the danger of finding the words or spelling them out can only be understood in the context of the relationship fraught at that time in that stage of development.

An example that made an impact on me was the development of a virtual paralysis of one leg by a five-year-old boy who the previous day had been playing football with his father on a picnic, using an empty beer can. If anything, the boy had performed better than his father. Why should this have proved pathogenic? I believe it was connected with the fact that on the day before the picnic, while playing on a climbing frame in their garden, the father was showing off by raising himself to the boy's level on top of the frame, using his arms only – something the boy could not do. While doing this, Father strained his shoulder and had to desist because of the pain.

My inference was – and of course there is no way of proving this – that competitive feelings between them thus came to seem 'dangerous'. It is a fact, however, that though the weakness of the leg cleared in a few days, the boy avoided competing with his father on his own ground for many years. Body language had made its mark. The boy was stuck with it till enabled to speak freely in therapy some years later.

Such conflicts are commonplace, and in psychotherapy become re-enacted in the transference relationship. In an analytic group such issues as competition and rivalry become – in Foulkes's words – *located in the matrix of the group*. Here they are seen to be universal human characteristics, and both impulses and defences are manifested in the verbal and non-verbal text of the group interaction and discussion. The ebb and flow allow impulses and defences to be seen as connected, and their manifold forms and manifestations demonstrated. The courage to admit to such feelings is facilitated by the example of others. The discovery that admitting them does not result in punishment, rejection or destruction permits new ways of dealing with them; because it is the feared response and consequence of our feelings in the family that led us to repress important parts of ourselves in early life, and thus continue to restrict ourselves or inflict neurotic suffering on ourselves. Inevitably this distorts our relationships with others and in turn gets built into our own family patterns a generation on.

It is in families which block emotional expression and communication of difficult feelings that childhood neurosis is more likely to persist into adult life and be handed on. Psychotherapy can thus be prophylactic as well as therapeutic.

Clinical practice

Clinical analytic practice endeavours to undo the damage sustained in early experiences in the family. It does this not only by deciphering the *text* of an individual patient's 'free associations' discovering the meaning of connections created by contiguity in an associational chain, which otherwise would not be decipherable from the isolated units of communication; but it does it by taking note of the *context* of the transference relationship, and the boundaries of the situation created, e.g. by weekend and holiday breaks. The same applies in group analysis, but here the equivalent of free association is free group discussion within the context of the group matrix, with a rich *texture* created by multiple transferences and many layers of communication as Foulkes has pointed out: (a) current relationships (or working alliance), essentially adult-to-adult in Eric Berne's terminology; (b) individual transferences, typically child-to-adult or, when members see each other as siblings, child-to-child; (c) shared and projected feelings, often bodily and from early preverbal stages of development; (d) primordial level of archetypal universal images.

Powerful and primitive feelings can emerge in a group through processes Foulkes termed condenser phenomena and resonance – the latter implying that individuals respond to themes and emotions at the level which is meaningful to them and at which they are able and ready to respond at that time. There is thus a range of responses which come to be seen as relative and not inevitable, and which can occur for a multitude of ultimately understandable reasons. This provides a flexible framework in which fixed fears and fantasies can be tested, modified and even discarded. What Yalom (1985) has called 'corrective recapitulation of the primary family' is an important part of the therapeutic process in groups. This is not the same thing castigated by many psychoanalysts in responding to Franz Alexander's promotion of 'corrective emotional experiences in psychotherapy' (Alexander 1975). That seemed to depend on a manipulative adoption of 'corrective' attitudes by the therapist, i.e. deliberately reacting in a way different from that feared by the patient viewing the therapist in transference terms, e.g. as a fearsome and punishing authoritarian father to any hint of challenge.

In a group trying to explore the meaning of two members having a kissing session in a car after a recent session, the topic spoken about (i.e. the text) turned to that of authority and dutiful submission. One man, emerging over recent months out of a rather inhibited but still somewhat split and secret sexuality, confronted an inhibited and guilt-ridden woman with a description of her as working on the ROD principle – Responsibility, Obligation and Duty. Others laughed, but like a flash, and with a twinkle she countered 'Rod?' This enabled the excitement of sexuality, symbolised by the phallus (which the inhibited man took a while to recognise in the ensuing banter) to be linked with the authority represented by a forbidding father. For several of the women incestuous feelings were highly charged, with consequent blockage to their sexuality, and the men were beginning to challenge authority, as represented in the group by me. They were needing to do this, especially the one who had been involved in 'acting out'. The phallus was thus both forbidden and forbidding – and for healing and growth needed to be superseded and overcome in relation both to the original paternal objects and, in the transference, in relation to me. This *text* could only be understood within the *context* of group associations and what was happening in the group setting both for individuals and for the group as a whole. And it was the richness of *texture* of the communications in the group matrix that allowed the play on words to resonate.

Institutional dynamics

Institutional dynamics illustrate well the importance of recognising the systems of which an institution is composed, and the larger suprasystems of which it is part – and the way systems overlap. Foulkes was very much a systems thinker in the way he recognised the social nature of the individual, and how the internalised intrapsychic family determined an individual's interaction with others, and also the way in which new transpersonal experiences in later life groups and especially therapy groups can modify the internal system through 'ego training in action'. The therapeutic community movement was the consequence of his recognising the powerful dynamic interaction between individuals, small working group and institution, so that change in one could initiate change in the others. Morale and health of individuals and of the hospital as a whole were improved when he restored a sense of autonomy and co-operation within the small groups at the Northfield Military Neurosis Centre. The energy flow established in one system flowed over into the others.

However, I believe it is true that the success of the second Northfield experiment, in contrast to the short-lived first experiment under the direction of Bion and Rickman, was due to the fact that there were no large meetings of the hospital as a whole – staff and patients. Foulkes himself embodied the hospital as a whole, integrating his awareness of the separate units and their interaction, and thereby not running the risk of speech being so free as to alarm the army authorities in the suprasystem of which Northfield was a part. The sound of mutinous anti-authoritarianism was not allowed to reach ears which were not willing to hear it because of the state of the nation and of the world at that time. I mention this to illustrate the difficulties of free speech being premature or unacceptable and uncontainable by the system it addresses – be this the individual not able to listen to his own unconscious, the group scapegoating an individual member, or an institution not willing to pay the price of knowing what it is doing to itself. Perhaps most commonly it is those in power who do not want to listen. Tom Main's paper on 'Knowledge, Learning and Freedom from Thought' (Main 1967), emphasised the way in which thinking can be stultified by rigidification and institutionalisation of principles, as the ego becomes supplanted by the superego.

The junior medical staff and paramedical staff of an institution I know were recently undergoing a ferment of free speech – saying things long hidden – partly as a result of the arrival of an outspoken senior member of staff. This ferment involved beginning to voice some criticism of the support which different disciplines gave to each other and received from those in hierarchical authority. Staff were beginning to discuss certain structural alterations in support meetings. At a staff meeting attended, relatively unusually, by a member at the top of such a hierarchy, a suggestion was made that in order to ensure enough staff for psychodynamic support and supervision, an external expert be invited to work with the staff of one ward. This led to an energetic rejection of the idea by the member ensconced at the top of her hierarchy, and a feeling in the staff meeting that change was unwanted or at least going too fast. Thinking about it later, it seemed to make sense that rejection of the idea of the outsider coming in was silenced by as yet unspoken feelings abut the boat being upset by the new senior member whose arrival had uncovered the uncomfortable ferment, and, I believe, about the intrusion of freer speech which dynamic psychotherapy represents. This system was not yet ready for free speech (if it ever will be with its present senior staffing). That is, the full text cannot be published within the present context, even though some of it can be discerned if the texture – the many levels of interaction – is taken into account.

Politics

I will not say much about politics, but I think that recent events in Poland[1] and within the Labour and Conservative parties provide obvious material for consideration within the context of the theme of this paper. An illustration from a slightly different field impressed me very much at the time of the 1978 World Cup.

Scotland were playing Peru in Argentina. The Scottish fans must have sacrificed much to travel there, their enthusiasm and loyalty providing the energy for the long journey. It was their behaviour when their team lost which revealed the desperate narcissistic roots of their loyalty. The television film showed the team members being jeered at and abused as 'rubbish' and 'scum' by really irate and contemptuous ruffians. The wish to identify, even merge, with the glorious, omnipotent conquerors was dashed. It looked as though the fans were left feeling themselves to be nothing but the bitter hate-filled hopeless dregs of society. We do not know their individual stories, inner worlds or social circumstances, but from their appearance it looked as though they were indeed the bottom of the social pile for whom the only activity to restore self-esteem in, say, a Glasgow slum, would be to turn the tables on the rest of society by joining the National Front, or making a fantastic journey to South America in search of gold – not in El Dorado, but in a vision of themselves as clean-limbed conquerors of the world. The tragedy was to see their free speech reduced to the spat-out words 'rubbish' and 'scum'.

I have illustrated the interaction of text, context and texture in individual development, psychotherapy, individual and group, institution and politics. In all these, words have a crucial role in fostering and blocking communications. Sometimes it evokes the wished-for response, sometimes it does not. Sometimes health and healing, of individual, group, institution and society, are fostered by the honest speaking of minds, sometimes the truth has imperatively to be out. But sometimes honesty and truth have to be modified

1 The author refers to the Solidarity movement and the change in political structure in Poland (ed.).

to get a hearing, to be accepted in a useable way. Is this free speech? Our expectations that patients in psychoanalysis should free-associate is an imposition which no analysand succumbs to without resistance; in that case can the analysand's speech really be free? Perhaps all patients need to keep some secrets; it might be very important for their development that they do, and that we understand the need to do so, particularly for some patients. Masud Khan's paper on 'Silence as Communication' in his book *The Privacy of the Self* (Khan 1974), illustrates this very well. If we are to develop freely we need to be protected from excessive intrusion and impingement. One of the advantages of a group for 'really free speech' is that patients can hide, take their own time and speak through other people until they are ready to speak with their own authentic voice. Speaking in itself is no sign of real communication.

This is something recognised by Jacques Lacan. He is, to some, a wayward narcissist whose uncomfortable speech proved intolerable to the ears of the International Psychoanalytic Association. But he has had some very sharp things to say about language and speech, though often written in an opaque and idiosyncratic style. In Chapter 3 of his *Ecrits* (Lacan 1966), entitled 'The Function and Field of Speech and Language in Pyschoanalysis', he uses Heidegger's distinction between 'empty speech' and 'full speech', and states that 'there is no speech without reply, even if it is only met with silence, provided that it has an auditor' (p. 40). Asking where the patient's frustration comes from, he replies: 'The silence of the analyst, or a reply to empty speech, even – or especially – an approving one?' (p. 41). This is vividly truthful and relevant to our clinical practice.

Writing of the unconscious, Lacan states: 'The unconscious is that part of the concrete discourse, in so far as it is trans-individual, that is not at the disposal of the subject in re-establishing the continuity of his conscious discourse' (p. 44). This reminds us of how other members of a group may speak for the subject's unconscious. Further on Lacan writes: 'That the unconscious of the subject is the discourse of the other appears even more clearly than anywhere else in the studies that Freud devoted to what he called telepathy, as manifested in the context of an analytic experience' (p. 55). Lionel Kreeger has reported impressive evidence of 'telepathic' experiences occurring within the context of an analytic group; though we do not need such extreme examples to know that group members speak unwittingly for each other. Lacan goes on in a sort of Messianic poem to Foulkesian transpersonal processes:

> The omnipresence of human discourse will perhaps one day be embraced under the open sky of an omni-communication of its text. This is not to say that human discourse will be any more harmonious than now. But this is the field that our experience polarises in a relation that is only apparently two-way, for any positing of its

> structure in merely dual terms is as inadequate to it in theory as it is ruinous for its technique.
>
> (Lacan 1966: 55)

But the text of communication, as spoken and (hopefully) heard, is spelled out in a relational field that is complex and many-layered, even when only two people are involved, as in psychoanalysis. Robert Langs, writing about the psychoanalytic process, has developed the idea of the bipersonal field, the temporal-physical space within which the analytic interaction takes place (Langs 1979). This clearly links with Kurt Lewin's Field Theory (Lewin 1952), with Winnicott's ideas about psychotherapy being a sort of playing that takes place in the space between analyst and analysand (Winnicott 1971), and with Foulkes's idea of the matrix, which he has defined as 'the hypothetical web of communication and relationship in a group. It is the common shared ground which ultimately determines the meaning and significance of all events and upon which all communication and interpretations, verbal and non-verbal, rest.' Langs explores with great subtlety the mutual interactions between analyst and analysand within the bipersonal field. He distinguishes between verbal and non-verbal communications based on manifest content and what he calls Type One and Type Two derivatives. Type One meanings and latent themes are relatively readily inferred; while Type Two are organised around what Langs calls specific *adaptive contexts* – 'The precipitant or instigator of the interactional and intrapsychic response' – which have to be recognised in order to discern the relevant meanings and functions. Every communication is seen as an interactional product, with inputs from *both* participants.

This way of thinking is very similar to Foulkes's, and for group analysts Langs is spelling out what we intuitively take for granted. An important difference, of course, is that in an analytic group all members are analysts (at least potentially), and we have, not a bipersonal field, but a *multipersonal* one; within this we perceive and participate in multiple transferences, multiple projections and projective identifications as well as, at times, shared regression to early, preverbal states involving symbiosis, loss of individuality and archetypal imagery. But Langs points to the different levels and *types* of communication in the bipersonal field which must be relevant also to the multipersonal field of group analysis. Recognition of these may help to clarify Foulkes's ideas of the value of communication in therapy. Langs' further classification enables us to see why some communications are more valuable than others; why some are destructive and detrimental to health and the process of healing.

He describes three styles of communication, each with a related form of interactional field. Type A uses *symbolic* communications, and the interactional field 'becomes the realm of illusion and a transitional or play space'. Type B is characterised by action and discharge; the main mechanisms are projective identification and living (acting) out – both language and behaviour are used for *discharge* rather than as means for symbolic understanding. While Type A fields are of a greater therapeutic value, both Types A and B entail positive communications. In contrast, Type C fields are negative and destructive of communication and meaning; they use 'falsifications and impervious barriers as the main interactions mode'. Here, language is used as a defence against disturbed inner mental contents. The Type C field is static and empty, and is further characterised by the projective identification of both emptiness and non-meaning, finding its only sense of meaning in these efforts to destroy communication, links and meaning itself. While resistances in the Type A field are characterised by the availability of analysable derivatives, and those in the Type B held are amenable to interpretation based on the defensive use of projective identification, defences and resistances in the Type C field have no sense of depth and possess a persistent, amorphous, and empty quality.

In developing the concept of the bipersonal field, Langs stresses the importance of the analyst's contribution to the type of field that develops. A Type C field cannot be attributed to only the patient's personal psychopathology. As Langs puts it, for the most desirable Type A field to develop, both patient and analyst must be able to tolerate and maintain a secure framework, and the analyst must be able to offer symbolic interpretations of the patient's communication. Neither falsifications and impervious barriers (Type C), nor projective identification and living (acting) out (Type B) must be encouraged by the analyst; still less should they be participated in or provoked by him. This is obviously true for the group analyst, who needs to keep on his analytic toes at all times, particularly as group members can be operating at many different levels and promoting different types of interactions field. In the texture of the group matrix, which type of field predominates at any time is his responsibility as much as anyone's.

If speech is to be 'full' rather than 'empty' (in Lacan's sense), the group's ears – including those of the conductor – have to be ready to hear. The counterpart of Lacan's 'full' or 'empty' speech is 'full' or 'empty' audition. Full communication calls for free speech responded to by free hearing, and perhaps further speech in a freer discourse or dialogue. The group will then be on its way to greater health and healing. But the institutional and political problems discussed earlier in this paper illustrate the necessity for a responsive openness to what is said for free speech to be effective.

Group analysts, as a professional group, need to be open to what others are saying in related fields in order to promote our own healthy development. This is what Foulkes was saying.

7

DIALOGUE FOR CHANGE

Dialogue is a particularly fitting subject for a group-analytic symposium[1] because it is the essence of group analysis and has many aspects. Here I shall reflect on five of these aspects: (1) The meanings of the terms 'dialogue' and 'conversation' and their relation to communication in group analysis. (2) The dialogue between psychoanalysis and group analysis. (3) The relationship between the individual and the group and its mediation by conscious and unconscious dialogue. (4) The role of 'genuine' dialogue in the therapeutic process. (5) The significance of dialogue in large groups, institutions and societies.

Meanings

According to the *Shorter Oxford English Dictionary*, dialogue (from the Greek διάλογος) is simply 'a conversation between two or more persons'. But while neither 'dialogue' nor 'conversation' appear as key words in the index of any of S. H. Foulkes's books, the many meanings of the words 'conversation', 'conversant' and 'to converse' that are to be found in the same dictionary (living and talking together; an 'At Home'; social intimacy in a circle of acquaintance; interchange; turning around and transforming) sum up well the aims and processes of group-analytic psychotherapy. They clearly link with Foulkes's idea of the central role of communication within the dynamic matrix of the group. Through free-floating discussion extending to deeper levels and becoming ever-more articulate, autistic and neurotic patterns are replaced by a sense of commonality and common sense.

Blocks to this process originate not only in 'individual' neurotic conflicts and reactions to early trauma, but also in wider assumptions and ways of being that are embedded in the original foundation matrix. This is based on the biological properties of the species, but also on the culturally firmly

1 This paper is based on the Opening Address to the Sixth European Symposium of Group Analysis, in Zagreb, Yugoslavia, September 1984.

embedded values and reactions. These have been developed and transmitted especially in the nuclear family, in the social network, class, etc., and have been maintained and modified by the intimate plexus in which the person now moves (Foulkes 1975: 131).

At this level, individual, family, society and culture can be seen as facets of a whole. Growth or therapy can be seen as the replacement of old and now inappropriate 'internal' dialogues that have prevented the emergence of currently valid and creative dialogue 'here and now'. The idea of internal dialogue has been clarified by psychoanalysts, especially object-relations theorists.

Dialogue between psychoanalysis and group analysis

Foulkes's greatest contribution was his ability to hold on to the essential discoveries of psychoanalysis – the significance of unconscious conflicts, drives and defences; the importance of early relationships in individual development and the power of resistances to change – while at the same time extending our understanding of how profoundly social human nature is. Conscious and unconscious dialogue, both external and internal, were the mainsprings of his creativity. A sign of his genius is the way in which the development of his ideas has been paralleled by developments in and beyond classical psychoanalysis. Malcolm Pines (1983) spells this out very clearly in his paper 'Psychoanalysis and Group Analysis'.

Some of the key developments in psychoanalysis during the time Foulkes was establishing his ideas about group analysis were Hartmann's (1958) adaptive model; the move from the original theory of instincts to a more social and psychological theory (Erikson 1965; Klein 1976); the flowering of object-relations theory; the understanding of the 'psychological birth' of the infant out of the mother–infant matrix (Mahler *et al.* 1975), and clarification of narcissistic and borderline pathology (Kohut 1971; Kernberg 1975). From the start, Foulkes's ideas about group analysis parallel or are consonant with all these developments in psychoanalysis. Moreover his emphasis on communication in therapy and on making this ever more articulate can be seen to link with the ideas on language and the structure of the unconscious which Lacan (1977) sees as the 'discourse of the Other', initially the speech of the infant's parents (Laxenaire 1983); and the ideas of Langs (1979) on different types of communication (symbolic, indirect and blocking) in the bipersonal field of individual therapy.

Much of this parallelism and consonance between group analysis and recent developments in psychoanalysis has gone unexplored: the dialogue has been largely unconscious, and largely among group analysts. A notably explicit example is Franco Paparo's (1982) work on 'Self Psychology and Group Analysis' in which he demonstrates how useful are Kohut's ideas about empathy and frustration in the development of the self, and describes the group functioning as a primitive self-object in promoting transmuting internalisations and structuralisation. One might add that the early development of communication between mother and infant, from preverbal modes and mimicry to articulate language, also has its parallel in groups. Much group work goes on unconsciously and unspoken.

The overlap between psychoanalytic and group-analytic ideas was discussed by Malcolm Pines (1982) in his elaboration and extension of Foulkes's concept of mirroring, showing how much theoretical mirroring and resonance can be discerned. Pines refers to Abelin's (1980) proposition that narcissism derives from the one-to-one mirroring nature of all relationships before the rapprochement phase of separation–individuation described by Mahler and can only be reduced by the recognition of early triangular identifications with both mother and father and the parental relationship. Only then can symbolic imagery develop, along with the 'knowledge that one is both subject and object in a world that contains subjects and objects'. This reminds us of Foulkes's model of three, and the truism that to be healthy we need to be both subject and object, I and me. The group setting allows and encourages recognition of both – even forces them at times, in a way that is sometimes impossible in the bipersonal field of individual analysis.

I do not need to emphasise the difference between dialogue in psychoanalysis and in group analysis – the asymmetry of the psychoanalytic relationship, and the limitation to two pairs of ears (analyst's and analysand's) and one pair of eyes (the analyst's), compared with the more equal and democratic nature of the group-analytic situation where the eyes and ears of many provide multiple perspectives. The group situation allows what Foulkes described as 'horizontal analysis' compared with the 'vertical analysis' of psychoanalysis (Foulkes and Anthony 1973: 42). This is worked out in the 'here and now' of a dynamic matrix involving a range of relationships that is nearer to everyday life, yet as potentially full of conflicts, distortions and illusions based on the past experiences of each individual member. The individual is confronted not only with his own transferences, projections and so on, but also with those of others. Being the recipient of such distortions heightens his appreciation of what his do to others.

This confrontation with multiple perspectives could be seen as related to the social birth of the infant, and to such sociological ideas as 'the looking-glass self' (Cooley 1968). The infant has to be born physically, then psychologically and finally socially. I believe that just as we need to deepen our dialogue with psychoanalysis, so we need also to develop a dialogue with social psychology if we are to do justice to the objective as well as the subjective facts of human nature. Some day these dialogues may be more reciprocal, with freer interchange with committed psychoanalysts and social psychologists.

The relationship between the individual and the group

The relationship between individual and group is full of paradox. As Diego Napolitani (1980) has put it: 'While the biological individuality coincides with the concept of identity (steadfastness of genetic store and rigorous uniqueness of the individual), the psychological individuality results from subjective components, expressed in terms of creative reflectiveness, and from relational components manifested as a continuity of others within its own experiential field'. He also states: 'If the biological grafting necessarily causes a complex organic reaction of pathological kind – the rejection – the process of identification, which can be metaphorically described as a psychic graft, is the ground of that typically human and indefinitely open phenomenon that is culture.' There is no group without individuals. Equally there is no individual without a group. Individuation requires the infant to differentiate himself from mother, for which at least a third person is required, or a group or society.

Early psychoanalysts viewed the individual as turning to others to satisfy instinctual drives, and basically at odds with society, but later object-relations theorists emphasised that the individual self is object-seeking from the start: at first 'there is no such thing as a baby, only a nursing couple' (Winnicott 1975); the baby emerges from a harmonious mix-up with mother (Balint 1959). Foulkes's belief in the deeply social nature of mankind is an extension of this, seeing social and cultural factors not just represented in the superego established with the resolution of the Oedipus complex, but influencing the child from the start through their effect on mother, father and the wider family and society in the foundation matrix. Lacan particularly related this to the acquisition of language, and saw the child as slotting into society and culture as it catches on to the mother tongue of the family, initially unconsciously. Through this process both mother and child submit to the 'law of the father' who acts as a spoil-sport (Rifflet-Lemaire 1970), depriving both of their desired possessive fusion with each other.

We might of course question to what extent preverbal communications are unconsciously influenced by language and vice versa. The group-analytic process of making communication more articulate presupposes earlier, more primitive levels – unshareable before shareable, unconscious before conscious, bodily and fantastic before abstract and intellectual.

Didier Anzieu (1984) has written persuasively about the relationship of individual and group, emphasising the role of unconscious fantasy. He says, for example: 'Human groups are the consequence of topographic, subjective projections; if the individual did not project onto the group, the result would be a mere aggregate of individuals, and not a group' (p. 100). We might see this as an overstatement since it does not mention such processes as identification and structuralisation. Indeed his statement would seem to apply only to the early stages of stranger groups, rather, for instance to family or work groups which provide a ready-made external structure which the baby or worker enters and adapts to. It is likely, however, that processes in therapy groups do throw light on more universal unconscious phenomena active in relating individual and group, whether in family or society.

Anzieu goes on to state: 'The only way a group can protect itself and make use of external stimulation, and the wishes and drives with which it is cathected by its members, is to fabricate an over-arching group psychical apparatus on top of those of the individuals composing it.' This is strikingly like Foulkes's idea of the dynamic matrix and fits in with Winnicott's notion of culture being created in transitional space. Anzieu's contribution to group theory is the idea of an 'envelope', which could be a superego function, a commonly held ideal ego as in the phenomenon of the group illusion (for example, that the group is perfect); or an id-derived wish associated with fantasies of the group as breast–mouth or womb–toilet; or fantasies of breaking apart; or of the group as a machine. To Anzieu the attraction of being in a group consists of 'sharing or of hoping to share with others pre-genital experience relegated to the back of one's mind or repressed at the genital phase' (p. 238).

But groups are not only fantasies, nor are they only held together by fantasy. Indeed, Anzieu later writes:

> All human activity aims at satisfying the needs of a living organism or of the social body by a mixture of phantasy and know-how. Those who are under what we might call the technical illusion resist phantasy; conversely those who are under what we might call the illusion of phantasy resist know-how.
>
> (Anzieu 1984: 229)

We would all agree that group and social fantasies exist both consciously and unconsciously, and that groups of all sorts, family and social, can only be viewed with true objectivity if the power of subjectivity is allowed for. I believe this could help us to promote the much needed dialogue between strict Kleinians and psychoanalysts who value the findings of Winnicott and Bowlby. Through our interest in systems we would have something to say about how internal and external realities interact.

The therapeutic process

Unlike family therapy, group analysis does not treat the group: it 'treats the individual within the context of the group' (Foulkes and Anthony 1973: 16). Yet in group analysis psychotherapy is 'by the group, of the group, including the conductor' (Foulkes 1975) and paradoxically, to the conductor, the group as a whole and its therapeutic functioning are as important as the individuals. Otherwise the move cannot take place from autistic symptoms to discovering the true and potential self through communication and interaction with others. The individual has to trust the group and not be abused by it (for example, scapegoated). The individuals have to value the group for the group to develop cohesion from which coherence can develop, allowing differentiation and valuing differences as well as similarities.

Caroline Garland (1982) has written persuasively about the importance of 'Taking the Non-Problem Seriously', whereby especially in the early stage of group formation a system is formed which is different from that from which individual members come and in which transformation follows the substitution of group non-problems for individuals' presenting problems. In this system, simulative play allows the negotiation and renegotiation of change between the inner world and outer realities, within himself, between himself and the group, and between the group and the outside world' (p. 14). This describes very well the process by which belonging to a group leads to the discovery of new priorities and opportunities. Other people's problems are seen to be as important as our own and to overlap with ours. Moreover, we come to share the problems of getting to know each other. Functioning well as a member of a well-functioning group has priority over old problems which are seen to have historically determined origins. 'We-go' comes to balance 'ego' (Klein 1976).

The classical psychoanalytic ideas of defence and resistance are obviously of value in understanding and working with blocks to this change. So too may be newer approaches, such as Eigen's (1983) adaptation of the ideas of Marion Milner (1952) in relation to psychic creativeness, which requires oscillation between differentiation and undifferentiation, separation and identification, objectivity and subjectivity, hard and soft boundaries. The ideas of Matte-Blanco (1975) may be very helpful in understanding how the part can stand for the whole, and vice versa. His concept of the unconscious as 'infinite sets' is based on a dual logic in mental life: asymmetrical in relation to discriminant functions, characteristic of 'secondary process thinking'; and symmetrical in relation to apprehension of sameness or equivalence, characteristic of 'primary process' thinking and intense emotional experiences. I think the group conductor is working with such ideas, albeit unconsciously, when he both empathises and attends to countertransference phenomena in relation to both individuals and the group-as-a-whole. He uses them to hold a 'dialogue' between these aspects of his experience in order, among other things, to discern interaction between individual members (including himself) and between them and the group-as-a-whole.

Agazarian and Peters in *The Visible and Invisible Group* (1981) have attempted to conceptualise this complex field with a purely asymmetrical scheme which encompasses four sets of dynamics, to do with an individual functioning as a person, as a group member and in a role for the group, and concerning the dynamics of the group-as-a-whole. Agazarian believes we need to keep all four perspectives in mind in order to follow fully what happens in a group. She envisages the therapeutic process as moving from group phases of flight and fight to confrontation with the authority of the conductor, from enchantment and disenchantment to what she calls the phase of valid communication between individuals. She believes that this final aim, which I would call 'genuine dialogue', cannot be fully achieved until the earlier group phases are worked through. Matte-Blanco's bi-logic could help us to understand how this formidable task is achieved.

Such a synoptic viewpoint might help to explain differences in the approaches of Bion and Foulkes, which I have explored in relation to Bion's group-as-a-whole concept of basic assumptions (Brown 1979, 1985b). I believe that basic assumptions functioning (dependent, fight–flight or pairing) is encouraged by conditions which discourage dialogue, including aloof mystifying group leadership, or where dialogue is feared and inappropriate as in some formal committee work.

Genuine dialogue in a therapeutic group does not develop easily. Much talk is defensive and 'empty'. But gradually unconscious and non-verbal communications come to be recognised and unconscious aspects of the self discovered through the interaction and discourse of others and with them. Much dialogue is indirect (for example, silent members identify with those who converse and respond as though they were talking or being talked to) so that the feelings and associations of all resonate at the various levels that Foulkes described – current relationships; transference phenomena; shared fantasies and projective identification, and both mental and somatic processes. New ways of experiencing and thinking about interactions and group phenomena are acquired. They are often extended and articulated further by members who have acquired them covertly, in a way that often comes as a surprise to us as conductors. One of the great satisfactions of our work is the pleasure and pride we feel in the therapeutic skills of our patients when, for example, they say things we had not thought of or in a better way than we could have done.

The fact that therapy in group analysis is affected by the group rather than by the conductor, who deliberately leaves as much as possible to the group, makes it imperative that while he keeps in touch with as much as possible of what the group is feeling and making him feel, he does not put it all into words. He must not attempt to be an omnipotent therapist always making accurate interpretations. In fact we could modify the title of the paper by Edward Glover (1931), 'The Therapeutic Effect of Inexact Interpretation', and talk of the 'Anti-Therapeutic Effect of Exact Interpretation'. This reminds me of Foulkes's characteristic trailing sentences ending in mid-air (and my own unconscious mannerism of ending in intervention in individual analysis with an 'or . . .').

Therapy involves encouraging genuine dialogue between group members, and between the conductor and both individual members and the group-as-a-whole, between different systems and subsystems, as it were. In addition

I think it is possible to see as dialogue the opening up of links between the different levels of functioning and communications in the individual and the group. (See examples 1 and 3 in Brown 1985a.)

In addition to processes of 'direct dialogue' between individuals, parts of individuals and the group-as-a-whole, and 'interactional dialogue' between different levels of function and communication in individuals and group,[2] it may be helpful to consider the structuralising role played by certain contents in groups. This is akin to the way individual psychic structure results from 'stable co-ordinations between inner urges and the representation of experience', and grows in the maturational process (Cohen and Kinston 1984). As groups progress, and the matrix is established, dialogue in the group comes to include both key individual memories and shared group experiences which act as representational reference points in the group. Such group structures function at times as foreground, often as background to changes in both individuals and the group-as-a-whole.

Large groups, institutions and societies

The case for developing a dialogue with social psychology as well as with psychoanalysis depends on showing the relevance of group-analytic ideas, including dialogue, to phenomena in large groups, institutions and societies. Any system has to balance 'ego' and 'we-go'. Cohesion and stability have to be sufficient if there is to be room for flexible differentiation, adaptation and creative change. On the other hand, stability maintained by denying dialogue is likely, sooner or later, to crumble. In relation to Agazarian's person, member, member role and group-as-a-whole systems, any group-as-a-whole has to work out how much autonomy it can allow its subgroups (including individuals) without their becoming threats. If they do become a threat the individual or subgroup risks being put in a retaliating member role (for instance, that of scapegoat) as a result of splitting and projection. This is more likely when an institutional or social system depends on something like Bion's basic assumptions, which I see as group-as-a-whole phenomena inevitably dominant in groups where dialogue is avoided or feared. Sometimes this happens to protect powerful but vulnerable individuals or subgroups, sometimes because of the rigidity of the system. If dialogue and change are to be risked, courage and a fair measure of trust are needed.

A graphic example of this was given by Ronald Sandison in 1984 at a

2 Since writing this chapter, I have been struck by its resonance with Loewald's comments on understanding: '. . . unless the patient feels understood we feel that we have not fully understood him. Understanding would seem to be an act that involves some sort of mutual engagement, a particular form of the meeting of minds. As applied to self-understanding, it would involve the mutual engagement of different mental levels' (Loewald 1980).

meeting of the Group-Analytic Society (London). He described his two-and-a-half years' work with a community of contemplative monks on an island off the coast of Wales. They lived according to the Rule of St Benedict written in the middle of the sixth century. Basic to this Rule is a vow of stability and lifelong commitment to the community. By taking the risk of allowing a sympathetic stranger to live with them, the community was able to move out of relative stagnation and demoralisation. The role of personal interchange and the importance of the feminine element in a completely male society came to be understood and harnessed to the general good. As Malcolm Pines commented at the meeting, by introducing and tolerating the therapeutic 'Lord of Misrule', the over-stable society was able to take on a new lease of creative development (Stephen 1984).

From the unstructured large groups in our own workshops we know not only the power of friendliness and fellowship, but also how powerful and even psychotic are the potential anxieties and fantasies. As group analysts we know we have to respect and allow for the destructive potential in individuals and therefore the groups of which they are composed, however theoretically 'ideal'. Pat de Maré (De Maré and Piper 1984) has proposed that dialogue in a large group is actually powered by hatred springing from the frustration of individual desires (some might add, the threat of psychosis and loss of self). We need clear boundaries and a real sense of containment if chaos is to be risked. This is true in so-called think tanks set up to allow brainstorming and the emergence of new and challenging ideas, as well as in small psychotherapy groups. Where boundaries, containment and integration are inadequate, we must beware. Dialogue can be dangerous as well as creative. Dialogue is not a panacea, a cure for all ills. It can be dynamite. We should consider its indications and contradictions, its necessary conditions and timing. In a previous paper (Brown 1982) I gave an example taken from a vulnerable psychiatric unit. The following example of personal vulnerability is taken from a therapy group.

A professional teacher, deeply damaged in his self-esteem, reported reading the book by Robin Skynner and John Cleese, *Families and How to Survive Them* (1983). He found it tremendously illuminating, though all it said to him had been said in the group. It was as though his self-esteem was less vulnerable when reading than when he participated in a direct dialogue. The book could less easily humiliate and shame him, it would not answer back or act unexpectedly. It enabled him to see what had been said in the group from an impartial perspective.

Many of the issues I have touched on so far are also relevant to learning and training (for example, holding and containment; identification; differentiation and integration; recognition of the multiplicity of perspectives of individuals' needs and vulnerability, and the importance of freedom of speech and thought for ideas to be accepted or rejected). If new ideas are to emerge and old ones discovered anew, we have to counteract the tendency for orthodoxies to become entrenched and unquestionable in the process Main (1967) has called 'hierarchical promotion'.

Summary

Dialogue, in the sense of intimate reciprocal communication at many levels, is an essential part of group analysis. The multiple viewpoints that are made available in group analysis open up possibilities for reassessing unconscious stereotypes and assumptions about the self and others that are based on the vicissitudes of individual development and on variations of family, social and cultural background.

Compared with psychoanalysis, with its two-body context, group analysis provides a multi-body context that more directly brings to life conflicts and distortions that are relevant to those family, social and cultural settings in which problems originate and continue to manifest themselves.

Communication in the matrix of an analytic group springs from and reinforces the deeply social character of human nature. Fundamental to Foulkes's view from the beginning, this has been gradually recognised within psychoanalysis with the challenging of a simplistic instinct theory, the development of object-relations theory, the understanding of narcissism, acknowledgement of the contribution of countertransference and the personality of the analyst and so on. The embryonic dialogue between group analysis and psychoanalysis could be balanced in the future by a dialogue with social psychology (begun by Foulkes in Frankfurt).

The relationship between individual and group has both developmental and systems components which are reflected in the twin needs for autonomy and belonging. Fantasy and identification resonate with the creation and maintenance of more or less structured interpersonal and social roles.

This is illustrated in the therapeutic process in group analysis, in which psychoanalytic views about the individual's inner world are augmented by interactional perspectives of what goes on between this inner world and that of others, and between these inner worlds and that of the group-as-a-whole and the objectivity and common sense of the group.

The importance of dialogue or its absence in understanding what goes on in large groups, institutions and societies is mentioned briefly, and the dangers as well as the opportunities they offer for understanding and change are touched upon.

Finally, because dialogue is intrinsic to group analysis, our training methods must embody it. True learning has to question and challenge orthodoxy if our 'received wisdom' is not to ossify or be incompletely understood; we have to work it out and discover it for ourselves, and if necessary change it.

8

CONFRONTATION IN THE GROUP-ANALYTIC MATRIX

Toward a classification

Confrontation in a bipersonal field is the first step in the classical psychoanalytic process in which one analyst helps one patient to become aware of something of which he or she was previously unaware (Greenson 1967). By confronting the patient with the possible meaningfulness of an act or omission, a statement of inconsistency, the analyst will then go on to clarify what is happening before making an interpretation. But as group psychotherapists we mean more than this. A group is a *multipersonal* field where several people meet face to face and at many levels. In group analysis we make the most of this field and of confrontations in it, particularly of confrontations in the sense of 'meeting' or 'bringing face to face', or 'setting side by side for purposes of comparison' rather than the more vernacular sense of 'facing in hostility or defiance' (*Oxford English Dictionary*). The latter, combative, sense I propose calling 'false confrontation', as it is largely based on projection and is common in everyday life, including politics.[1]

Confrontation means many things in clinical practice, as Adler and Myerson (1973) richly detail. We need to be aware of the *negative* as well as the positive aspects of confrontation, its dangers (especially with borderline patients, and where it is based upon countertransference errors) as well as its urgent necessity at times (for example, where there is the danger of destructive acting out). Here I shall concentrate more on confrontation's positive aspects, and assume that it is reasonably accurate and appropriately timed, that it is balanced by enough empathy and support, and that the person confronted is sufficiently ready to receive it. Only then can an unwelcome truth be taken in.

1 In everyday life, where there are conflicts of interest and struggles for power, hostile confrontation can be a function of these differences of interest, and not of projection; they can, therefore, be 'true'. But in an analytic group, where there is a shared interest in and struggle toward truth, hostile confrontation is, I submit, more likely to be based on projection and, therefore, a way of avoiding the truth. Hence, in the *context of an analytic group*, I choose to call it a 'false confrontation'.

In the multipersonal field of an analytic group, more than in the bipersonal field of psychoanalysis, confrontation, clarification and interpretation merge and overlap among themselves and with processes of identification, mirroring, resonance, socialisation and communication at many levels (see Foulkes 1964). Indeed these group-specific factors can be seen as aspects of confrontation which are basic to the therapeutic effects of being in a group, and which often do not proceed to interpretation. They belong more to the *direct response* end of the continuum between interpretation and direct response described by Karl König (1986).

A central concept in group analysis is that of the group matrix. Foulkes (1964) has described this as 'the hypothetical web of communication and relationship in a given group . . . the common shared ground which ultimately determines the meaning and significance of all events and upon which all communications verbal and non-verbal rest'. The processes in the matrix are *trans*personal as well as interpersonal. 'Its lines of thought may be conceived as passing right through the individual members and may therefore be called a transpersonal network comparable to a magnetic field' (Foulkes 1973). The richness and allusiveness of this concept has been explored and developed by several group analysts (Lintott 1983; Roberts 1982; Ahlin 1985; Van der Kleij 1985).

I would like to emphasise the characteristic difference of group analysis from 'psychoanalysis in the group' and from 'analysis of the group-as-a-whole', the former represented by the work of people like Slavson, the latter by the Tavistock School, including Wilfred Bion. In contrast to these approaches, group analysis involves 'psychotherapy *by* the group, *of* the group, including the conductor' (Foulkes 1975); that is, the conductor is part of the group as well as separate from it, and is inevitably permeated and affected by it. Group analysis aims to increase the capacity of the group-as-a-whole, as well as individuals in it, to act as therapists. This involves becoming more fully aware of themselves and others and of clarifying and confronting similarities and differences at the many levels that Foulkes (1964) describes:

(a) the everyday level of current relationships;
(b) the extrapolations of the past we call transference phenomena;
(c) the deeper level of shared and projected feelings and fantasies; and finally
(d) the more primordial and universal level of images and myths akin to Jungian archetypes that Usandivaras (1986) has developed in relation to therapeutic groups.

Level (a) corresponds approximately to the level of social psychology and interactionism; (b) to classical psychoanalysis; (c) to Kleinian part-object psychology and to self-psychology; and (d) to Jungian archetypes and universal images and myths with a primordial, even phylogenetic basis.

The role of the therapist, or conductor as group analysts prefer to call themselves, leaves as much as possible to the group. The conductor is the servant of the group, like a self-effacing musical conductor who keeps the beat as timekeeper and ensures that everyone gives of their best. The conductor steps in when needed to say something others seem unable to say – sometimes an interpretation, sometimes a clarification, quite often a confrontation. But confrontations can be painful to the recipient, so the conductor must be ready to apply first aid if a group member needs it, especially a very vulnerable (for example, borderline) patient. One of the well-known strengths of a group is that while some confront and might even in a sense 'knock down' a member, others will almost inevitably 'pick him up'; the conductor may be in either camp!

I shall offer a tentative classification of confrontations in group analysis in order to demonstrate their multidimensionality. They can be seen as occurring at one or several of the relationship levels and often linking them. They are more often spontaneous than 'by design' and are more often than not gentle but pervasive rather than rough and invasive, more often by the group and other group members than by the conductor (see 1–4 below). Sometimes the conductor chooses deliberately to confront an individual or the group (see 5 and 6), but often his or her role (actively reticent, therefore seemingly passive) invites attacks by patients seeking authoritarian leadership, dependence and gratification, and leads to confrontations with the conductor (see 7). The relationship levels (a–d) at which confrontations are likely to occur in each dimension are indicated after each type.

1 Confrontation of an individual by otherness (group-as-a-whole) – a/b/c/d.
2 Confrontation of an individual by others – a/b/c.
3 Confrontation of an individual by the self in others (mirror phenomena) – b/c.
4 Confrontation of an individual by others-in-relationship – a/b.
5 Confrontation of an individual by the conductor – a/b/c.
6 Confrontation of the group by the conductor – a/b/c/d.
7 Confrontation of the conductor by an individual or group – a/b/c/d.

Some brief examples of each type of confrontation follow.

1 Of an individual by otherness (group-as-a-whole)

A patient in individual analysis for several years became stuck in a primitive symbiotic self-object transference despite very great effort on my part. Reluctantly, she eventually agreed to join a twice-weekly group with a colleague, while I went on seeing her for a smaller number of sessions a week. Finally we were able to finish the individual analysis while she continued in the group. In her individual sessions I was able to see that the changeover led to alterations in her experience of herself and her relationship with others, though at first she found the group, as she put it, 'terrifying – it was like them or me. I'd not give an inch, or give everything so as not to be found out'. I think that the group provided space to test out these primitive anxieties associated with separation and individuation and sharing, and finally to overcome them to a considerable extent. The change in context provided the necessary leverage and could be seen as a form of confrontation with a context which did not collude with her search for a primitive symbiotic self-object fusion, nor concentrate on analysing her frustration. The group in this situation was acting like the analyst who allows himself or herself to be used as the 'mother of separation', a concept of Stone (1961) cited in relation to confrontation by Shapiro (1973).

2 Of an individual by others

We frequently see group members resisting transference distortion or projective identification, sometimes, for example, in exasperation, declaring, 'I am not your mother/father, brother/sister' or by simple feedback in which characteristics of the individual are discerned in a person complaining of it in another group member. Also confrontation can be indirect, such as when a patient talking about her love for her hated mother leads to another member reflecting on whether he might perhaps at some time have loved his mother whom he thinks of still only with hatred.

3 Of an individual by the self in others

This represents an example of the mirror reaction described by Foulkes and developed by Pines (1982). Foulkes likened the group to a hall of mirrors. People not only get direct feedback in terms of what other group members see in them or understand by what they say or do, but members discover by identification how other people are experienced as containing parts of themselves which they find difficult to own. An example is the 'group time-keeper', who habitually attacked latecomers with self-righteous intolerance. He continued with this until confronted by others with his anxiousness to please and be the conductor's ally. Then he came to recognise that this covered his own healthy rebelliousness and competitiveness with the conductor. Once this was acknowledged, his self-righteousness gave way to a more relaxed concern for the group. In other words, his combative confrontationalness, a 'false confrontation' based on projection of his own noncompliant rebelliousness, was modified by his being confronted by others with an understanding of his defences.

4 Of an individual by others-in-relationship

The direct experience of jealousy toward others who are in a relationship is something not directly encountered in individual analysis. In a group it is common in a variety of forms. For example, a woman in a group, whose father had died before she was born as the only child of a narcissistic artist mother, took a very long time before she could tolerate attention shifting from her without feeling annihilated or narcissistically damaged. Eventually she was able to use confrontation with this pattern by the group, who had become very sensitive to her sense of hurt. In another group, a middle-aged professional woman, who had been pressured to join by her individual therapist who subsequently died, brought into the group a powerful resentful silence which induced the group's concern, and a pattern of talking *about* her that provoked more resentment and panic. Confrontation with this facilitated her understanding how she experienced the group as the family of her aunt to whom she was sent after her mother's death when she was seven; her father would visit but talk *about* her, not *to* her. The confrontation here was not so much a single challenge as a living through and bearing the pain. The previous week she had walked out of the group; but this week she stuck it out to the point that the confrontation led to an almost spontaneous group interpretation.

5 Of an individual by the conductor

The group-analytic conductor will hope that the individual will be sufficiently confronted at the foregoing dimensions (1–4), whether verbally or non-verbally, consciously or unconsciously, as in the last example. But at times the communications will be blocked by various forms of anxiety or collusion. Then the conductor needs to open them up, using his or her analytic understanding and example to model the way in which communications can be understood. At both this dimension and the next (6, confrontation of the group by the conductor), the conductor will feel free to use countertransference feelings and fantasy, including bodily feelings (Yassky 1973; Brown 1985a, 1985b). The conductor might be more able to make a confrontation than group members because of his or her (perhaps) greater knowledge of how much confrontation an individual might be able to tolerate, and, because of his or her marginal position, to take a broader view of the opportunity a particular group session allows for an individual breakthrough.

For example, the second session after a new man joined the group started with the theme of competition between male members. A woman member spoke of identifying with them, sensing that sibling rivalry meant a lot to her. She went on to say that she felt tearful, as though it had to do with the birth of her sister when she was three, though she had no conscious memory of feeling this at the time. I had a hunch that this was particularly relevant to perhaps the most narcissistically damaged and longest attending member of the group, so I confronted him (in a way I had learned to do particularly gently) with his being stuck in a painful preoccupation with being up or down in relation to other people *and* his often spoken of search for vengeance on women, which for a long time had prevented him from getting close to them. I interpreted these as a cover for grief, like that of this woman member. (At the age of two, during the war, when a brother had been born, he had been sent away from his mother and family to stay with grandparents and was not even allowed to take his teddy bear with him.) This interpretation of his defence allowed him to report weeping whenever he drives through the suburb where his family had lived, and, for example, watching on television the grief of a mother whose son had been hanged in the East for drug trafficking. It also enabled him to link his narcissistic vulnerability with his grief and bitterness.

I quite often use countertransference feelings of fearfulness as well as such feelings as boredom, sleepiness (Brown 1977) and irritation. On extremely rare occasions and after careful, if rapid, consideration I have used countertransference to 'act out' in the group. For example, I once threw a cushion at a particularly inhibited passive-aggressive member. This had the effect of vividly confronting the patient with his effect on others, and linking it with his fear of expressing himself directly rather than through projective identification. This 'shocking' behaviour on my part could be called 'planned acting out' (Klain 1986) though in reality it was more intuitive and instantaneous than that would imply. But as Ormont (1984) has put it, 'The right expression of counter-rage, in the right dose, at the right time, can save a group that would otherwise remain lost and unsettled.' A sense of fun is a great help in enabling and tempering such confrontations. Indeed humour can be seen as a form of confrontation between different levels of reality.

6 Of the group by the conductor

Although group-as-a-whole interpretations are less often made by group analysts than by some other group psychotherapists, it can be very helpful to confront the group with, for example, joint manic evasion of painful feelings, scapegoating of an individual, or (rarely) so-called basic assumption configurations (Bion 1959; Brown 1985a).

7 Of the conductor by an individual or group

A trainee in a group of patients and trainees told of a dream in which she was attacking me for not seeing things as clearly as she did in the previous session, and the attack only stopped when I stood up – with which she had phallic associations. She related it to difficulty in attacking her father, who needed to maintain his authority even when he did not deserve it. I was able to acknowledge her disappointment and rage, but also to point out that indeed she might well have seen things more clearly, and this was all right – her potency didn't actually destroy mine. We were all confronted by the difference between real and fantasy fathers inside transference (dimensions 1 and 2).

In practice these different types of confrontation (1–7) often overlap and coincide in a single session. For example, one session was started by a member speaking of the loss of the house she had sold which had represented an idealised self/mother. She added that she was thinking of taking up training as a group analyst. She had fairly recently been talking about finishing her therapy in the group about this time, and I made what was perhaps a premature or inappropriate interpretation of this thought as a way of avoiding separation and loss. This had the eject of a harsh confrontation (5) that 'knocked her off her perch' as she later put it. A male member spoke about his anxiety about being 'tamed' by his impending marriage. Then another man 'confronted' me (7), saying he was puzzled by my role in the group of which he had been a member for some 18 months. He complained that I did not explain my role or recommend books to read. As I was reflecting on his frequent indirect challenges alternating with apparent dozing withdrawal, he began talking about anarchist bombs or opting out as two alternatives. Another member likened him to a defensive winger in rugby who ran right across the field to score without being tackled (2). The woman had spotted his evading my question about what *his* welling tears were about after he had identified with *her* welling tears about relinquishing her house (2). I confronted him (5) with my countertransference of feeling frustrated by his not having a stand-up row with me, asking him if he had ever had a stand-up row with his father. He replied, 'Twice.' The last time he was 11; when his parents were rowing he defended his mother. At the next session this man commented that the last session was the first he remembers my talking like that. It had made an impact on him, and he described how in the meantime he had found he was able to be aware of and to contain his anger at a disparaging client.

It would seem that my apparently confronting interpretation to the woman activated a transference configuration in the group for this man, who then confronted me indirectly as if re-enacting his puzzlement at the relationship of his mother with his father, who used to be away for long periods from the family during the war. The lack of directness had then led to the countertransference feeling that I was able to confront him in a way that brought this transference into consciousness. The greater openness and tolerance within the group seems to have provided him with a model which he could use in a difficult 'confrontation' in real life.

These confrontations mainly occurred at levels (a) and (b) – in terms of current and transference relationships. However, it seems likely that confrontation with the woman's narcissistic deflation resonated with anxieties in the man about to be married which belonged to the more primitive projective level (c), or even the primordial level (d) of an archetypal suffocating mother. It is interesting to note that he was asthmatic and had gradually overcome markedly counterdependent character traits – hence his marriage!

Conclusion

It will have become clear that confrontation, in the sense of meeting, setting side by side and bringing face to face, is an essential part of the therapeutic process in group analysis. Hostile confrontations based on projection and projective identification take place also, but these have to be recognised for what they are and worked through. I call these 'false' confrontations.

Hopefully, this classification of confrontations, by indicating who confronts whom within the group matrix, will prove clarifying, especially when linked up to the different levels of relationship described by Foulkes. It might prove helpful to add further parameters to provide a more complete classification, such as how much force or apparent hostility is used or, in the case of confrontation by the conductor, whether a confrontation is based on so-called subjective or objective countertransference reactions (Spotnitz 1979).

9

CHANGE IN THE GROUP-ANALYTIC SETTING

In *Psychotherapeutic Techniques in Medicine*, Michael and Enid Balint state that: 'After a successful psychoanalytic treatment a patient is definitely less neurotic but not really mature; but on the other hand, after a successful treatment by group methods the patient is not necessarily less neurotic, but is inevitably more mature' (Balint and Balint 1961).

How does group treatment promote maturity? What is maturity and its relevance to the therapeutic change? Hopefully this contribution will shed some light on these questions, taking in turn the three elements of *setting, relationships* and *change*, as they interact in the therapeutic processes of group analysis (Foulkes 1948, 1964, 1975; Pines 1981). I believe these are complementary to those of psychoanalysis, both theoretically and practically.

Setting

In psychoanalysis we view dynamic change in an individual's unconscious (or conscious) relationship with themselves and others as more important than mere symptomatic change. The work of David Malan (1979) detailing this in individual psychotherapy is of great importance. In group analysis, with a more open setting than that of the hermetic bipersonal field of psychoanalysis (Langs 1979), we have a multipersonal field. Here there is space, in the Winnicottian sense, to play (Winnicott 1971b), to fantasise, act-in, have acting-out recognised, reverse roles, and explore the interplay of subjectivity and objectivity and the intricacies of intersubjectivity, in a setting that involves several people, and is nearer to the mutuality of family and everyday life. For example, we can see individual transference and projective identification interacting in vivid ways that promote illumination for other group members as well as for the protagonists as their recognition gives rise to mutual understanding and tolerance, and respect for differences as well as similarities. These can be seen as aspects of maturity.

In a clinical vignette I have described elsewhere (Brown and Pedder 1979), two men got caught in a patterned mutual hostility that dominated the group for several sessions. On the surface, they were very different. One, recently married, had been dubbed 'the bear in the cave' by the group, because of his severity and the hint of fierceness that had kept others at bay (his marriage had been seen as a move away from this defensiveness). The other man was an effeminate homosexual who 'wore his heart on his sleeve' and was touchy and sensitive. Work in the group led the homosexual to recognise that he reacted to 'the bear' as to the rejecting and inhibiting father of his childhood, who had, in fact, been very much like 'the bear's' father. But 'the bear' instead of defying his father and his father's standards as the homosexual had done, had identified with his father and rejected his longings for affection from him and projected them as dangerously homosexual into the other group members along with the associated hurt and rage. In the group, the two men were able to reconcile themselves to each other and these painful and dangerous parts of themselves, in a way that all members of the group were able to learn from.

Such multiple synchronous gains in understanding and the related modification of transference and projection are dependent on the group setting. But this setting also promotes levels of interaction that go further in transcending individual boundaries, to those areas of malfunction such as fusion, premature closure, and exploitation of the emerging individual by the family network where much pathology originates. Agazarian and Peters (1981), in *The Visible and Invisible Group*, describe four sets of dynamics contained within the group setting. They relate to the individual (1) as a person; (2) as a group member (e.g. part of a competing pair or subgroup); and (3) in a role for the group (e.g. scapegoat); as well as to (4) dynamics involving the group as a whole (e.g. so-called basic assumption phenomena – Bion 1961; Brown 1985a). The group therapist needs to keep all four sets of dynamics in mind.

In group analysis, six or eight patients of both sexes and with a variety of backgrounds and problems sit face to face in a circle with a conductor, all on equal chairs. They have a free-floating discussion for one and a half hours once or twice a week over a long period of time. The conductor's first task is to create, maintain and protect this setting, and to attend equally to what is going on in individuals and in the group, and to both what happens in the group and at its periphery – what Foulkes called 'boundary phenomena'; events before and after the group starts, possible meetings outside, issues of time-keeping, absences and (in private practice) fee-paying. As an analyst he has to attend to his own countertransference and how he is being used by individuals and the group as a whole. The fact that he is sitting in the circle means that he is exposing himself to real scrutiny as well as projected fantasy as in psychoanalysis, and it is very important that he keeps to his analytic role in order to represent the analytic attitude, so the group can gradually identify with it. As the group matures, members gradually become more analytic themselves.

For the patient, confrontation with being a group member poses a dual pull between wishes to belong and to be independent of the group. Wishes for acceptance, support and help are countered by wishes to remain independent and free from the fear of exposure, humiliation, attack or rejection. The needs of the ego may be seen as in conflict with those of what George Klein (1976) called the we-go. Sitting in a circle allows these conflicting pressures to be faced up to, and the realisation of interdependence and the respect for both similarities and difference that are the basis of mature family and social life to be arrived at. Sitting face to face promotes such processes described by Foulkes (1964) as *resonance* (in which common themes are picked up and developed by individuals according to where they are at that time) and *mirroring* (in which people not only get feedback from others about how they come over, but discover in others aspects of themselves they have difficulty in owning – as in the example I gave earlier). Foulkes likened the group to a hall of mirrors, where distortions can be alarming or funny, and accurate reflections disturbing or reassuring. Often they say as much about the mirror as the people reflected in them. The group provides a way of recognising such distortions in a way that is more difficult in the psychoanalytic dyad.

Relationships

Group analytic theory marries well with general systems theory in which individuals, the group and wider social groupings can be seen as open systems formed and informed by information and meaning (Bertalanffy 1968; Durkin 1982). Among the principles of group analysis described by Foulkes (1948) in his first book, written hard on the heels of his experiences in Birmingham at the Northfield Military Neurosis Unit, were that (1) *the essence of man is social, consciously and unconsciously*; (2) *the idea of the individual is an abstraction*. Groups are the matrix of individual development. Every individual is part of a series of networks, internally and externally. In these networks, the individual is like a neurone suspended within the tissues of the nervous system – a metaphor springing from Foulkes's two years studying with the neurologist Kurt Goldstein. Just as they do in football crowds, institutions, nations and families, *transpersonal* processes operate in therapeutic groups. Hence, group-as-a-whole phenomena take place, and different aspects of everyone can be personalised in individuals. Apparent opposites represent ends of a continuum to which every individual contributes opposing aspects of themselves.

To extend Winnicott's famous dictum 'There is no such thing as a baby, only a nursing couple' (Winnicott 1975) one could say that there is no such thing as an individual, or a couple (including a therapist–patient couple) or a family or a social group (including a therapeutic group); there is only a series of interacting systems. The group enables regression *to*, but also progression *from* dyadic dependency, towards reliving triadic (Oedipal) relationships, social awareness and a recognition of the complementarity of different roles and stages of development as maturation takes place.

When we create 'artificial boundaries' to study relationships in a particular system and its infrasystems, we can choose to ignore information penetrating from the adjacent suprasystems. In group analysis, these are acknowledged in the concept of the *foundation matrix*: 'based on the biological properties of the species, but also on the culturally firmly embedded values and reactions. These have been developed and transmitted especially in the nuclear family in the social network, class etc; and have been maintained and modified by the intimate plexus in which the person now moves' (Foulkes 1975: 131).

This contrasts with the new dynamic matrix we aim to establish in a therapeutic group: 'the hypothetical web of communication and relationship in a given group . . . the common shared ground which ultimately determines the meaning and significance of all events and upon which communications verbal and non-verbal rest' (Foulkes 1964). The processes in the matrix are transpersonal as well as interpersonal. 'Its lines of thought may be conceived as passing right through the individual members and may, therefore, be called a transpersonal network comparable to the magnetic field' (Foulkes 1973). It develops from a set of conductor-directed dependent transferences, with other group members a vague but intriguing threat and scarcely recognised as themselves. Gradually a rich network of relationships between all members develops. Finally, experience of the group-as-a-whole interplays with individual dyadic and triadic relationships. Each is available for comparison and contrast, alternating as foreground and background within a space safe enough for primitive anxieties to be tested out, contained (in the Bionian sense – James 1981) and digested, and for play and innovation. Fantasy and reality are discovered to interplay, and identity can be merged and discovered anew.

It may be helpful to remind ourselves that there are several levels of relationship in the matrix: (1) everyday current relationships; (2) transference relationships; (3) projected and shared images, often bodily; and (4) primordial universal images and myths; roughly corresponding, respectively, to the moulds of social psychology, Freudian, Kleinian and Jungian psychology. A discovery of their coexistence and interaction is part of the therapeutic process that promotes change. Of course, there are many transferences in a group, to other group members as well as the conductor, and to the group-as-a-whole which can represent, for example, a womb or mother or family. These inevitably coexist.

The different levels of relationship also coexist, e.g. transference and projective, even in processes involving the same individual. For example, in one group latecomers were habitually attacked with self-righteous intolerance by somebody who came to be seen as 'the group timekeeper'. He continued with this behaviour until he was confronted by others with his anxiety to please and be my ally. This enabled him to recognise how his behaviour covered his own healthy rebelliousness and competitiveness with me as a father. Once this was acknowledged and the anxieties behind this defensive behaviour overcome, his self-righteousness gave way to greater freedom in his relationship with me and a more relaxed concern for the group. This, of course, can be seen as a move towards maturity.

Change

In group analytic theory neurosis and immaturity are correlated. Neurosis is seen as an autistic expression of feelings and fantasies, those aspects of relationships which could not be expressed within the relationships in which the developing individual experienced trauma and conflicts (Foulkes 1948). An essential part of the therapeutic process is the discovery, communication and increasing articulation of these previously isolating aspects of themselves, within a network of relationships that at times seems to resemble the original family, but ultimately does not react like it. Indeed, they come to be seen as part of the human condition which can be integrated within the individual and used as a basis for empathy and identification with others.

In classical psychoanalysis, insight is seen as the prerequisite for change. In group analysis we see insight and change as interacting. Indeed, Foulkes regarded insight as the consequence of change. For insight to be full, and for it to be recognised and adjusted to within oneself and relationships with others, there has to be a readiness to receive and respond to a new way of seeing things. Hence, patients will often say such things as 'I now know what you were getting at'.

Despite much psychoanalytic work, some patients cannot overcome deep resistances to change, nor apply what they learn in the dyadic relationships to wider relationships outside. For example, I had a patient in individual analysis for several years without being able to help her move from a primitive symbiotic self-object transference. Reluctantly, she eventually agreed to join a twice-weekly group with a colleague while I went on seeing her for a reduced number of sessions per week. Ultimately, we were able to finish the individual analysis while she continued in the group; but in the meantime I was able to see that the change of setting led to alterations in her experience of herself and her relationship with others, despite finding the group as she put it, 'terrifying – it was like them or me – I'd not give an inch, or give everything so as not to be found out'. I think that the group provided space to test out these primitive anxieties associated with separation and individuation and sharing, and finally overcome them to a considerable extent. The group provided the necessary leverage, and could be seen as a form of confrontation with a context which did not collude with her search for a primitive symbiotic self-object fusion, nor merely concentrate on analysing her frustration.

In group analysis we attempt to select a group of individuals with a variety of problems from a range of backgrounds. For Foulkes (1948) the group represents the norm from which individuals deviate. It has long been known that one of the special therapeutic advantages of groups is their capacity to challenge ego-syntonic defences (Guttmacher and Birk 1971), but Robin Skynner (1986) has recently thrown light on why a heterogeneous group could be so effective in promoting change. 'At the start, each person's different family pattern exists only inside his head, but each member will bring his family to the group in the form of projections: e.g. projected expectations based on his own typical family experience, together with a family pattern of non-verbal signals by which he will seek to manipulate other group members into joining into his particular family "cover-up".'

For example, someone from a family where jealousy was denied and avoided may seek to persuade group members to 'take turns' and avoid competition by sharing out time equally. Another member, from a family which denied and avoided dependence by emphasising self-reliance, may instead push the group towards fierce competition.

The classical psychoanalytic ideas of defence and resistance are, of course, still crucial in understanding and working with blocks to change, and there are group defences and resistances as well as individual ones. But group collusion is rarely total and the example and pressures of others and 'otherness' can be of inestimable help – as in the patient I had to move into a group. Moving from autism to communication, from defensive self-absorption to deeper relatedness to others, implies, in psychoanalytic terms, firstly, a move from the paranoid-schizoid to the depressive position (Klein 1975/1935); but also, secondly, an ability to modify one's relationship with internal objects, so that primitive persecution and guilt are replaced by concern for them, and parents and siblings can be understood as having their own conflicts and problems; they can be blamed less and forgiven more.

These moves provide some of the most crucial and poignant moments in group analysis as well as in psychoanalysis. And their achievements, in both forms of treatment, are ultimately dependent on the capacity of the therapeutic relationship in the setting to provide the necessary understanding, containment and holding (Bion 1967; Winnicott 1971a; Casement 1985). Only then, can the individual move in a deep sense.

Such are the similarities. But maturity implies respect for differences too, between forms of treatment as well as between individuals. Psychoanalysis – 'vertical analysis' – provides a setting where the detail of primitive dyadic relationships can be re-experienced and reconstructed with great precision. Group analysis – 'horizontal analysis' – provides an environment where blocks to moving beyond early trauma at that level can be released, even bypassed, so that they cease to have such a distorting effect on development. Caroline Garland (1982) has described the benefit that the group provides by forming a system with different rules from the system the individual comes from. Because the system of the group is nearer to that of everyday life, it is often easier to transfer changes to the outside world from the group setting than from that of psychoanalysis. It is this, perhaps, that makes the group a particularly potent setting to help people move towards that aspect of maturity that involves an enjoyment of what Enid Balint (1972) has called 'fair shares and mutual concern'. Seeing people make this move is one of the great joys of group analysis.

I hope we are nearer to answering some of the questions raised by the Balints' aphorism which I quoted at the beginning: What *is* maturity and its relevance to therapeutic change? How does group treatment promote maturity?

The last words will be left to a patient in a current group. He is a middle-aged ex-submarine commander turned management consultant whose early contributions were simple prescriptions as to how others could solve their current everyday problems. Gradually he came to acknowledge his own problems, past as well as current, and to recognise the complexity of his own and other people's natures, including the balance between strength and weakness, particularly expressed through his need of others. During one session he described to another member how he had come to realise, by being in the group, the importance of getting a full and proper balance between selfishness and compassion. 'That's how the group works, it enables you to be *really* selfish, and *really* compassionate, together.'

10

SELF DEVELOPMENT THROUGH SUBJECTIVE INTERACTION

A fresh look at 'ego training in action'

Introduction

As a psychoanalyst who came later to group analysis, I shall attempt in the present chapter to describe and explain a process characteristic of well-functioning small stranger groups, and not of individual analysis. It contributes, I believe, an important element to what are experienced as 'good sessions' in group work. It forms the basis for actually becoming more fully oneself in reciprocity with others. Psychoanalysis can be only a preparation for such a move. The most concise term I can find for this process is 'self development through subjective interaction'. It is more specific than Foulkes's expression 'ego training in action', and nearer to the clinical experience I wish to describe. Later in the chapter it will be illustrated with three vignettes: The Man Who Could Not Understand, The Woman Who Would Not Feel Understood, and The Drowsy Group Including the Conductor.

Exploration of the process requires consideration of the concept of intersubjectivity. While the development of intersubjectivity is indirectly recognised as important in modern psychoanalysis, e.g. in the emphasis now given to countertransference and unconscious interaction between the personalities of analysand and analyst, I will argue that in group analysis the achievement of awareness of intersubjectivity with a *range* of other personalities, not restricted to the analyst, and in their presence, powerfully promotes maturity and a capacity to engage in mutually validating relationships.

Others come to be treated as subjects rather than objects, partly because they demand it. The exploration of each individual's private inner world occurs against the background of the inner worlds of others within the developing matrix of the group (Powell 1994). It is augmented by tacit encouragement to discover how internalised relationships, rooted in the past, can distort and limit engagement in new and more satisfactory relationships based on the actuality and potentiality of the experiences of self and others.

Ego training in action

Foulkes characterised psychoanalysis as 'vertical' analysis, conducted in an asymmetrical relationship and emphasising the detailed reconstruction of the past of the individual patient. In contrast, group analysis is 'horizontal' analysis, conducted within a circle of equals, amongst whom problems rooted in the past can be played out and modified (Foulkes and Anthony 1965: 42). This allows what Foulkes describes as 'ego training in action':

> 'Action' here does not mean doing or, literally, acting or role playing; nor is it the equivalent of 'acting out' in psychoanalysis. The group provides a stage for actions, reactions and interactions within the therapeutic situation, which are denied to the psychoanalytic patient on the couch. However, the ego to which we refer is the ego in the psychoanalytic sense, the inner ego as a metapsychological concept, which is activated and reformed.
>
> (Foulkes 1964: 82)

Foulkes's description of the process of therapy as 'ego training in action' originated in the prominence of Freud's structural theory during his training in Vienna, and in his early professional practice in Germany and Britain. According to this theory, the personality is divided into the instinct-dominated id, the conscience-carrying superego and the adaptive and mediating ego. The ego is the seat of conflict resolution, signal anxiety, defence, and of reality testing: appraising stimuli from within and without the individual.

Gradually Freud had moved some way from a purely one-body psychology. He had written of the character of the ego as a 'precipitate of abandoned object-cathexes' (Freud 1923: 29) and realised the importance of identification (Freud 1921: 105ff). In the ego defence mechanism of 'identification with the aggressor', Anna Freud (1936: 109ff) pointed to the interchangeability of self and object representations, later to be described in detail by Jacobson (1964). Recently Bollas (1987) has written about the ego embodying rules for relating to the primary object, mother. It 'develops "rules" for processing intrapsychic and intersubjective experience . . . as mother and child negotiate paradigms for processing all of a life's experience' (p. 72). We could also say, however, that it comes to embody rules for relating to various constellations in the family network, and to the social context, to differentiate but also to connect and belong.

Thus, in a review of modern views of the ego, Padel (1985) draws attention to four ego functions, which will be strikingly familiar to a group analyst: (1) scanning of the field; (2) dividing it with alternation of attention between at least two features, and exploration of each from the vantage point of the other; (3) reuniting it and viewing the field from a third position; (4) refinding each object by identifying with the other.

This last function is especially interesting as it involves moving beyond 'asymmetrical' discriminatory functions towards the complementary 'symmetrical' thinking included by Matte-Blanco (1975) in his theory of bi-logic. The latter allows the discernment of analogies and connectedness, and thus the possibility of self-object de-differentiation (Milner 1987). This type of thinking is necessary for empathy, intuition, and the experience of being part of something that includes oneself, whether a dyad, a group, a species or the cosmos (Blackwell 1994; Powell 1994). It could be considered as playing a part in what Foulkes called resonance in groups.

As a psychoanalyst, Foulkes was ahead of his time with his ideas of the individual as an abstraction, a nodal point in a network, of the interchangeability of figure and ground, or context and what happens in it, of inside and outside, and of disturbance being located between people. However, during the time Foulkes was developing the theory and practice of group analysis, and not involved in the development of psychoanalytic theory itself, the latter was being radically affected by object relations theory and to a lesser extent by self psychology. Like group analysis, both of these emphasise relationships, and the interactional and contextual element in individual development and functioning. In that sense they have moved further away from a one-body, purely biologically based theory towards a theory of interacting systems: intrapersonal, interpersonal and – in the case of group analysis – social. Both types of analysis – group and individual – are increasingly being seen as occurring in overlapping subjective worlds. Indeed it is interesting that the psychoanalyst Klauber (1987: 24) recently and quite independently of Foulkes, distinguished between vertical analysis, based on the individual patient's history, and horizontal analysis, based on transactions in the present between patient and analyst.

Self development through subjective interaction

I propose that Foulkes's visionary views, laid out in his first book (Foulkes 1948), and the subsequent advances in analytical thinking, call for the idea of 'ego training in action' to be amplified to allow for a circular and spiral movement that includes: (1) discovering how we experience and relate to others in terms of our inner worlds of internal object relationships; (2) discerning how these experiences rooted in the past can be transformed into more flexible new experiences in the shared world of 'here and now'; and (3) learning to attune ourselves to other people, and to make sense of them and their experience as well as our own. Such learning requires the development of a capacity for empathic sensitivity that increases our relatedness to others, through both identification and differentiation. This final achievement is, paradoxically, near to the point from which we all, to varying extents, start. It involves the unfolding of capacities central to the early infant–mother relationship, as Stern (1985) has argued on the basis of developmental research. Mutual responses between the subjective experiences of infant and mother are the building blocks of the baby's sense of self. This three-phase process is what I shall refer to as '*self development through subjective interaction*'. It involves the recognition and development of a sense of intersubjectivity.

Intersubjectivity

Conceptualising the processes of discovering of inner worlds, discerning new opportunities to transcend blocks rooted in them, and learning to relate to others in empathic mutuality, can draw not only on developmental studies but also on both object relations theory and self psychology. Foulkes acknowledged neither directly. However, as Malcolm Pines noted in his foreword to Foulkes's selected papers (Foulkes 1990b), Foulkes thought not of internal objects – isolated intrapsychic representations of key figures to whom instinctual drives are directed – but of internal object relationships. Although he never wrote specifically about object relationships or subjectivity, his work is pervaded by the idea of *subject–object relations*, or even *intersubjective relations*. This might need some explaining.

In an examination of the close parallel between the views of Foulkes and those of the French phenomenologist Merleau-Ponty, Cohn (1990) points out that experience of oneself inevitably means experience of oneself in the context of relationships with others – as Foulkes said (1948: 10), the isolated individual is an artificial abstraction. In phenomenological terms, meaning and significance occur not inside people, but between them, i.e. in intersubjectivity. Merleau-Ponty (1964: 134) puts it as '[the] subject is no longer alone, is no longer conscious in general or pure being-for-itself. He is in the midst of unconsciousnesses'. In dialogue between one person and another, 'my thought and his are interwoven into a single fabric, my words and those of my interlocutor are called forth by the state of the discussion, and they are inserted into a shared opinion of which neither of us is the creator' (Merleau-Ponty 1976: 354). Cohn points out the correspondence between Merleau-Ponty's 'single fabric' and Foulkes's idea of the group matrix: 'the common ground which ultimately determines the meaning and significance of all events and upon which all communications and interpretations, verbal and non-verbal, rest' (1964: 292).

Gordon (1991) has recently written persuasively about the role of intersubjectivity in group psychotherapy. This 'union or contact of the subjectivities' demands reformulation of traditional ideas of subject–object, I–you. Gordon writes: 'In the intersubjective realm there is no inner or outer, only a body of contact and experience which expresses itself in a "consummate reciprocity" in which we discover ourselves through the other.' This describes very vividly the everyday experience of life in an analytic group.

In Chapter 26 of his collected papers (Foulkes 1990), dictated in his last year of life and entitled 'Concerning Criticism of Inner-Object Theory', Foulkes argues for a distinction between experiential and metapsychological processes. He states that internal mental processes are not created by individuals in isolation, but originate in a context of a multipersonal network of interaction. The individual is stamped with these experiences in the primary family, and tends to re-experience and recreate them in later contexts. But, Foulkes insists, 'the more mature and free a person becomes to function as a *whole* person in relation to other persons, the more will these processes lose in importance and significance'.

The mediator for the encounter between self and other, Merleau-Ponty argues, is language. This accords with the primacy of communication in group analysis, of making articulate what could not previously be put into words: 'It is only retrospectively, when I have withdrawn from the dialogue and am recalling it, that I am able to integrate it into my life and make it an episode in my private history, and that other recedes into his absence, or, insofar as he remains, is felt as a threat' (Merleau-Ponty 1976: 354–5).

However, as I see it, integrating the dialogue established in intersubjectivity plays a part in transforming old structures based on rigid internal object relationships, and reduces that threat. Sharing promotes recognition that others are not just objects to be desired or feared. They have their own valid viewpoints and feelings. This recognition opens the way to empathy, withdrawal of projections and stereotyping, and the attainment of mutual concern between members of the group.

George Klein, in his influential attempt to formulate a clinical as opposed to a metapsychological theory of psychoanalysis, pointed out that psychoanalysts had lacked a concept of 'we-ness'. This has its prototype in the mother–infant unit and continues as an essential part of identity. He states:

> The terminology of subject and object has contributed to misleading conceptualisations of selfhood and especially to obscuring its 'we' aspect. The traditional view of man as becoming gradually aware of himself as 'subject' confronting others as 'object' may be applicable *morphologically* but it does not describe dynamic wholes. Identity must always be defined as having aspects of both separateness and membership in a more encompassing entity, and as developing functions that reflect one's role in a relationship to that larger entity.
> (G. Klein 1976: 178)

This 'Janus-faced view' of the relationship of the individual to the other, contrasts markedly with Bion's view of the inevitable struggle of the individual in the group as corresponding to that of the infant in relation to the breast, and of the group as only an illusion (Bion 1961); a view I have contrasted with that of Foulkes (Brown 1985a). One could just as well say the individual is an illusion, or that both the group and the individuals in it are illusions. It is here that the idea of intersubjectivity proves useful. Groups can certainly share illusions, but a therapeutic group provides a way of exposing illusions, and of modifying them by intersubjective validation.

Atwood and Stolorow (1984: 41) have pointed out that individual psychoanalysis can be viewed as 'a science of the *intersubjective* focused on the interplay between the differently organised subjective worlds of the observer and the observed'. Group analysis can also be approached as a study of intersubjectivity, focusing on the interplay of the subjective worlds of group members, including the conductor. According to Atwood and Stolorow (1984: 52), negative therapeutic reactions in psychoanalysis can be seen as 'most often a product of prolonged, unrecognised transference-countertransference disjunctions and the chronic misunderstandings that result'. Just as this can occur in the 'bipersonal field' of psychoanalysis, so it can occur in the 'multipersonal field' of group analysis. But here it is less likely, as harmful collusions between individual patient and therapist can be observed and challenged by others. This might be one reason why groups can help people who have become stuck in interminable individual analyses – intersubjective impasse is open to scrutiny by others.

Intersubjectivity is an important aspect of relationships from early infancy onwards, but the notion of internal object relationships seems unavoidable in the present state of our understanding. To make sense of this, philosophical ideas have to be augmented by ideas originating in infant observation and clinical experience.

The development of internal object relations

Turning to the early development of the individual, it is reasonable to suppose that the groundwork of a coherent subjective sense of self precedes the establishment of internal representations of the self in relation to others (Stern 1985). Empathic mirroring and containment by mother precede the infant's experience of her as a clearly separate object. Whether she is the object of instinctual drives or the focus of powerful wishes is a distinction which can still be left open as pointed out by Greenberg and Mitchell (1985) in their thorough examination of the contributions of the principal object relations theorists – including Balint, Fairbairn, Klein and Winnicott in Britain, Jacobson, Modell and Mahler in the USA. It is relationships that are internalised.

Kernberg (1980), attempting to integrate the work of these pioneers with ego psychology, has built up a case for viewing internal object relationships as composed of subject–object–affect units. These units gradually develop into more complex substructures, such as real and ideal self and object representations in the internal world. These internal representations and relationships originate in the subjective experience of self with other, in a world not yet sharply split into internal and external. One could add that it is likely that the nascent self, emerging from a barely differentiated unity, experiences objects as essential parts of itself, e.g. as the confirming (mirroring) and motivating (idealising) selfobjects, the antagonist and twin selfobjects described by Kohut and his followers (Kohut and Wolf 1978). They continue to influence perception of outside relationships, largely unconsciously, so that inner and outer worlds resonate and mutually recreate each other.

However, beyond the family the personality is sustained, for good or ill, through significant relationships with others, including work, pastimes and identification through membership of groups that give one a continuing sense of 'we-ness'. Rouchy (1987) has written about the importance of such 'belonging groups' ('groupes d'appartenance'). These are only now beginning to receive proper attention from psychoanalysts and group analysts. They can be taken for granted until they – and their function for the individual – are disrupted by migration and other exigencies. They can be viewed as serving transformational (Bollas 1987) and transitional functions for the individual (Winnicott 1971a), and provide opportunities for sublimation of instinctual drives, and for such necessary functions as reparation and idealisation. But also they act as links with sociocultural norms and values, with the world outside family. They provide alternative belonging groups.

In the course of development we internalise relationships between important people in our universe: the primary dyad, family and wider social groups, all in turn impregnated by and thus to varying degrees internalising values, customs, standards, history, myths and aspirations of the prevailing culture or subculture in which we are embedded. (Le Roy). The individual internalises automatically and unconsciously what is at first neither internal nor external. Culture is both between people and encompasses them, binds them and defines them to each other. However, the significance of each to the other, and thus the nature and quality of the subjective feelings and fantasies evoked by the interaction at any point in time, will depend on the total configuration of relationships within the system – or the matrix within the multipersonal psychological field. Foulkes's way of understanding Oedipal phenomena illustrates such a systemic viewpoint (Brown and Zinkin 1994). The arrival of an infant leads to regression in *all* members of the family, so that both parents as well as the infant instigate the Oedipal conflict. Moreover, identification is not 'undirectional'. As Rouchy (1982) puts it, 'the subject is created in the desire of the parents and through reflections. A lack or an ambiguity in the eye of the other is a source of deficiencies and disturbances in the constitution of identity and the social link'.

How each family member manages and manifests this regression, and how they look at and respond to the baby, will depend on their own history and personality. What each member has 'internalised' is composed in the first place of relatively fixed mutual relational patterns between self and parents, siblings, and often members of the wider family, family friends and pets. Represented as images and fantasies, these are essentially unconscious because of repression and infantile amnesia, but also because their earliest form is adumbrated by purely somatic strivings and experiences, at a pre-reflective stage that Bion (1961: 101) called the protomental level of development. Many people continue to manifest difficulties in relationships at this level throughout life, especially at times of stress, leading to psychosomatic disorders (McDougall 1974; Brown 1985, 1989; Taylor 1987). At this protomental level the infant, or physically ill adult, functions at the level of beta-functions (Bion 1962b: 35) before the alpha-functions of fantasy and imagery appear (see the cases of Richard and the drowsy group below).

It is those relationships which are forgotten, repressed or based on as yet unimaginable, beta-element experiences that increase in power in regressive states, e.g. as a result of anxiety and stress, including the given-up/giving-up states of despair and withdrawal that can lead to physical illness (Engel 1962: 392). They are therefore less available for correction and modification by accurate appraisal of external, consensually validated reality. They lead to transference distortion of external relationships, and interfere with individuals' engagement in new and more mature relationships (A. Freud 1965: 39), as will be evident from the clinical material described later.

In a recent examination of the psychoanalytic concept of internal object relationships Sandler (1990) proposes that our need to cling to the internal object relationship is a source of severe resistance in analysis. This often becomes clear in the matrix of the analytic group as a shared problem. What do we do if our sense of self and safety, or that of another group member depends on maintaining, e.g. the role of victim or of omnipotent controller, of independent 'coper' or entertainer? These and other roles can block the development of the individual or group. For example, mature dependence (Fairbairn 1952) may fail to replace infantile dependence or counter-dependence (see the case of Kim below).

Development beyond internal object relations

These relationships and roles can be incorporated into character traits and inhibitions of personality such as alexithymia (McDougall 1974; Taylor 1987). They become manifest in the therapeutic situation, not as isolated internal objects, but as relationships or 'presences' which allow a reconstruction of each individual's past life and their consequent 'internal baggage'. At the same time, structures based on internalising certain types of object relations that were not present at crucial times in development can be built up later during therapeutic regression (Loewald 1980: 376–7). These include relationships in which other group members and the whole group can be said to function as the selfobjects described earlier. Other new opportunities for identification and internalisation are offered by the therapist's 'analytic attitude', and healthier experiences of mothering, fathering or sibling relationship that provide a more appropriate balance of confrontation and support, frustration and compensation.

They occur in a group-analytic group without any conscious 'corrective emotional experience' (Alexander and French 1946); indeed they are an important part of the therapeutic and maturing effects of membership of an analytic group (Brown 1987a). Pines (1990) has argued for replacing the term 'corrective emotional experience' by 'the appropriate response, the good-enough gesture, which enables the patient to move from an embedded defensive position towards intersubjectivity, being with another in a shared state, that is being understood in a proper sense of being with one who stands underneath the other'. This experience enables us to know more about ourselves in a way that makes us better able to make that knowledge part of a firmer foundation for the self as locus of experience. In a therapeutic group, most people want to feel understood and to understand themselves better. Eventually they usually do, and in the process understand others better. Members of a group become more capable of engaging empathically with each other. However, as Nitsun (personal communication, 1992) has emphasised, the empathic gulf can be extremely difficult to bridge, and can be accentuated rather than diminished in groups. Indeed Nitsun has suggested that such 'misattunement' may lead to the 'anti-group' experiences he has so valuably highlighted (Nitsun 1991). Thus it is important to bear in mind the dangers of failed intersubjectivity at the same time as clarifying the significance of aiming for intersubjective relatedness.

It will be seen that we have now moved through the three stages outlined near the start of this chapter: (1) discovering inner worlds of object relationship; (2) using new opportunities to transcend blocks rooted in them; (3) learning to relate to others in empathic mutuality. In the clinical situation these stages are reached in a fitful and recurrent progress towards intimacy and empathic understanding. When achieved they carry the group and its members forward towards a greater degree of experienced intersubjectivity.

Clinical material

I shall present and comment on clinical material following these three stages.

1 The man who could not understand

In an earlier paper (Brown 1989) I described the struggles of a group with a patient stuck at a protomental level, before any awareness of an inner world. It illustrates the interplay between understanding, being understood, the role of empathy, and the need for *intersubjective validation* to create a solid enough self for interaction with others to be meaningful. It could be seen as a paradigm of the sort of construction through 'transmuting internalisations' (Kohut 1971) that this degree of self-deficit requires.

Richard came to therapy because of his inability to present himself verbally before groups of colleagues at work. He also complained of a constriction of feelings which made his marriage sterile for his wife in a way that he himself *could not understand*, in contrast with his intense emotional attachment and concern for his young son. From joining, his involvement in the twice-weekly group was precarious and puzzling. He constantly felt *unable to understand* what 'people were going on about'. However, after a while it became clear that he longed for attention, waited for it, and raged inwardly when it did not come. He came to appreciate his own needs and wishes.

After one such occasion he did not return. In a letter he said he despaired of being able to use the group. I offered him an individual session in which we explored his feeling of being forgotten and defeated in the group. Though formerly denying early memories he had gradually uncovered some in the group, and this time he talked of being put aside by his mother when his sister was born and father returned from the army; also of mother's suppression of his feeling, saying 'boys don't feel' while the sister was allowed her tantrums. In the session he acknowledged with pleasure my telling him of the projected tearfulness I felt. After recognising the group was experienced as a family in which he could not find a place and afford to be spontaneous, he decided to return to it. He fleetingly appreciated how he had externalised his experience of his internal family.

When he did so, he spoke of realising he *needed the group every day* and feared he would fall flat if not picked up. One could thus see that an important part of his character defence was against dependence and abandonment. At the next session he reported fury with me for not 'bringing him out' despite my declared knowledge of his need, but did so only after someone else had been talking about leaving and wishing to be special. For a while Richard had been sitting impassively, but flicked a speck off his tie once and glanced quickly at his watch. I withheld indicating that I had observed these signs, and the man who had been talking asked him how he was. Richard replied, 'Furious, there is no point. I nearly walked out.' He could not 'understand' what was being talked about. He saw no point in coming if I was aware of his needs and did nothing about them. Another member expressed his anger at Richard, but explained that he also identified with him, realising that he covered his own needs by *talking* rather than by *silence*. This exposed him to the possibility of intersubjectivity, begun by the other member.

Again, this time in the group, I pointed out my own tears, recognising them as well as the anger, as his and that of others in the group. At this confrontation with empathy or exchange of subjectivity he was deeply and dramatically moved, felt intense pain in the neck and shoulders '*as though being choked*'. When I commented that he was choking his own feelings, he began to cry. One member passed him the tissues and another put her hand on his shoulder, but he could not talk about it until the intensity had worn off. Asked how it related to feelings in the family, he could clearly see it was, especially in situations of being ignored and overlooked, of which he gave graphic examples. After this opening up, and the discovery that his rage and tears could be accepted and understood, for the rest of the session he was able to keep up with the ebb and flow of conversation and understanding in the group. He left his isolated internal world and joined the intersubjective world of the group for a while.

What happened here seems to correspond with that stage of development of the nascent self calling for a responsive selfobject (Kohut 1971). Here the group was able to take on an empathic and maternal role, sufficient for Richard to open himself to it. He discovered he had, like others, an internal world, understandable by others, and he was able to take part in the ebb and flow of shared experiences.

This is the basis of intersubjective validation. By this I mean that the person's sense of themselves in relation to others is confirmed by those others' responses in a mutual process of self-discovery. This entails each discovering something new about themselves and the other, which confirms and changes views of self and other. In this way it deepens the sense of relatedness. In a well-functioning group, each member discovers their inner world and discerns how it colours their view of others, and their inner worlds. Similarities and differences can then be clarified and respected, as projections are reduced, transference distortions based on internal object relationships are modified, and prejudices transcended in the direction of mutual empathy. Individuals then become less defensively self-absorbed. The negotiation and holding together of deep ambivalences allows the development of concern, which recognises the fragility of these achievements. Working through within the group, or in relationships outside, strengthens confidence in these achievements. But in a group that does not function well, or one that fails to meet the needs of an individual, such intersubjective validation through empathic attunement does not occur, or not sufficiently to promote the developmental spiral. It might require a change of group, move to individual therapy totally or in augmentation, or even acceptance that the individual cannot be helped further at this time. In fact Richard dropped out of the group, as he had dropped out of individual therapy before. In a sense he had defeated us. One might question whether his baffled response of 'not understanding' as it were identifying with a misattuned parent who did not understand, was a response to misattunement in his early life, or to disrupted partial attunement – a defensive post-traumatic refusal to trust that was stirred up by the moments of apparent attunement experienced in the group and in his individual sessions.

Nevertheless, in a group one often finds that those members who are most defensively self-absorbed to start with are the ones who are later capable of the greatest empathic sensitivity to others. The opportunity for learning through such experiences in group analysis gives it a special advantage over individual psychoanalysis, where empathy is almost the perogative of the analyst. The latter then has to rely on changes in the patient's transference, and his or her reports of changes in relationships outside the treatment setting. Indeed the group setting not only provides the opportunity for observing others in interaction, and of having oneself observed in interaction with others, but it also models the triangulation that is the basis of both Oedipal and social development (see Brown and Nitsun 1991: Chapter 9).

2 The woman who would not feel understood

At this later stage of development, experiencing oneself as having a valued place in a family that supports and challenges is also important for development. Individuation involves recognition of others in relation together as well as to oneself. In this stage, late Oedipal and sibling jealousy and rivalry are added to, and to some extent supersede, separation anxiety and insecurity springing from environmental failure, infantile envy of the breast and of mother and the parental couple. In Lacanian terms, la loi, 'the name of the father' and entry into the world of language and society and its symbolic order, demand and assist a move from fusion in a dyad (Benvenuto and Kennedy 1986: 133). The sense of belonging gains new horizons and boundaries. The sense of 'we-ness' develops through extension and differentiation.

Kim was a 30-year-old Oriental immigrant, a helping professional who denied her own needs in the group for a long time. Her counter-dependence was fiercely maintained, as was her single marital status, to such a degree that it stood out at times as a troubling and puzzling foreground to the general background level of expressed neediness in the group. The group confronted her with her extreme position, which she nevertheless clung to, even after she had shared childhood experiences of being dropped as an infant, and choosing after the birth of her brother to spend a lot of her childhood nights at the home of a grandmother.

From early on in the group she attributed to me a dislike of her, which echoed (in reverse) her dislike of men from her country of origin, clearly connected with her father who spent long periods away from home and denied her affection and a sense of being valued as a girl. For a long time she insisted that I was unable to understand her because she came from a different culture.

Her counter-dependence gradually softened, but broke down in a group session when intense rivalry emerged between her and another woman member over 'secrets' withheld from me after a session when I had been away. After her rival had told me more about this 'secret', I took the issue up. While I was still speaking, Kim stormed out of the group, leaving us upset and concerned.

Reflecting on this next time, she was able to relate what happened to walking out of the homes of both her parents and her grandmother, making each feel the rejection she found it so painful to feel herself – as in projective identification. Further she was able to see, and have understood, that the hurt was especially keen because she had felt betrayed by the woman in the group she most liked, and by me for seeming to favour her. Kim's dependent longings were now further revealed also in her painful recollection of seeing her brother breastfed by her mother; and her telling us that she only went to her grandmother to sleep, as grandmother did not cook as well as mother. In the same session, other group members, associating to these events, and to the discovery of powerful needs behind defensive indifference and detachment, reinforced the awareness of such processes in themselves. Kim had become more human and knowable, more a member of the group, which gained a deeper understanding of the wishes and defences of all.

The example shows how the group can confront strong character defences by stimulating the emergence of repressed object relationships. Here their recognition allowed them to become part of a greater awareness of commonality. This reinforced the sense of empathic attunement the need for which Kim had previously denied, and unblocked her development.

3 The drowsy group including the conductor

Drowsing is a common and insufficiently attended to phenomenon in groups. Drowsiness in the conductor, in individual members of the group, or in the group as a whole, can often be understood as a defensive avoidance of feelings stimulated by the situation, just as disturbing affects provoked by a theatrical performance can sometimes explain the boredom or sleepiness experienced by members of the audience. Drowsing may occur in either patient or therapist, when blocking off their own emotional responses. Equally however, I often find that my own countertransference drowsiness represents a failure of empathy which can be triggered by a patient withholding from themselves and from me powerful and often primitive affects. These can be the very early, protomental affects illustrated by Richard; the reason why so many 'alexithymic' patients provoke boredom in their interviewers (Wolff 1977). I have previously described countertransference drowsiness playing a crucial role in individual psychoanalysis (Brown 1977). Until its significance was realised, it was merely a block to progress.

Countertransference drowsiness occurs more often in some groups than in others, particularly those that are emotionally inhibited or in which several people exhibit alexithymic features, but even then it will tend to happen during certain phases in the group.

In one group, I felt intensely drowsy on two consecutive sessions. In the first session, it persisted for a while. It disappeared when John, normally rather bouncy and frequently insisting he no longer needed to be in the group, talked about his mother not having had a photograph of him on her wall. He became aware of a sense of outrage at her omission, which he associated with not knowing why she had agreed to his being evacuated in the war between the ages of two and three. The strength of his feeling seemed to lift my drowsiness, but, surprisingly, I felt an intense pain in my stomach.

In the next session, another member, Tom, reported that he had experienced a pain in his stomach since the last session, and felt it had to do with his own emotional deprivation as a child, when he had very troublesome eczema. In his usual emotionally flat way, Tom recounted how he would rock his pram so violently that his father had tied it down and put his hands in splints. Despite the distressing content of his story the whole group appeared drowsy and inattentive. When I pointed this out it was acknowledged, and lifted somewhat as members spoke about their fear of expressing dangerous feelings.

This led on in the next session to the group exploring, with considerable animation, issues of power and powerlessness, and the fear of having their emotions 'played with'. It seemed that by identifying with Tom's example they had lowered their defensive barrier against communicating their experience. Intersubjectivity replaced concealing their individual vulnerability.

Having observed drowsiness develop in individuals who were disturbed by feelings stirred up by another group member's experience, I do not think it is inappropriate to equate this group drowsiness with countertransference drowsiness of the subjective type, contrasting it with Winnicott's 'Objective Countertransference' (Winnicott 1949). That is, it is particular to that person or group, and is saying something covert about their subjective experience; not something that anyone or any group would feel in that situation. It corresponds to withdrawal in hurt from the 'ebb and flow' of the group, or missing sessions when the longed-for interest is withheld or seems to move to another group member. The difference is that for the drowsing to be evoked the other person has to be physically there but emotionally and empathically absent.

Concluding discussion

The matrix of the group, with its personal, interpersonal and transpersonal functions, is a multipersonal field in which subjects and objects appear, interact, interchange and transform. In the early stages of a group, the individual tends to get drawn into anxious opposition or self-denying fusion, treating the group and others in it as objects to be submitted to or possessed. Later, they tend to be desired or feared. As the group and its members mature, this gives way to recognition of similarities and differences, and to a sense of intersubjectivity that permits real communication. The self, or ego, finds itself through communication with others, as the infant finds itself through the mutual attunement of infant and mother. Internal representations of self and objects are recognised through their action and enactment in the group matrix. They emerge there, and can be modified there in the struggle to be understood and to understand. To be growth promoting, yet allowing benign regression when necessary, the group needs to feel secure and function well. This is the ultimate responsibility of the conductor.

As each member's inner world of internal object relationships is played out in the group, old object relationships (what Kernberg call subject–object–affect links) are clarified in a public light that makes them less easy to forget. Their modification by empathic understanding and insight is aided by the *new* subjective interrelationships provided in an increasingly mature group. In the process of exposing and clarifying these residues of early experiences, and the sharing of new experiences within the common ground of the group matrix, mutual understanding can develop. At its deepest I believe this is rooted in what Merleau-Ponty called collaboration in 'consummate reciprocity' (Merleau-Ponty 1976: 354). As Gordon (1991) argues, this is not only developmentally primitive. Mahler's symbiotic phase (Mahler *et al.* 1975), selfobject functioning (Kohut 1971), and the intersubjectivity of the infant–mother dyad (Stern 1985) may underlie the need and capacity to relate intersubjectively. But intersubjectivity is also part of relating fully in adult life.

At fleeting moments Richard seemed capable of it. Kim increasingly established this capacity, bringing together an enlarged subjective experience which intercommunicated with that of others in the group. The group where drowsiness was a prominent problem, by working through it, functioned more fully, and sharpened its awareness of each other's subjective experience. These changes are subsumed in my understanding of an important aspect of what Foulkes called ego training in action, which I call self development through subjective interaction.

Hans Cohn (personal communication, 1992) has questioned the possibility of integrating phenomenological notions with psychoanalytic theory, as the latter is flawed by a Cartesian split that the notion of intersubjectivity overcomes. Am I therefore mistaken by seeing intersubjectivity as providing the first building blocks of the sense of self in infancy, and yet a goal to achieve in mature relationship? I think not, if we take the view that the 'internal world', internal objects and object relationships reflect subjective experiences that have been split off and 'privatised' as a result of defensive manoeuvres, as well as representing the seat of imagination and creativity. They make the inner world a subjective reality. I think it is reasonable to suppose that while the 'internal world' of psychic reality has been discovered through psychoanalysis, emphasis on it reflects the individualistic nature of modern socio-economic philosophy and Zeitgeist, underplaying and even denying the connectedness underlined by existential phenomenology.

Intimacy is often a prominent characteristic in the final stages of development in experimental group dynamic situations, reviewed e.g. by Whiteley and Gordon (1979: 77–83), and seen in group-analytic and other workshops

– sometimes as wished-for or pseudo-intimacy. In slow-open group-analytic groups it is more a recurrent phase, repeatedly and more deeply experienced each time round, as in a spiral. My impression of how it progresses is that the experience of mutual empathy allows the development of enough sense of security to promote another turn in exploring and sharing private inner object worlds, and so to allow the middle phase of achieving a more flexible relationship to them. This will often entail turbulent confrontation of transference distortions and projections, but when worked through will lead to a renewed mutual understanding and intimacy.

A once-weekly group had met once in my expected absence. On my return they reported that they had had a good meeting, patching up the violent transference-based confrontation between two members occurring the previous week. Gradually they realised the apparent resolution had been partly motivated by fear, and that they needed the safety afforded by the conductor's presence to face the potential hatred between members, itself based on intense rivalry for my attention when I was there. My verbal interpretation of the conflict was scarcely necessary, but it helped them to see that the integration of the experience of the 'bad' uncomfortable session with the pseudo-'good' session was necessary to achieve a deeper sense of empathic relatedness, both between the couple and between them and others in the group who could identify the issues as also their own.

The spiral I have described can move in both directions. Members starting in the group with little insight or introspectiveness can begin to develop a sense of their own inner world by witnessing and participating in the moves others make towards mutual empathic understanding, and by tuning in to similarities with them through what Foulkes called resonance. In other words empathy can come before an awareness of an 'internal world' of relationship.

While something akin to the spiral process happens in individual analysis, the final phase of reciprocity does not fit in with customary psychoanalytic techniques. This might explain some of the caution psychoanalysts show in publicising what they actually do. One of the advantages of group analysis therefore is that the final phase can be explored and exploited by the group without the conductor relinquishing a necessary degree of analytic detachment.

In the transitional space of the group there is opportunity for recognition and modification of restrictive or distorting object relationships, and for new identifications and selfobject usage as individuals allow themselves to be seen more fully and to look at and be seen by each other in different ways through empathic attunement. Much of this is subsumed in what Foulkes called mirror reactions, but the wider view allows one to see how object relations theory and self psychology could be integrated into an understanding of 'self development through subjective interaction'.

In summary, it is proposed that the process of self development in group analysis is circular and spiral: the experience of being empathised with and failed enough – as in early infancy – sets in motion the three stages enumerated at the beginning of the chapter: fuller *discovery* of our inner world, which allows us to *discern* the difference between old internal object relationships and new ones, and in a step towards maturity to *learn* to attune ourselves to *other* people's experience as well as our own. On the way to more mature, intimate and reciprocal relationships with others, we mitigate the effects of earlier empathic failure and ossification of internal object relationships. I call this *self development through subjective interaction*, and believe its attainment during group analysis is a test of how well the group is functioning.

Acknowledgements

I am grateful to Hans Cohn, Morris Nitsun and Louis Zinkin for very helpful conversations and correspondence about earlier drafts of this essay.

11

FAIR SHARES AND MUTUAL CONCERN

The role of sibling relationships

In 1972 Enid Balint published a paper entitled 'Fair Shares and Mutual Concern'. This was based upon discussions that she had had over several years with her husband Michael, who had died a short time before. In thinking about the origin of concern for others, she noted that there were two main theories: the first related to patriarchal moral law and the second was based in the relationship of infant and mother during early demand feeding. In patriarchal law, fairness is the same as equality. (Note the concept of equality before the law, so that even with such obvious 'unfairness' as primogeniture, whereby the oldest son inherits the estate, or the different treatment of boys and girls, the equality extends equally throughout the whole of society.) During early demand feeding fairness is not the same as equality; frustration, anything or anyone standing in the way of greedy self-satisfaction is experienced as unfair by the infant. Balint noted that the child needs a relationship with a law-giving father to move beyond this simple equation (i.e. triangulation has to occur), and it also needs to experience the way parents continue to be concerned for each other despite their differences of interest. This was connected, I believe, with Enid Balint's impatience with simplistic feminist ideas; but obviously things are very different today, when lone parenting, and even parenting by homosexual couples are approved of by at least some in our society. Other phenomena, much commoner today than in 1972, and often prominent in family therapy, are those of step-parenting and step-sibships.

It is striking that Balint neglected to develop the role of *sibling* relationships in her article, though as I will later spell out, she recognised the crucial role of peers. 'It isn't fair!' is such a typical verbal complaint of rivalrous children. It is expectable in a relatively powerless child, but parents have also to cope with the child in themselves. As Winnicott pointed out, it is natural for parents to hate their children at times when they feel that unfair demands are being made. Parents have to cope with their own frustration and residues of their own Oedipal and sibling rivalry, stirred up even before the birth of a new baby. This can be extremely difficult if the parental relationship is poor, or their own personality is not mature enough. In this regard Eloise Moore Agger (1988), a psychoanalyst with a social work background, made the interesting observation that disturbed borderline parents split their children and actually promote sibling rivalry. I shall return to this contribution shortly.

Freud believed that social feelings arise in the individual 'as a superstructure built on impulses and jealous rivalry against his brothers and sisters' (Freud 1923: 37). He believed that reaction formations, reversals and identifications are other important pathways leading to a sense of fairness and social justice. 'If one cannot be the favourite oneself, at all events nobody else shall be the favourite' (Freud 1921: 120). In this short paper I am proposing that development from primitive greed and rivalry towards mature relationships – perhaps even towards social justice – requires the integration and transformation of three elements: *maternal, paternal* and *sibling*. It is the last-named that has been the most neglected in our attempts to understand peer relationships. There is a big gap between primitive rivalry and the attainment of a capacity for mutual concern. We need to begin to fill it.

It is particularly surprising that sibling relationships have been neglected in *group analytic* literature. Although Foulkes acknowledges sibling transferences within the group, e.g. towards newcomers, siblings do not appear in the index of any of his books, nor in the 1991 cumulative index of the journal he founded, *Group Analysis*. Nor have there been relevant papers in subsequent issues. However there have been two notable contributions to the theme, presented as part of their authors' qualification with the Institute of Group Analysis in the 1980s. One is by Gloria Hope-Price called 'Sibling Rivalry and the Therapy Group' in 1982, and the other by Diana Kinder entitled 'Sibling Rivalry and the Analytic Group' in 1989. I am indebted to both of them for important insights and ways into the literature. I shall limit my review to some articles relevant to our theme of 'Fair Shares and Mutual Concern'.

In a review of the psychoanalytic literature on siblings Colonna and Newman (1983) highlighted Freud's awareness that with the appearance of another child the Oedipus complex becomes a family complex. (More radically Foulkes 1990b saw it as such from the start; issues of rivalry are stirred up in both parents even before the first child is born, related to the Oedipal issues that each parent brings from their own family of origin.) Freud described sibling rivalry in *The Interpretation of Dreams* (1900). Later he drew attention to how a girl's hatred of her older sister can be greater than that of her mother (1916–17) and that hostility to older brothers can lead to homosexual love objects by transformation of hate into love (1922). But most analysts since Freud have reduced the vicissitudes of sibling relationships to displacements from the primary Oedipal parental objects. Indeed this is true of many group psychotherapists such as Ezriel (1973) and Stein and Kibel (1975).

Kohut (1971) from his vantage point in self psychology saw the effect of sibling relationships on the narcissistic enmeshment with mother, and the role of siblings in functioning as parent substitutes and as self-objects. And in recent years group therapists have begun to challenge the view that sibling relationships are of secondary interest to Oedipal ones. Horwitz (1977) and Rabin (1989) argue that peer and sibling history, transferences and theory construction should be considered in their own right.

If we look into our own and our patients' lives as well as those of our professional father figures, the importance of sibling relationships is obvious. Graham (1988) reviewed all his 35 psychoanalytic cases, and found sibling transference material *in every one*. One might say he found what he was looking for, but what is particularly interesting is that he used the material to illustrate his own countertransference difficulties in appreciating their significance. Graham discovered a range of patterns in sibling relationships that I think will resonate. He pointed to the way sibling rivalry can distort separation–individuation from mother and the development of a secure identity. He also showed how much more pathogenic is the arrival of new siblings when it is close to the first year (as in Freud's case) or late in latency or early adolescence. As well as illness and death of siblings, recognised by Freud, he describes the impact of frustrating and incestuous relationships. Sibling love can become a specific ideal model for relationships, including providing a model for reaction formation against the negative emotions of envy, rivalry and destructiveness. Children can come to play a mediating role in families, for example, consoling bereaved parents and stepping into the role formerly played by a lost sibling. Separation from siblings can also be an important developmental task to free the individual from assigned roles, e.g. as a polarised complement to a sibling's qualities. I would add the need to understand the special problems of not having siblings. The *only child* has to cope with fantasies about the dead or unborn siblings; and bears all the expectations of both parents, without the assistance of sibling 'division of labour', and without an ally against parental 'abuse of power'. He or she has to struggle alone with Oedipal conflicts.

Sharp and Rosenblatt (1994) have recently drawn our attention to the existence of what they call 'Oedipal Sibling Triangles'. They distinguish between what they call pre-Oedipal, *dyadic* sibling rivalry, in which the sibling is unambivalently experienced as an intruder (in fact a clash of two dyads), and more advanced Oedipal rivalry in which ambivalence and therefore conflict and guilt are experienced. They also point to the 'twinning reaction' of twins or siblings very close in age: 'in which the mother becomes excluded as the primary love object and a symbiotic dual unity is formed by the siblings. In these reactions, rivalry is almost totally stifled or takes a sado-masochistic form, and the siblings do not develop individual identities' (1994: 497).

Sharp and Rosenblatt postulate a *developmental line* for sibling object relationships. This is similar to the phases of symbiosis and separation–individuation described by Mahler for the mother–child relationship, never complete, but reworked in new and more integrated forms. They propose: 'the continuation of a developmental progression between and among siblings that would move from dyadic to triadic Oedipal constellations and then follow new editions of separation–individuation and Oedipal issues through latency, adolescence, and adulthood in a parallel but intertwined fashion with the child's internalised and interpersonal relationships with the parents' (1994: 156).

Sharp and Rosenblatt finish with speculation about why Oedipal sibling relationships sometimes emerge as more important than Oedipal experiences with parents. These include (1) an Oedipal defeat with one or both parents leading to compensation with another sibling; (2) failure to develop idealisation of one or both parents because they are 'too neglectful, incompetent, vicious, absent, or denigrated by the other parent'; and (3) one parent's relationship with a sibling being too much like a spousal relationship, so that this sibling becomes a surrogate parent.

In my view sibling and child–parent relationships might be seen in a reversible figure–ground relation to one another. Its absence might be one of the disadvantages that only children suffer. Only children of lone parents can then be seen to have a double disability if deprived of the rivalries that stimulate identification and so contribute to the process of separation and individuation.

Finally, I wish to draw attention to an important series of papers in the *International Journal of Group Psychotherapy* that are specially relevant to group psychotherapy. Grunebaum and Solomon (1980, 1982, 1987) reviewed work relating to the significance of sibling and peer relationships in optimal personal and social development. Secure attachment fosters the early development of peer relationships, though they can develop despite its absence, but *both* contribute to the establishment of self-esteem. With age, interpersonal skills increase in complexity, along with the ability to perceive and empathise with others, and behaviour embodying increasingly sophisticated moral principles. They found that *popularity among children relates to their ability to perceive and comprehend the behaviour, feelings and motives of others*. I think this resonates with our experience in therapy groups. Indeed Grunebaum and Solomon state: 'The developmental phases of peer-orientated group therapy can be expected to recapitulate the ontogenetic growth that characterises the child's progression from a parent-child focus to peer group relatedness' (1982: 299–300).

Perhaps this is implicit in Pat de Maré's idea of Koinonia: impersonal fellowship in larger groups transcending family relationships (De Maré *et al.* 1991). I think it is related to what, at a social level, Norbert Elias meant when he described the importance of *mutual identification* and a *capacity for empathy with peers*, as part of the civilising process and moral development in all cultures (Mennell 1989). What is considered fair and just in a particular society is also embedded in cultural patterns, e.g. laws of inheritance (Todd

1985). A sense of injustice about such laws is mitigated by recognising that all younger siblings or females are treated equally badly; in the same way as being a member of a sibship can mitigate a sense of injustice in relation to parent power or misbehaviour.

It is obvious that there is a relationship between the resolution of difficulties within sibling relationships, and the development of satisfactory relationships with peers. Of course the actual sibling relationship may remain uneasy and prone to regression, but the pattern of relations with peers, formerly based on sibling relationships, can be modified and transformed. A more negative balance can shift to a more positive one as ruthless competition and hatred – however hidden and reacted against – are joined by co-operation, solidarity and concern. The capacity for mutual identification and empathy form the basis of moral development. It is implicit in the sense of the 'brotherhood of man', political as well as religious idealism, and the idea of a sane society (Fromm 1991). Intersubjectivity, 'I–Thou' rather than 'I–It' (Buber 1970), is part of the religious sense of interconnectedness and concern for others. It forms the basis of an awareness of what is transpersonal as opposed to unreflectively egocentric.

The capacity for concern involves arriving at what Melanie Klein called the depressive position, which was not referred to by Balint in the article I started with, though I have no doubt that she was fully aware of deeply ambivalent impulses and, having had an analysis with Winnicott, knew the importance of the object surviving the intense hateful rage of frustration, or stemming from narcissistic damage. Without this we are doomed to live in a paranoid-schizoid world. This is now recognised by sociologists and historians with a Kleinian view (e.g. Rustin 1991, in *The Good Society and the Internal World*, and Alford 1989 in *Melanie Klein and Critical Social Theory*).

So how does all this relate to our clinical work? I propose three areas of consideration. First of all we need to pay special attention to the importance of sibling and peer relationships of our patients and their parents in our history-taking, and note how these are illuminated in interactions within the group matrix; e.g. in response to the arrival of a new member, the departure or discomfiture of another and all the manifestations of envy, jealousy and rivalry.

Second, destructive rivalry – sibling as well as Oedipal – has to be fully acknowledged and worked with in the group before it can be transformed and transcended. We need to ensure that projections are withdrawn, ambivalence recognised, and the capacity for concern and mutuality realised. Eventually a well-functioning group provides the experience of mutual empathy, even in those who did not experience it in earlier life, via the working through not only of conflicts with parental objects, but sibling objects also.

Finally, interplay of subject and object can allow the 'decentring' of the self as the human matrix of intersubjectivity is taken on board by each individual in the group. This is furthered by taking others in the group seriously, including the whole group, moving beyond taking seriously only the problems of our own isolated self, stuck in the repetitive patterns with our own primitive early objects, parental and sibling. This is one of the things that Caroline Garland (1982) meant when writing about 'Taking the Non-Problem Seriously'. It is also what I meant when I wrote about 'Self-Development through Subjective Interaction' (Brown 1994). Selfishness can then give way to a wider sense of fairness and concern based on empathic identification and mutuality.

It is impressive how groups are able to move from (and regress back to) demanding equal shares of time, to allowing for members having needs for differing shares of available time at different periods, e.g. at times of crisis. This is helped by recognising that one can gain through identifying with another and resonating with their experience. That is, a well-functioning group can replace rigid equality with flexible fairness.

To return to the paper by Enid Balint I spoke about at the beginning, I think her final remarks sum up remarkably what I have been trying to say. She refers to Winnicott's description of the child's relation to the *object mother*, who has to survive the infant's destructive rage, and the *environmental mother* whose presence is necessary for the development of a sense of guilt and reparation and the consequent capacity for concern. (As we know the environmental mother can be represented by the group matrix.) Balint questions whether a capacity for concern can develop in a two-body relationship alone, or does not also need 'a certain kind of multi-person relationship' to develop fully. She then jumps from this statement to considering, not a sibship, but the *group therapy* situation. The group, she writes, is very sensitive that time and consideration are given to each member in fair (not equal) shares. She also quotes the famous aphorism in her 1961 book with Michael Balint:

> After a successful psychoanalytic treatment a patient is definitely less neurotic (or psychotic) but perhaps not necessarily more mature. On the other hand, after successful treatment by group methods the patient is not necessarily less neurotic but inevitably more mature.
>
> (1961: 5)

In *psychoanalysis* the patient receives full and individual attention, while in *group therapy* every patient must become accustomed to the idea of fair shares. They are helped by becoming aware that other people also have to tolerate tensions.

Balint asks whether the toleration, even enjoyment, of witnessing the satisfaction of another at our own expense can be established without a *multi-person relationship*, where laws are developed by a group of equals, not given by one 'superior' individual. While in a family and in a therapy group the presence of a parent or therapist is essential, the climate of concern results more from relations *between group members*, and not only as a reaction-formation to jealousy as Freud (1921) had suggested. She suggests that: 'In a quiet almost imperceptible way, group members will show concern for each other and will help the group leader to give more or less what each member needs (and will include the needs of the group leader in their endeavours)' (Balint 1972: 71).

Finally she says that a child's wish *not only to get* is helped if the mother's wish to give is not over-strong. *The group conductor is helped by group members because his or her need to 'cure' is shared by others.*

In concluding, I want to remind us of the value of balancing compassion with selfishness. Group conductors, like parents, need to survive. There is a limit to the usefulness of selflessness. Those of us who believe it is fair to ourselves to have a half-term break can observe that group members often appear to behave better towards each other when the conductor is away. In an 'immature' group this can result from fear of mutual destructiveness between siblings – reported as a 'social' or superficial session. But in more mature groups, in which the role of therapist has been internalised by members, it is a genuine consequence of growth in individuals and group, akin to siblings surviving their parents' death.

Part 3

TRANSCULTURALITY AND METAPSYCHOLOGY

12

CONTEXT, CONTENT AND PROCESS

Interrelationships between small and large groups in a transcultural workshop

The European Association for Transcultural Group Analysis was set up in 1982 by a group of psychoanalysts and group analysts from France, Germany, Belgium, Holland, Italy, Switzerland and Britain (Le Roy 1987b). Its aim is the study of those aspects of the Self which are constructed from and expressed through the collectivism of cultures and subcultures of which each individual is a part – aspects reflected in what Foulkes (1975) called the Foundation Matrix. The Association's first workshop came to fruition in July 1985 in the city of Maastricht, Holland, where 45 participants from France, Britain, Belgium, Switzerland, Holland, Germany, Greece, Italy, Norway and Poland joined 13 members of staff.

Because numbers precluded having national groups as originally planned, it was decided to set up two Anglophone and two Francophone groups and a fifth group of mixed language. Each group had a conductor and an observer from different countries. The conductors' role was to bring to their everyday group-analytic practice a special sensitivity to the transcultural phenomena expectable within this context; the role of the observers was to observe silently and later report, attending to countertransference as well as transference and other group dynamic processes. All staff participated in the large groups, only the observers again remaining silent until the final plenary meeting.

Working hypotheses

The working hypotheses of Rene Kaës, the principal researcher, were that: (a) an undifferentiated zone exists in both individual and collective psyches in every culture, based on the earliest exchanges between mother and infant as well as on cultural codes and rules, but only discernible when confronted by people of another culture; and (b) cultures vary in the degree to which they protect members against primitive anxieties and/or repress expression of wishes.

A recent recruit to the staff team, the author had not had a chance to participate in the development of these hypotheses, and had no knowledge of them until after the workshop. As a British observer in a group conducted by Ursula Keller-Husemann of Germany, my observations were based on brief notes written after each group session and completed within the subsequent week. They were therefore uncontaminated by a previous knowledge of these hypotheses.

From my understanding of Kaës's hypotheses, I prefer to conceptualise the so-called 'undifferentiated' zone as an 'unindividualised' zone; because if synonymous with the Foundation Matrix of Foulkes we would expect it to be structured according to complex unconscious patterns of relationship, both of internal objects and of social expectations and traditions. Individual and cultural history will interact in this unconscious Foundation Matrix.

Description of the small group

There were nine members: two Greek, two British, two Swiss and one each from France, Germany and Holland. Five of the nine had 'transcultural histories', for example: living in a different country from that in which they were born and brought up; marrying somebody from another continent; marrying into another European country; spending the formative years in a prisoner-of-war camp in another continent; and born in a Middle Eastern country of European parentage and moving to another European country which became the main source of identification. Only two of the nine were male. The group worked well together. The conductor was group-analytic in her approach and relatively reticent, only stepping out of this role in the initial introductions in the first small group, and in her closing words in the final one.

Summary of sessions in small and large groups

In the following pages small groups (SG) are summarised on left-hand, large groups (LG) on right-hand columns. Note that the sessions extended over four days, with eight small group sessions interpolated by six large group (plenary) sessions, as indicated. The small and large groups are reported on opposite columns to facilitate an examination of their separate but interacting developments. These developments are the basis of the commentaries in bold, which were added afterwards.

Day 1 Small group sessions	**Day 1 Large group sessions**
9.30 am. SG1 Paranoid anxiety about observer and (at this stage) only one male member ('a staff ploy'). Helplessness in relation to staff. Image reported from a film of man being buried by landslide and rejected by wife when eventually extricates himself. Fantasy of Greek men stealing your women but killing you if you steal theirs. Theme of chaos versus order. *11.00 am. SG2* Regrouping into national subgroups. Discussion of defensive identification and stereotyping. Retreat from discussing feelings about Germans and conductor–observer couple. Transcultural themes used defensively to counter personal exposure.	
Paranoid anxiety in SG reflected in LG. Language battle corresponds to basic assumption fight/flight (Bion 1961)? leading to sexualisation, basic assumption pairing? leading to polarisation between paranoia and reconciliation, paranoid-schizoid and depressive positions (Klein 1935)?	*2.30 pm. LG1* Warm welcome to Maastricht versus report of people excluded from municipal swimming pool/open versus closed boundaries. Battle between Anglophones and Francophones leads to explosion of conversation in 'small' languages, that is those excluded. Evidence of curiosity about observers followed by sexualisation of creative play. Hostility to German language expressed by our French member countered by peacemaking protectiveness by our Swiss member.
4.30 pm. SG3 Our French member, 'forced' to sit next to German conductor, attacks her for not speaking her native language. Other women express envious attachment to the French member. Unconscious themes seemed to be jealousy, envy, mistrust of speech and deep ambivalence to mothers and mother-tongues.	**Forced reconciliation in SG where ambivalence seems related to mother and mother-tongue.**
Day 2	**Day 2**
9.00 am. SG4 Silence, expression of despair about change and much intense personal pain, One member's intellectualising attempt to avoid pain countered by group holding on to it, so she moved a lot (becoming a 'lost little girl'). Escape into sexuality only transient, and personal pain shared. Unconscious themes	**Attempt to find place for and rescue suppressed, stereotyped, scapegoated German(s) in LG through attacking 'bad' staff. Non-verbal link with 'absent' silent observers corresponds with basic assumption pairing or dependence?**

continued overleaf

seemed to be mistrust of families and culture which do not recognise personal pain. Group holdings allows deep sharing and benign regression.

11.00 am. LG2 Issue of why no German group. Hierarchy pointed out (a) mulitilinguists, (b) Anglophones and Francophones, (c) the rest, who have to speak to one or other of these two. Criticism of staff for structure and lack of clarity, inviting research but not allowing them to do their own, that is 'subjecting' them to research. Others defended staff. 'Absent' observers raised, and one of SG members spoke of non-verbal communication with me. 'Good' and 'bad' staff related to national differences – French staff accused of infantilising them.

Depressive position achieved in SG, lost in LG.

2.30 pm. LG3 Powerful session. Myths of Garden of Eden and Tower of Babel – jealous God punishing us for over-reaching ourselves by making us sexually ashamed and polyglot. African walked out when confronted with myth of God giving each country a language except the Sudanese (Barbarie) who were given 'any old language'. Film mentioned about search for a father when mother and daughter in a strange country. Differentiation of mother tongue from others related to origin of former in nipple-in-mouth. But this could be dangerous, and communication with mother poisonous. Several participants spoke of changing their language or struggling to renew benign aspects of their mother tongue with their own children. Need for father to facilitate this. There seemed to be a hidden wish that mother and father could speak the same language or congruent languages.

Issues of authority and power, identity and identity diffusion. Need for third person (father) to help negotiation and integration between good and bad. Hinted temptation of basic assumption dependence.

4.30 pm. SG5 Very personal development of themes of LG3. Paternal failure/ absence, fear of failure as father. Mistrust of easy speech, and use of silence to express anger. Unconscious theme of rectifying loss and failure of early relationships through children.

More personal development of issues of need for alternative authority of father and use of children to rectify early deficiencies.

continued

Day 3

9.30 am. SG6 Transference to observer as missing father/the father never known. Search for father, women sharing men, perversion of sexuality. Need for boundaries for both contact and protection from impingement. Withdrawal into timelessness seen as linked with impending end of workshop.

Day 3

Issues developed within transferences to observer as well as conductor. Problem of sharing and perversion. Need for boundaries. Sense of time boundary and impending end.

Acknowledgement that boundaries containing identity exclude excitement as well as fear of otherness.

11.00 am. LG4 Boundaries explored. African who walked out from LG3 explained he had done so because no one was translating (he was Francophone). Breaking rules by bringing in waste-baskets as ashtrays. Strangeness/otherness can be reduced to waste-baskets or ashes. Alternatives of maps based on boundaries or (as in parts of Africa) rivers, channels of communication. The stranger as exciting and seductive, perhaps as defence against incest. Need for clear self-identity for safe exploration of otherness.

Reluctantly face shadow of historical trauma and guilt associated with overdependence on exclusiveness and projection into scapegoated others. Ambivalence emerges.

2.30 pm. LG5 Reluctance to discuss anti-Semitism. Its relation to failure of mutual empathy when concern and gratitude not expressed. Ghettos as prisons for outcasts or envied havens of exclusiveness. Need for own language as basis of identity. Resentment of exclusiveness of staff group not admitted to, but in other areas envy expressed or hinted at of power, of boundlessness and of exclusivity.

4.30 pm. SG7 Theme of identity and need for containment developed through personal incidents and intimate revelations – theft of bag containing passport, purchasing a big bag to contain diverse experiences. Deep feelings emerge about loss, separation and death, guilt at survival and fear of never getting involved. Intimacy, love and mutual regard expressed. Need for someone, a parent or analyst, to stand 'endless' weeping.

Anxieties about personal dangers of attachment and loss. Struggle to face without empathic support, the vulnerability threatened by transcending defensive boundaries.

continued overleaf

Day 4

Projection and scapegoating overcome as they are recognised, allowing reconciliation and integration. Differentiation and autonomy allow for more honesty and less defensive identification ('pseudo-identification'?) Paranoid-schizoid position gives way to more firmly established depressive position and more realistic (?) hopefulness. This seems more than the messianism of a basic assumption pairing.

Day 4

9.00 am. LG6 Move from rejection and denigration towards reconciliation and growth. Foreigners can be enriching as well as threatening. Silence tolerated. Paucity of Germans and avoidance of German language, their association with defeat and excretion recognised as a universal experience of projection. Reconciliation between Germans and Jews challenged if based on denial of historical and personal experiences. Need to work through hatred to overcome it, and gratitude reported about this being achieved within transference in SG. Facing ending of workshop. View expressed that this needs to be experienced by individuals, not 'stage-managed'. Some members expressed realisation that love for other cultures represented way of escaping restrictiveness of their own.

11.00 am. SG8 Struggle to acknowledge sadness about separation and ending, defences against it in individuals' pasts described, giving way to expression of gratitude and new beginning springing from encounters and working through of transferences in the group. Some blocks to this worked through, particularly envy and competitiveness. For one person murderous rage turned into idealisation of political terrorism, but now allowed for heroines to be vulnerable. Regret at losing closeness of group as much mutual perceptiveness and intuitive understanding revealed.

The processes in LG6 as well as those in SG7 seem to have developed and become more intimate and personal. Envy and competitiveness are acknowledged and transcended and the paranoid-schizoid remains subordinate to the depressive position. But for at least one member, idealisation of political terrorism suggests that this can change, and basic assumption fight/flight can always re-emerge. Personal movement and growth seem to have paralleled motivation in the workshop as a whole.

2.30 pm. LG7 Final plenary, summing up in English and French by the two principal researchers was appreciated, and wishes to repeat and extend the experiences of the workshop were expressed.

Notes on interactions and parallels between small and large groups

The themes and dynamics of the small and large groups were frequently seen to flow from one to the other or to reflect similar processes on another level. Here are a few examples.

1. Initial paranoid anxiety in SG1 was followed in SG2 by regrouping in nationalities and the discussion of defensive identification and stereotyping, with a retreat from talking about Germans and the conductor–observer couple. Themes of cultural differences were used defensively to counter personal exposure. In the subsequent LG1 these themes were seemingly reflected in the battle between Anglophones and Francophones and the idea of creative playfulness in the large group being sexual. In the next SG3 our French Jewess was 'forced' to sit next to the German conductor whom she attacked for not speaking her native tongue, and there was some evidence of envy of the conductor–observer couple. Defence against paranoid anxiety in SG2 by national grouping and avoidance of personal contact was paralleled in LG1 by a language battle. Group 'sadistically' forced reconciliation in SG3 between Jewess and German conductor; the former retaliated by attacking her for not speaking her native language (transference).
2. Discussions of the problems of a multilingual world, and the advantages and disadvantages of being multilingual in terms of self-identity, forced identification and the wish to avoid destructive identification with the mother, talked about in the third large group, led in the subsequent small group (5) to the problems of the absent or unavailable father, and the use of silence to attack destructive or negative communication; and in SG6, to the 'perverse' sexuality an external search can lead to. The need for boundaries to define and protect the self with was followed in LG4 by exploration of the dangers and excitement of foreigners – the wastebasket and the dual image of countries which have boundaries on the one hand, or internal flowing communication on the other. In the subsequent LG5, positive and negative aspects of ghettos were explored. In the subsequent SG7 a powerful image was the need for a container to hold what is valuable, but the fear of it then being lost, including an analyst-parent who can contain one's vulnerable self. Issues of identity, boundaries and containers, need for father as well as mother in SG6 were paralleled in LG4 by ideas of national identity and foreigners as both threatening and exciting.
3. The theme of reconciliation, of accepting similarities and withdrawing projections, the need to protect against the pains of trauma and of national humiliation, and the toleration of silence in the sixth large group were followed in SG8 with sadness at ending and regret at excessive

defensiveness, toleration of murderousness and ambivalence. The pain of powerlessness in the face of the conductor–observer couple was perhaps the last thing to resolve.

Transcultural phenomena and their interaction with personal processes

Three examples are drawn from individual members of the small group: (1) changing national identification to an idealised grandiose form in order to avoid deeper internal identification with a parent impossible to compete with, or unusable because degraded and shameful; (2) transforming personal murderous violence into idealised courageous fight against tyranny through political terrorism; (3) the search for the missing self/object through involvement with partners from different cultures.

Note that these are positive phenomena and contrast with Husemann's view of the traumatic nature of a break in the continuity of culture and language in refugees and emigrants (Husemann 1986).

Discussion

The prominence of language in the workshop probably reflects its structure by language rather than by national groups, but also perhaps the language use of staff groups in which only two members were very fluent in both main languages of the workshop. It was interesting to note that as the workshop proceeded people were able to discover a greater fluency in languages which previously they had not used, or used very diffidently.

Initially languages seemed to be categorised as good and bad (particularly German), and which was the most influential (French or English). Dominance granted their users the power to communicate and mystify, leaving others helpless, confused and excluded. These splits were readily available for the splitting and projection provoked by the initial paranoid anxieties in both small and large groups, the basic assumption fight/flight, and the paranoid-schizoid position. The split in languages seemed to represent a split between the familiar and the strange, and between maternal and paternal tongues, between early identification with mother and 'otherness'.

One wonders whether despair about a universal language is based on an unconscious recognition of the enormity of the internal struggle to heal these splits. A powerful image in one large group was of an old man visiting his village peddling books in Esperanto to an uninterested populace. Aggressive hostility between groups can represent a fight against the threatening 'other', with a defensive assertion of power to avoid annihilation. On the other hand, sexuality (at least heterosexuality) could be seen as a fascination with and attraction to otherness to escape threatening and stultifying sameness, as well as a reaction against hostility.

There seemed to be a gradual move throughout the workshop from the paranoid or paranoid-schizoid to the depressive position (Klein 1975/1935), and from basic assumption state functioning to confrontation, differentiation and reconciliation through dialogue (Bion 1961; Brown 1985a). These moves were parallel in the small and large groups, but seemed to establish themselves sooner in the small groups. One wonders if work in the small groups fostered that in the large groups. Certainly, as one would expect, themes and dynamics flowed from small and large groups and back again as well as through each separate series.

In the large groups projection and scapegoatism continued longer and more prominently, in relation to the staff as well as to other linguistic and national subgroups. Issues of intimacy were commoner in the small groups, issues of authority and power in the large groups. Historical, geographical and cultural references were also more significant in the large groups, which thus seemed a more fruitful setting in which to study the cultural Foundation Matrix described by Foulkes.

Summary and conclusions

The structure of a transcultural workshop based on language groups is described. Small groups were relatively homogeneous linguistically, large (plenary) groups were diverse. Themes and developments in the small and large groups reflected each other, though as might be expected *small* groups appeared to function at a more *personal* level, *large* groups at a more *cultural* level. Issues of identity were prominent in both, but in the small group observed by the author personal history and the struggle with ambivalently cathected parental introjects while moving towards individuation and intimacy were uppermost; in the large plenary meetings, *cultural* history, language, and identity were most prominent. The fear of non-recognition and annihilation gradually gave way in both as the paranoid-schizoid position was superseded by the depressive position, and basic assumption phenomena were replaced by differentiation, reconciliation and mutual concern (Balint 1972).

These observations tend to support the first working hypothesis about an undifferentiated or unindividualised zone in individual and collective psyches stated at the beginning of this paper. Certainly the individuals and cultures represented found common areas in the workshop in which they could discover a deep sense of commonality as well as begin to differentiate without resorting to too much projection. The parallels between developments in the small and large groups suggest that anxieties and defences based on early individual development are evoked and reflected in large group experiences, and presumably in wider social and cultural phenomena.

The *second* hypothesis, that different cultures protect their members to different degrees against primitive anxieties and/or repress expression of wishes, could not be tested in the structure of the workshop as it was. The original plan to have national cultural groups rather than linguistically based groups needs to be carried through on another occasion to begin to approach this hypothesis. However, the examples drawn from individual members of the small group suggest that individuals use aspects of national identity to reinforce or modify aspects of their own personal identities, to externalise internal conflicts and sublimate drives of different types, both libidinal and destructive. These processes in specific individuals could be seen as supporting this second hypothesis.

Language is a crucial part of the various foundation matrices, or undifferentiated/unindividualised psychic zones of individuals and groups. In this workshop, where different linguistic and national groups confronted each other, the power of languages to unite, differentiate and confuse was revealed. They contributed to the context, content and processes at a profoundly primitive level, and to their development and growth.

Postscript

After writing this paper I came upon the following passages in *The Human Province* by Elias Canetti (1986), and felt they would be of value if one were to review the findings of the workshop:

> The various languages you ought to have: one for your mother, which you will subsequently never speak again; one which you only read but never dare to write; one in which you pray but without understanding a single word; one in which you do arithmetic and to which all money matters belong; one in which you write (but no letters); one in which you travel, and in this one you can also write your letters.
>
> The fact that there are different languages is the most sinister fact in the world. It means that there are different names for the same things; and one would have to doubt that they are the same things. All linguistics hides the striving to reduce all languages back to one.
>
> (Canetti 1986: 7)

13

VIEWS OF MAASTRICHT AND HEIDELBERG

Some questions arising from two transcultural workshops seen by observers with different roles

Introduction

The European Association for Transcultural Group Analysis (EATGA) had held three workshops up to 1991: the first in Maastricht in 1985, the second in Heidelberg in 1989, and one in Oxford in 1991. The Maastricht experiences have been described by Ancona (1987), Brown (1987b), Foulkes (1989), Husemann (1987), Kaës (1987), Le Roy (1987a, 1987b) and Rouchy (1987).

The present paper adds an account of what happened at Heidelberg, to facilitate study of our developing experiences in these workshops. It also emphasises the similarities and differences between the two workshops as seen by Le Roy and myself, filling different roles in each.

At Maastricht, Jaak Le Roy, a Belgian whose professional life is spent in Maastricht, Holland, was a researcher on the staff team. He participated in the large groups and the staff group meetings, but not in the small groups. I was a silent observer, British, in a small English-speaking group, composed of people of various nationalities, conducted by a German (Ursula Keller). At Heidelberg, Le Roy was a small group conductor and one of the staff team. I was an ordinary participant and an English speaker with poor French in a French-speaking small group.

Maastricht

(a) In his account of this workshop, Jaak Le Roy noted the prominence of what he called the 'specific intercultural phenomena': language issues; paranoid anxieties and persecutory images; splitting (e.g. between Francophones and Anglophones); defensive national stereotyping; initial avoidance of the German issue and German language; and a wishful fantasy of oneness, e.g. abolishing language differences through a common language (related to the myth of the Tower of Babel). He proposed that the *difficulties*

experienced in this workshop were related to traumatic *individual* agendas motivating both staff and participants into this area of study; and to the lack in the workshop organisation of formal *structures* to contain linguistic and national groups, i.e. what he calls secondary groups, or 'groupes d'appartenance secondaire' (Rouchy 1987), as opposed to natural or primary groups. Le Roy postulated that groups denied self-expression within formal structures, seek to belong to transcultural groups in which cultural differences are dissipated, using a fantasy of oneness as a defence against anxieties of annihilation and loss. Finally, he pointed out that historical traumas such as war, genocide and emigration, when denied and not processed within primary family groups, can produce family and individual trauma that is passed on from generation to generation. The workshop format of alternating small and large groups was containing enough to allow these traumas to be exposed along with a lot of pain and distress, in a way that seemed to allow some relief and resolution. This was true at a national as well as an individual level.

(b) At Maastricht, as a silent observer in both small and large groups, I found that issues of identity were uppermost in both: personal identity in relation to the primary, family group in the small group; national, cultural and linguistic identity through secondary groups in the large group. As in the large group, the small group had a 'paranoid' start, with transient national subgroupings, and the conductor–observer couple were avoided for a while; it will be recalled that the conductor was a German woman, the observer a British man. For a time transcultural themes were used defensively. Soon, however, deep pain emerged to do with the primary family group. The holding and containing function of the group allowed regression and the expression and exploration of intimacy, ambivalence, reparation and loss, particularly felt in the last two group sessions.

Themes and dynamics were seen to flow between small and large groups (Brown 1987a). In both, maturation occurred from initial mistrust, paranoia and splitting towards more genuine dialogue and intimacy. In Kleinian terms, there seemed to be a real shift from the paranoid-schizoid to the depressive position and the capacity for concern, which I would view as synonymous with a *moral* or *ethical* position. This seemed to require recognising the value of one's own identity as well as that of others – i.e. valuing differences as well as recognising similarities, taking responsibility for one's hatred, envy and guilt, and moving towards reparation and forgiveness. (Some theoretical implications of these processes will be discussed in a subsequent paper, Brown 1992a.)

In the small group, there were instances of individuals using cultural change to carry out internal work on their own personal identity, for example (1) changing national identification into an idealised grandiose form to avoid deeper internal identification with a parent impossible to compete with, or unusable because degraded and shameful; (2) searching for the missing self or object through involvement with partners from different cultures; (3) transforming personal murderous violence into an idealised courageous fight against tyranny through political terrorism (Brown 1987a). It was thus seen that breaking the continuity of one's cultural, national and linguistic background can serve a positive psychological function for some individuals, even though when forced such breaks can be very traumatic, as pointed out by Husemann (1987) and Grinberg and Grinberg (1989).

My large group observations were very similar to those of Jaak Le Roy. After the 'paranoid' initial stage its organisation into the battle for supremacy between Anglophones and Francophones seemed to represent a struggle for power and control that everyone could identify with as a way of avoiding exclusion and annihilation. The denial of a German voice might have been a way of maintaining at least some moral superiority. When the Germans found their German voice it seemed to provoke anxiety as well as relief. Perhaps this was why the issue of anti-Semitism and ghettos took longer to emerge, and the Holocaust was only hinted at – as though its traumatic violence would re-emerge in talking about it (as in Le Roy's comments about unprocessed family traumas).

However, like the small group, the large group did mature from the paranoid-schizoid to the depressive position. The battle to speak only English or French gave way to a situation in which both were spoken along with German, and other languages. This necessitated tolerating *not* knowing, in order to be fair and respectful of others. Defensive stereotyping lessened as the universality of narcissistic trauma and pain were recognised, between groups as well as between individuals. The parallels suggest that anxieties based on early individual development known to us through psychoanalysis are reflected in large groups and through social and cultural phenomena.

Much could be said about the way the issues of language were explored at considerable depth in the large group, but I shall merely mention two themes, which I see as connected: (1) that of the foreigner or stranger, expressed e.g. as the barbarian who does not have his own language; and (2) that of maps as showing containing boundaries or, as in Africa, the lines of rivers as channels of communication. Shared language allows communications to flow. These can be desired or feared. The danger to divine power and authority if we all talk the same language was expressed through the frequent mention at Maastricht of the myth of the Tower of Babel.

Heidelberg

(a) At Heidelberg Jaak Le Roy, now a small group conductor rather than a researcher, felt very much more in the middle of the experiences. His accounts of his small group and the large group parallel each other. On Day 1 anxiety and distress were quickly felt in both, with apparently defensive idealisation of the Maastricht workshop.

On Day 2 he describes how in the small group the empty chairs of the missing Russian and Yugoslav acted as a focus for ambivalence and loss. Later, after they had moved towards each other – telling their names after the conductor interpreted the wish to transcend nationality as a wish to transcend their families of origin – they were able to attack the staff for being inadequately supportive. Regressively they invested the small group as a containing primary group, in which primitive and bodily needs and sensations were manifested. In the large group, perception of the staff as cold and unreasonable evoked anxieties about Nazis and the Holocaust. Thus in the larger group, in Germany, issues suppressed at Maastricht emerged fully.

By Day 3 the primitive regressive theme emerged more strongly in the small group, with acting out by refugees from the Nazis, or their children, acting out their oral needs with German gateaux! In the large group, in a German environment, Germans were able to speak of and explore their own and their families' suffering during the Nazi period, and the large group became more containing for all. The split between victims and victimisers lessened.

On Day 4 the same themes were continued, though in the small group the traumas spoken of were to do with the primary family group, and in particular it was seen how denial of aggression and of traumatic events in the family's history and the subject of historical social trauma often ran parallel. By the end, Le Roy described how primitive bodily digestive sensations were transformed into grief which could be spoken of and placed in history. (I would add that this is a graphic example of how a group-analytic approach can deal equally with somatic, psychological and social processes.)

Jaak Le Roy commented that while the small group moved in the course of the workshop from a regressive primary family to a space in which to think, the large group became a new secondary group, containing and (in the Winnicottian sense) transitional (Winnicott 1971b).

(b) My position at Heidelberg was also different from that at Maastricht. No longer a silent staff member, I was flung straight into the experiences of both large and small groups. Without the sense of detachment and control that being a member of staff can promote, I was quickly in touch with persecutory anxiety, heightened by the location of the workshop in Germany, by hearing students chanting in the streets the first night, and by the rapid assertion of the Germans and German language in the first large group. In fact I told the *large group* about my unease the night before, reflecting on the position I would have been in, 50 years ago, as a Jew. Like Jaak Le Roy, I was struck by the defensive idealisation of Maastricht at the start of the Heidelberg workshop, seemingly functioning to differentiate those who had been there from the newcomers, and avoiding the more problematic difference between Germans and non-Germans. By the second large group, stereotyping of 'bad Germans' was established, giving rise to a struggle to differentiate those Germans present among staff and participants. By the

third day this differentiation broke down with an explosion of fantasies that some Germans present were Nazis (expressed particularly powerfully by a Jewess whose family perished in the Holocaust) and equally moving accounts of German suffering in the war. It took a young man from Switzerland, neutral in the war, to quote the British poet of the First World War, Wilfred Owen, through the imagined words of a dead German soldier: 'I am the enemy you killed my friend.' ('Strange Meeting' was one of Owen's last poems before he himself was killed. He had been planning a volume of poems appealing to the conscience of England against the continuation of the war.)

This epitomised the move in the large group towards mutual responsibility and guilt, away from simple stereotyping and blame. Jaak Le Roy comments that the small group revealed our cultural complexity, the large group exposed simplistic nationalism. However, it is clear to me that the large group did work, painfully and turbulently, towards a more mature mutual understanding between national groups.

Of the *Francophone small group* I was in, I can mainly speak of my own experience, as the least proficient French-speaker. It was a disturbing and illuminating experience, giving me a vivid insight into being both an immigrant (as my grandparents had been in England) and what it is like for all of us to be an infant, without enough words.

Again, as in the large group, there was defensive talk about Maastricht at the first meeting, until eventually people gave their names and reluctantly told something about their backgrounds and why they had come to the workshop. In the next session, language and the difference between generations were important topics. My presence in the group was challenged – why was I in the group when I spoke so little French? As I had been a staff member at Maastricht, was I a staff spy here? (My presence seemed to touch off universal paranoid anxieties about the stranger in our midst.)

On the second day two women, relatively poor French-speakers, became very distressed and described feeling excluded. (Perhaps I did not do so because of my *self-appointed* role of participant-observer, thinking that however uncomfortable I felt I would reflect on it and put it to some use, such as writing a paper!) One member spoke of a dream that there was only one nation, others of identifying with a locality and of defiant subgrouping. After the violent large group had been talked about, there was discussion of asserting the right to use one's own language and taking responsibility (whatever the staff said) of asking each other for translation. Gender conflicts emerged, and the need to take responsibility for one's own internal violence. For a while destructive fantasies developed, the damage done to the environment by cars being linked with Nazi gas chambers. Violent *personal* reaction to an earlier rejection surfaced when one man admitted that he realised in the large group his intention to hurt the woman who had 'set herself up' to be stereotyped as the daughter of a Nazi, by saying he preferred the German woman who acted as convenor of the large group. He explained that he had done so in retaliation for her seeming to have pretended not to recognise him when they had met somewhere else between the time of the Maastricht and the Heidelberg workshops. This led to such a flight into sexual excitement that the group was reluctant to stop! (The event seemed to be a good example of how social processes can be harnessed to deal with individual narcissistic needs.)

On the third day resentment at sexual stereotyping was prominent, but when expressed and worked through, greater awareness of the resentment of both sexes led to a good deal more closeness and liveliness between group members. After a powerful large group had led to some international reconciliation, there were more personal revelations in the small group, which was able to explore the complexity of identity and of relations between the generations.

Finally, on the fourth day, this move to intimacy in the small group was expressed and explored through the use of 'tu' and 'vous', recognition of how projected images block empathy, and how different attitudes, supposedly characteristic of the north and south of Europe, related to control and passion are potential in all of us. There was even discussion of the role of education in promoting communication and toleration of intimacy. This was connected, I think, with the return to the group, to our great relief, of our 'good grandmother', an epitome of European integration, who had been absent through ill-health the previous day – a German living in Italy but a member of this French-speaking group, fluent in all three languages *and* English.

Her transculturality made the *British national group* seem an indulgent and parochial place. Because I believe that sooner or later our workshop format needs to take them seriously, I will say something about ours. The three British national groups were friendly, informal affairs experienced, I think, by everyone as oases of familiarity and safety, free from the need to work very hard. It was as though we could sink back into a certain amount of comfortable self-satisfaction and teasing rivalry amongst ourselves. The first one on Friday concerned itself with looking at how British each of us was, resulting in the complexity of British nationality being revealed, and the strength this provides despite the 'appeal of purity'. The second one was even more informal, as the two-man Scandinavian group usurped our room and we went off to a café to order drinks and snacks. In fact we became quite noisy, behaving I thought rather as one imagines Germans might do when holidaying together in the south of Europe, or British football hooligans abroad. However, we enjoyed ourselves and allowed ourselves a little fun at the expense of the hardworking staff group in the corner! On the final day the national group was a little more serious and insisted on the two-woman Irish group joining us and retaking possession of the large room. We shared our ideas about how the English are perceived in Europe in general and the group-analytic fraternity in particular, e.g. the vestiges of imperialism and envy contrasting with our feeling of having a lot to learn from our European colleagues, and from the sort of intercultural and transcultural explorations that the workshop format allows.

Discussion

In summary, it is possible to see that in both workshops there was a development from paranoid anxieties to a more depressive recognition of mutual responsibility, guilt and concern. This was true in both small and large group settings. In the small groups, as one would expect, issues to do with personal and family histories predominated, including their manifestation through both defensive and creative cultural dynamics. Jaak Le Roy's observation of parallels between the denial of aggression in the primary group of the family and denial of traumatic events in both family and social histories was striking. Profound pathology can originate in this denial and consequent repression of psychological trauma, as is now widely recognised in the field of child abuse.

In the large group, again as one would expect, issues to do with social and cultural issues were more to the fore. Historical traumas and the narcissism of secondary groups aroused very strong feelings. What is interesting is the way these resonated at personal primary group levels, including the preverbal – especially at Maastricht, where the significance of having different languages was explored. The vicissitudes of our search for a secure and valued identity seemed to underlie both types of group in both workshops. The issues of German history and identity were opened up, particularly in the large group, parallel to the release from repression of painful areas of personal and family experience, particularly in the small group.

Discovering oneself more fully requires finding yourself in others, and differentiating yourself from them – enabling projections to be withdrawn and fuller responsibility taken. This involves finding things in common with apparently very different people and groups, so that stereotypes and prejudices are modified. As mentioned at the start of this paper, these processes can be seen as having *ethical* implications which will be examined in a second paper.

This paper has been based on observations in the two workshops by two colleagues with similar theoretical but different cultural backgrounds. We also filled different roles in each of the workshops, and I want to finish by questioning how much this fact can explain the differences between our accounts. These questions occurred to me only in preparing this final version of the paper, over two years after the second workshop and the completion of my notes. They could only have had unconscious influence on my observations.

In Maastricht, Jaak Le Roy was very aware of general workshop processes, and the problems arising from not having allowed formal structures to contain linguistic and national groups. Was this connected with his overall research role and his responsibility in the planning and unfolding of the workshop? Does the nature and degree of his sense of responsibility, for example, reflect an interaction between his role and personal and cultural factors?

At Maastricht I was very aware of identity issues. Was this heightened by the threat to my own identity by not having a role allowing communication and exchange? A chief requirement was that I was silent. This too is likely to reflect personal and cultural issues for me.

Did our different roles in Heidelberg, mentioned at the start of this paper, affect our observations and experiences there? I think this is now obvious. As a small group conductor, Jaak Le Roy seemed much more aware of processes he was immersed in, from direct experience. While he felt attacked for not being sufficiently supportive, as the staff as a whole were in the large group, he saw how the small group itself was experienced as containing at a primitive even bodily level. He could also see how frequently parallel were denial of aggression and trauma, at both family and social levels.

At Heidelberg where I was an ordinary participant, my own experience was of being more directly part of what was going on. I felt drawn into a more personal involvement with my own transculturality, and the paranoia this can induce – both in me as a Jew in Germany; and in other members of the French-speaking group where I was an Englishman speaking poor French, yet who had been a member of the staff at Maastricht. (These experiences illustrate two contrasting aspects of the paranoiagenesis of the concept of a chosen people!) Speaking French poorly, I initially felt infantilised and powerless in the small group. But this stimulated me to struggle and make use, as well as sense, of what was going on. One outcome was my taking on an additional unofficial observer/research role, which led to my keeping rough notes of my observations and experience, culminating in this paper. Could this be a small-scale paradigm of immigration, and one way of coping with it?

Could one of the principal functions of such workshops be the revelation of personal and cultural trauma and their interaction, in part by provoking the re-experiencing of them in a new setting? This exposes old ways of coping with them, and brings new ones to light.

14

USE AND ABUSE OF CULTURAL DIFFERENCES

Analysis and ethics in transcultural workshop settings

Introduction

Transcultural work provides an opportunity to understand powerful processes in individuals and in the sociocultural groups to which they belong, when confronted by other sociocultural groups during migration and political upheaval. Their potential destructiveness is only too well known. Cultural differences can be the pretext for the grossest inhumanity. This can be viewed as abuse, in the sense of using them improperly or wrongfully, with implications of violation and damage (*Shorter Oxford English Dictionary*). Such abuse is committed by individuals and social groups and subgroups in what I have called 'false confrontation' (Brown 1988), based on projection rather than genuine differences, as well as on hostility arising from conflicts of interests and struggles for power. Workshops such as those of the European Association for Transcultural Group Analysis provide an opportunity to study it in ourselves, and thus to put cultural differences to positive use, and reduce their capacity to violate and destroy.

Reflecting on the workshops at Maastricht and Heidelberg described in the previous chapter, this suggests the need for a *moral* and *ethical* concept of maturity in group analysis. Such a concept would complement the psychoanalytic concept of *genitality* between individuals. The latter (according to Erikson 1964) combines strivings of sexuality and love pointing to 'one of those basic mutualities in which a partner's potency and potentialities are activated even as he activates the other's potency and potentialities'. However, Balint (1957) pointed out that 'genital love' is a fusion of disagreeing elements: of genital satisfaction and pre-genital tenderness. The reward for bearing the strain of this fusion, he stated, is the possibility of regressing from time to time to an infantile fantasy of oneness (as noted in the workshops).

From projection to mutual responsibility

The apparent move from paranoid-schizoid to depressive positions commented on several times in my account of the Maastricht and Heidelberg workshops seems insufficient, especially as a general guide to understanding intergroup behaviour as opposed to individual development. But when there is a reverse move, as happens in war or mob violence, the primitiveness of the process becomes clear. In Chapter 5 I gave an example from the 1978 World Cup between Scotland and Peru. The Scottish fans must have sacrificed a lot to travel to Argentina. The deep narcissistic roots of their secondary group loyalty were revealed when their team lost. 'The television film showed the team members being jeered at and abused as "rubbish" and "scum" by really irate and contemptuous ruffians. The wish to identify . . . with the glorious, omnipotent conquerors was dashed. It looked as though the fans were left feeling themselves to be nothing but the bitter hate-filled dregs of society.' They were confronted with an image of their own defeat, as a subgroup and (I imagine) as individuals and did not like it. Faced with an unwelcome similarity they turned it into a difference. The identification was turned into a 'dis-identification' as though the ego-ideal was transformed into 'faeces' that had to be expelled.

In a more recent paper (Brown 1987b) I have argued that group analysis can activate mutual responsibility and concern, and that the move from the paranoid-schizoid to the depressive position parallels a move from autism to communication, from defensive self-absorption to deeper relatedness to others. Greater individual maturity implies a move from *primitive* persecution and guilt to concern for parents and siblings (Winnicott 1965b). These can now be more realistically assessed. We can be concerned about them as we come to understand them as having their own problems and conflicts. We can blame them less and forgive them more. We are less inclined to confuse new relationships with these old ones; we can see how similarities can blind us to differences, and differences to similarities.

Greater social maturity contains all these elements which, it will be observed, have distinct ethical overtones – guilt, concern, blame and forgiveness. Once we are into the realm of group behaviour, particularly, sociocultural and national groups, ethics become a matter of life and death on a large scale. They can guide us towards mutual responsibility.

Moral and ethical development

Erik Erikson (1964) in his book *Insight and Responsibility* makes an important distinction between morals and ethics. He proposes that the former are more primitive, based on submission to threats, the latter more mature, based on ideals, rational assent and some promise of self-realisation. He envisages an 'epigenetic' progression from childhood development of *morality*, through adolescent perception of universal good in *ideological* terms, to adult *ethical* powers.

As he describes it, a true ethical sense in the young adult goes beyond moral restraint and ideal vision, while insisting on commitment to intimate and working relationship through which we hope to share a life of productivity and competence. But, as he says (p. 226), 'young adulthood has its own dangers. It adds to the moralist's righteousness and to the ideologist's fanatic repudiation of all otherness, the *territorial defensiveness* of one who has appropriated and staked out his earthly claim and who seeks eternal security in the super-identity of organisations. Thus what the Golden Rule at its highest has attempted to make all-inclusive, tribes, nations, castes, classes, moralities and ideologies have consistently made exclusive again – proudly, superstitiously and viciously denying the status of reciprocal ethics to those "outside".' One could add to this list football fans and schools of psychotherapy.

The dangers of projection and primitive moralising are well summed up by the Polish writer Czeslaw Milosz (1968) in his book *Native Realm*: 'Perhaps all nationalities seen as wholes and not assortments of individuals, are odious and their neighbours uncover in them only what are unpleasant truths about human societies in general. It may well be that what the Poles know about the Russians the Russians know about themselves but are unwilling to acknowledge and vice-versa.'

If there is a way forward for the world, the various forms of the ethical Golden Rule need to be *actively* followed – the Jewish 'What is hateful to yourself, do not to your fellow man', the Christian 'Love thy neighbour as thyself', The Hindu 'He who sees all beings in his own self and his own self in all beings', Abraham Lincoln's 'As I would not be a slave, I would not be a master.'

I like to think that the European Association for Transcultural Group Analysis is pioneering this progress by exploring and publicising the damage we do to ourselves as well as each other by denying our mutuality, and using sociocultural differences for projection, silencing, oppression and annihilation between groups and subgroups. International Psychoanalysts Against Nuclear Weapons have actively warned of their mortal dangers (Levine 1987; Segal 1987). We also must remember that wars and genocide *do* take place (the Holocaust and the Bomb are not just metaphors), that nuclear weapons, officially condoned torture, football riots, gulags and apartheid are facts of life that we should have something to say about.

Certainly there was in the workshops much evidence of paranoia, silencing, disavowal, and of the consequences of historical trauma and subjugation. But by using group-analytic methods in both small and large groups, these could be worked with, pain shared and understanding fostered. The paranoid-schizoid gave way to the depressive position, and moralistic and other rigidities were modified. I think we have some evidence that ideological

Utopianism functioned as a wishful avoidance of differences, as in the fantasies of a universal language and of one nation. But there were signs that toleration of differences can increase – e.g. between Germans and Jews, Northern and Southern Europeans, English and French.

The mature use of cultural differences in the light of theoretical developments

Therefore I am proposing that the mature *use* of cultural differences parallels genitality. To paraphrase the passage from Erikson quoted at the beginning of this paper, it combines the struggle for a clear and worthy identity, the hostility aroused by threats to this, and recognition and concern for the rights of others to differ. *Abuse* results from the breakdown of this process and the denial of the mutuality implicit in the Golden Rule of ethics. An important cause of this is heavy reliance on projection and projective identification. This involves excluding significant parts of individual and cultural identity from a narrowly restrictive 'envelope' (as Jaak Le Roy describes it) – projecting them into the 'poubelle' (waste-bin) of other individuals, groups and cultures.

To further our understanding I believe we need to develop and integrate new concepts as well as old ones. The Kleinian paranoid-schizoid and depressive positions, rooted in early infancy, enable us to grasp some of the changes observed in the workshops, but Erikson's idea of an epigenetic progress in ethical development helps us to understand later individual and sociocultural phenomena in relations between individuals and groups. At some point we have to comprehend the details of an individual's need to belong to a group to sustain a worthwhile and stable sense of self (or not to belong), to belong to another group, or even to seek to destroy a group. Self psychology (Kohut and Wolf 1978), and the French analyst Anzieu's work on psychic envelopes (Anzieu 1984) provide us with some useful working ideas. For example, self psychology makes sense of the behaviour of the Scottish football fans in Argentina described earlier; and the common metaphor of the 'poubelle' in the large groups at Maastricht can be linked with the unconscious group phantasy of a 'toilet-breast'.

Within the European Association for Transcultural Group Analysis significant theoretical concepts have been developed. Kaës *et al.* (1975) propose that a group psychic apparatus compensates for the lack of a group *body* analogous to the *physical* roots of the individual psychic apparatus. Rouchy (1990) explores the triple functions of 'belonging groups' or 'groupes d'appartenance' – containing and providing both transitional space and identificatory images.

The effects of gender differences in the development of moral values might also prove important. Gilligan (1982) has argued that a male moral orientation emphasises individual rights and abstract principles; while a female orientation emphasises attachment, connectedness and sensitivity to the needs of others. This suggests that if rights and caring are to be given equal weight in a moral system, both sexes need a voice and to respect what the other stands for. As group analysts, we value the fact that overlap blurs an absolute difference in the connection between sex and moral orientation (Gilligan *et al.* 1988). One wonders if the rigid lines of fundamentalism are the consequence of overemphasising male moral elements in a culture. Our work in future might help us to answer such pressing questions.

Work so far has shown that the matrix of a group-analytic workshop can provide, for groups as well as for individuals, a 'transitional space' in which to question the unconscious envelopes we protect ourselves with, to redraw our boundaries, and move towards more mature and mutual relationships. In other words, we are learning a way of *using* cultural differences rather than *abusing* them, of respecting them rather than denying their value.

The move to intersubjectivity and mutuality

Malcolm Pines, in the discussion of an earlier version of this paper,[1] pointed to our lack of a new language to take us beyond the Kleinian view of the infant developing in terms only of *internal* object relationships, and to the need to include the idea of *intersubjectivity* in a more comprehensive view of mutuality. I agree with this. Perhaps that is why the psychoanalytic concept of genitality seems so relevant. But while the driving force behind genitality is sexual, Eros, or sexual love is less relevant in mature group behaviour, except in the sense that Freud used it in explaining the origin of group formation (Freud 1921). It might be more profitable in explaining the search for and attainment of group and intergroup bonding and tolerance to think of *brotherly love*, the Agape of the early Christian 'love feast', or *impersonal fellowship*, Koinonia, described by de Maré in *Large and Median Groups* (De Maré *et al.* 1991). Emmanuel Diet, also discussing my earlier paper, raised the need of the 'word of the father', 'la loi', to ensure the third position necessary to allow a perspective which allows two protagonists to move beyond seeing each other only as objects, to integrate two perspectives.

Such integration is necessary for an intersubjective mutuality; it requires that we be outside someone else as well as inside them, i.e. that we be differentiated, as an infant from its mother.

Intersubjectivity has been given a central position in psychoanalysis by Atwood and Stolorow (1984: 6). They state that 'The intersubjective field of a case study is generated by the interplay between transference and countertransference; it is the environment or "analytic space" . . . in which the

1 Read at a Study Day of the European Association for Transcultural Group Analysis, May 1990.

various hypotheses of the study crystalise.' Again, they state that 'The analyst is aware of the nature of interpretation as "the rediscovery of the I in the Thou" (Dilthey) and therefore knows that each of his ideas is grounded in and limited by the finite perspectives of his own personal world.' It is interesting that Atwood and Stolorow quote Dilthey (1961/1926), a German philosopher-historian who wrote about *transpersonal* processes, later emphasised by Foulkes.

'Fair Shares and Mutual Concern' in families

The issue of mutual concern and consideration has been worked with very interestingly by Enid Balint (1972) in a paper based on notes of discussions she and Michael Balint had over many years, and entitled 'Fair Shares and Mutual Concern'. It distinguishes between two contrasting theories on the origin of concern for others: (1) springing from obedience to a patriarchal moral law, originally conceived of by Freud (1921) as based on a group's relationship with its leader and a way of dealing with jealousy between peers; (2) originating in the relation with mother during early demand feeding, when the child creates the laws and the mother obeys them. But in the pre-Oedipal phase any frustration is felt as unfair. The theory of the fully developed superego implies that fair shares are the same as equal shares. But equal shares are not necessarily the same as *fair* shares according to the theory of demand feeding. The child, in order to achieve a full sense of mutual concern through the relationship with the mother, requires a relationship with a law-giving father, and an awareness of the way the parents continue to be concerned for each other despite *their* differences of interest. They function as both introjects and external objects. The Balints conclude that the quality of the object relationship between mother and father, as perceived by the child, is crucial in its development of a capacity for mutual concern and fair play.

In a therapy group, as in a family with more than one child, equal shares are not the same as fair shares – peoples' needs vary from time to time. Patients became aware that other people also have to tolerate tensions. While in a group, as in a family, the existence of a therapist or parent is necessary, the Balints comment that the climate of concern arises from the relation between the group members. Fairness takes priority over equality. All share a wish to help as well as for help. The Balints point to three factors essential in education: (1) tolerance of spontaneous development of 'natural' control and discipline; (2) normal emotional life in the parental couple; and (3) not too much primitive satisfaction sought from the child by the parents.

From families and small groups to cultures

This can be seen as an analogy of group life and the development of ethical concern in the group. But is it possible to see a line from relation between individual and group to the level of relations between large cultural groups and subgroups? Once we get to this level we need to take into account political, social and cultural history and structures. I have been impressed by the apparent explanatory value of the work of the French sociologist Todd (1985). In his book *The Explanation of Ideology: Family Structures and Social Systems* he correlates the geographical embedding of different political ideologies – even within a particular country – to different types of family structure (authoritarian or libertarian), inheritance rules (primogeniture or 'latifundia') and endogamy versus exogamy. One would expect that the extent to which a politico-economic system is perceived as fair by its citizens will depend on such culturally embedded ideological values. This raises the question of the 'democratic ideology' of group analysis, and its resonance or dissonance with the prevailing cultures in which it is practised. Whether or not it harmonises with the foundation matrix (Foulkes 1975) may determine where transcultural group analysis can function and establish its usefulness.

An ethical concept of maturity in group analysis[2] would take into account the need of individuals to belong to sociocultural groups, to respect that need in others and to value differences as well as similarities between cultures. Such a concept, with a generous view of fairness, would undermine the narrow 'moral' authority of fundamentalism. It would side with the inclusiveness of the Golden Rule against the exclusiveness of immature fanaticism, as described earlier in Erikson's epigenetic view of moral and ethical development. I think it would need to allow for the struggle towards maturity and for regressions from it, as in the concepts of genitality and genital love.

It is proposed that we tentatively use the term *transculturality* to describe the ideal relationship between cultures. This would imply the transcending of culture-bounded prejudices and projections. It would acknowledge at least some similarities between different cultures, and some processes which cross over and through them, and so bind them together in a common humanity.

2 The recent appearance of two papers on moral and ethical issues in the same issue of the *International Journal of Group Psychotherapy* (Larkin 1991; Mullan 1991) suggests a reawakening of interest in this area.

15

GROUP ANALYSIS, TRANSCULTURALITY AND ETHICS[1]

The Foundation Matrix

Group analysis exposes even more than psychoanalysis the way we live in a transpersonal and intersubjective world. In acknowledging our object-seeking nature, group analysis also stresses the deep significance of context, including the cultural matrix in which our relationships are embedded. This is what Foulkes called the foundation matrix, 'based on the biological properties of species, but also on the culturally firmly-embedded values and reactions'. Foulkes goes on: 'These have been developed and transmitted, especially in the nuclear family, in the social network, class, etc. and have been maintained or modified by the intimate plexus in which the person now moves' (Foulkes 1975: 131–2).

In using the term foundation matrix, Foulkes brought together biological factors and elements intrinsic to being a human being, along with specific cultural factors in a loose and general way. He did not consider in *detail* the cultural norms, values, traditions, expectations, aspirations, myths, and shared history, traumas and consequent anxieties and defences. However, we are familiar with these from the workshops of the European Association for Transcultural Group Analysis, where we have also had to face up to the consequences of social change and disruption such as migration and social trauma – and the problems that arise when cultures clash or threaten each other.

Transcultural workshops

Even sophisticated professionals, like the members of the European Association for Transcultural Group Analysis and others coming to its workshops

1 Based on paper read at 1st Symposium of European Association for Transcultural Group Analysis, Bologna, 1992, on Identity and Cultures. Several papers from this symposium have been published in *Group Analysis* 28, 2, 1995, and others will be published in subsequent issues.

– usually drawn to this field of study by relevant personal, family and social reasons – can get caught up in primitive processes that deny and dehumanise others, as shown by the accounts of such workshops (reviewed in Brown 1992a; developed in Le Roy 1994): the battle for supremacy between Francophones and Anglophones, and the denial of the German language at Maastricht; the explosive struggle for acknowledgement of their suffering during the Second World War by both Germans and Jews at Heidelberg; and the painful feelings associated at Oxford with unacknowledged experiences of racial oppression based on differences of colour. What was striking in all the workshops was the way in which the group-analytic format provided a safe-enough space in which to expose traumatic and painful experiences, and to move at least some way from initial paranoid anxiety to a sense of concern and mutuality.

It was the coexistence of these negative and positive experiences that led me to consider the need for an ethical dimension to understand and guide our work. I hope it is not wishful thinking to suppose that human beings are capable of recognising and at least partially overcoming their prejudices based on primitive anxieties and defences. This implies that some responses to perceived differences are more primitive and less good than others. For it to make any difference at a social level, such values need to become an increasing part of an expanding worldwide foundation matrix.

Looking around us we can see how easy it is for cultural differences to be used to deny other people's humanity, and as a pretext for inhuman behaviour towards them. As psychoanalysts and group analysts we know how individual and group projection and defences against anxiety can distort our perception of other people, and how such anxieties can be manipulated and exploited by leaders and influential subgroups at times of social instability.

How can the lessons we learn in our workshops help us to understand what happens in the world around us? We can see that even we are not immune to prejudice, stereotyping, failures of generosity and empathy, *at least in imagination*. We can see that confrontation in a multicultural setting can lead to disturbance, even hostility, that, *when contained*, can enlarge our sense of ourselves and of our connectedness.

Historical evidence

We know from history, ancient and modern, that social structures and conditions can play a crucial part in determining whether the outcome of such confrontation is destructive or capable of resolution and healing. Voices need to be heard and interests balanced. Resistances and practicalities can make this difficult to achieve. At Maastricht the battle for supremacy between English and French speakers gave way to both being spoken, *and* Norwegian, when the needs of others were respected and the inability to understanding *everything* was tolerated. But we had to wait until Heidelberg for German to be spoken openly, and the suffering of Germans in the war to be heard about.

The repression of unwanted dissenting voices can be hugely destructive, and be built into a cruel 'fundamentalist' morality. The history of Spain in the last thousand years is instructive (Roth 1969). Islam and Christianity, if rarely tolerant towards each other, were at times very tolerant to Judaism, though usually at times when the other was not. The expulsion of the Jews 500 years ago was at a time when Christianity had become increasingly intolerant and authoritarian. As Moore (1987) has shown in his book *The Formation of a Persecuting Society*, crucial changes took place in the Church between 950 and 1250 AD, a period of great cathedral building. The Church began to promote the persecution of heretics (including Jews, 'lepers' and homosexuals). Before that time, in parts of Europe, priests and rabbis conducted public theological disputes, often followed by large-scale voluntary conversion to Judaism.

Paranoid and depressive positions

Institutions and the values they promulgate can promote an atmosphere that encourages paranoia, idealisation of one's own, and denigration of the values of others. In Kleinian terms, they encourage social groups to operate in the paranoid-schizoid rather than in the depressive position. This contrasts with what Alford (1989), in his book *Melanie Klein and Critical Social Theory*, calls *reparative morality*, which he sees as other-directed and other-regarding: 'The key of Kleinian insight is that greed, avaricious individualism, possessive individualism, and the like are not given; they are responses to fear (ultimately of our own aggression) and a fear that stands in the way of *caritas*. It is this, I have argued all along, that makes Klein's view tragic. Our potential to love and to care for others is real: it is an expression of a desire whose power is exceeded only by its extreme susceptibility to fear' (p. 179).

There have been societies, like that in Ladakh, described by Norberg-Hodge (1991), in which co-operation, frugality and a sense of connectedness with nature are more conducive to mutual concern and gentleness. They are vulnerable however to the incursion of exploitation and alien values. Nevertheless one might ask which form of society is the more advanced and mature, which fosters mature personalities, 'suffused by benevolence' as Melanie Klein characterised them.

Ethics and morality

Erik Erikson (1964), in his book *Insight and Responsibility*, makes an important distinction between morals and ethics. He proposes that the former are more primitive, based on submission to threats, the latter more mature, based on ideals, rational assent and some promise of self-realisation. He envisages an 'epigenetic' progression from childhood development of *morality*, through adolescent perception of universal good in *ideological* terms, to adult *ethical* powers.

As he describes it, a true ethical sense in the young adult goes beyond moral restraint and ideal vision, while insisting on commitment to intimate and working relationship through which we hope to share a life of productivity and competence. But, as he says (p. 226), 'young adulthood has its own dangers. It adds to the moralist's righteousness and to the ideologist's fanatic repudiation of all otherness, the *territorial defensiveness* of one who has appropriated and staked out his earthly claim and who seeks eternal security in the super-identity of organisations. Thus what the Golden Rule at its highest has attempted to make all-inclusive, tribes, nations, castes, classes, moralities and ideologies have consistently made exclusive again – proudly, superstitiously and viciously denying the status of reciprocal ethics to those "outside".' One could add to this list football fans and schools of psychotherapy.

The dangers of projection and primitive moralising are well summed up by the Polish writer Czeslaw Milosz (1968) in his book *Native Realm*: 'Perhaps all nationalities seen as wholes and not as assortments of individuals, are odious, and their neighbours uncover in them only what are unpleasant truths about human societies in general. It may well be that what the Poles know about the Russians the Russians know about themselves but are unwilling to acknowledge and vice versa.'

Such projection and stereotyping contrast with the various forms of the ethical Golden Rule, expressed in such words as the Jewish 'What is hateful to yourself, do not to your fellow man', the Christian 'Love thy neighbour as thyself', the Hindu 'He who sees all beings in his own self and his own self in all beings', and Abraham Lincoln's 'As I would not be a slave, I would not be a master.'

Early psychological development: The concept of fairness I

At an infantile level, what Melanie Klein called the depressive position promotes the emergence of reparative wishes and the capacity for concern within the mother–infant dyad. Klein (1975: 252) comments: 'We know from Freud that pity is a reaction to cruelty. But reactions of this kind do not set in until the child has attained some degree of positive object-relationship – until, in other words, genital organisation has come to the fore . . . as soon as the child's sadism is diminished and the character and function of its super-ego changed so it arouses less anxiety and more sense of guilt, these defensive mechanisms which form the basis of a moral and ethical attitude are activated, and the child begins to have consideration for its objects and to be amenable to social feeling.'

The importance of this achievement has implications for the whole of later development, though I believe that wider contextual factors play a formative role in the development of the capacity for mutual concern, both within the family network and wider society.

The issue of mutual concern and consideration within the family has been worked with very interestingly by Enid Balint (1972) in a paper based on discussions she and Michael Balint had over many years, and entitled 'Fair Shares and Mutual Concern'. It distinguishes between two contrasting theories on the origin of concern for others: (1) springing from obedience to a patriarchal moral law, originally conceived of by Freud (1921) as based on a group's relationship with its leader and a way of dealing with jealousy between peers; (2) originating in the relation with mother during early demand feeding, when the child creates the laws and the mother obeys them. But in the pre-Oedipal phase any frustration is felt as unfair. The theory of the fully developed superego implies that fair shares are the same as equal shares. But equal shares are not necessarily the same as *fair shares* according to the theory of demand feeding. The child, in order to feel a full sense of mutual concern through the relationship with the mother, requires a relationship with a law-giving father, and an awareness of the way the parents continue to be concerned for each other despite *their* differences of interest. They function as both introjects and external objects. Balint concludes that the quality of the object relationship between mother and father as perceived by the child is crucial in its development of a capacity for mutual concern and fair play. Elsewhere I have proposed that beyond this, relations with siblings and peers play a crucial role in this development, which may be extrapolated into social attitudes (Brown 1998a).

The social unconscious: The concept of fairness II

The idea of the Social Unconscious is implicit in Foulkes's concept of the foundation matrix, mentioned at the start of this paper (Foulkes 1975: 131). Foulkes (1964) had written that 'the group-analytic situation, while dealing with the unconscious in the Freudian sense, brings into operation and perspective a totally different area of which the individual is equally unaware. Moreover, the individual is as much compelled and modelled by these colossal forces as by his own *id* and defends himself as strongly against their recognition without being aware of it, but in quite different ways and modes. One might speak of a social or interpersonal unconscious.'

Elsewhere I have drawn attention to some of the ways in which the Social Unconscious is manifested: (1) assumptions – what is taken for granted and natural in society; (2) disavowals – disowning knowledge or responsibility for unwelcome things; (3) projections – what is defended against by projection, repression or avoidance; and (4) structural oppression (Brown 1994). All these manifestations can contribute to the perpetuation of injustice and unfairness. They point to the areas in which the struggle for justice and fairness has to be waged.

Within sociological research I have been impressed by the apparent explanatory value of the work of the sociologist Emmanuel Todd (1985) which can be seen as providing the social infrastructure of the sense of what is fair, contributing to unconscious social attitudes. In his book *The Explanation of Ideology: Family Structures and Social Systems* he correlates the geographical embedding of different political ideologies – even within a particular country – to different types of family structure (authoritarian or libertarian), inheritance rules (primogeniture or equal division of property among the descendants) and endogamy versus exogamy. One would expect that the extent to which a politico-economic system is perceived as fair by citizens will depend on such culturally embedded ideological values.

Todd examines the relationship between family structures and political ideologies throughout the world. He sees Tuscany and Emilia-Romagna, which have traditionally elected left-wing representatives, as especially interesting: 'They dominate the national culturally through their universities which are the most important on the peninsula: Bologna and Florence have defined the language and the law of Italy' (p. 123). He categorises Italy as a country whose family structure is largely 'egalitarian nuclear', ensuring that there is (1) equality of brothers as laid down by inheritance laws; (2) no cohabitation of married children with their parents; and (3) no marriage between the children of brothers. This type of family structure predisposes to a concern for *equality and liberty*. But its central region, Tuscany and Emilia-Romagna, is dominated by the 'exogamous community' family form, which emphasises both *equality and authority*. This type of family structure also stresses equality of inheritance between brothers, and forbids marriage between their children, but married sons continue to live with their parents. Paradoxically, the fundamental values based on the extended family and springing from it, are consonant with communist ideology, but in the many countries in Eastern Europe and Asia where communist regimes became established, extended families conflicted with the regime's attempts to create a super-family. Perhaps this paradox explains the inner contradictions that have destroyed communism as we have known it: people might want their own families, not be forced into a huge impersonal one.

Maturity in relationships: The self and others

An ethical concept of maturity in group analysis would, I believe, take into account the need of individuals to belong to sociocultural groups, to respect that need in others and to value differences as well as similarities between cultures. Such a concept, with a generous view of fairness, would undermine the narrow 'moral' authority of fundamentalism. It would side with the *inclusiveness* of the Golden Rule against the *exclusiveness* of immature fanaticism as described by Erikson. It would need to allow for the struggle towards maturity and for regressions from it, as in the concepts of genitality and genital love.

We can consider full relating as encompassing the appreciation of the coexistence of both similarities and differences (acknowledging them and enjoying them), allowing an interplay between differentiation and de-differentiation, as in the relationship between mother and infant. The relationship between the sexes also provides a key example of differences being enjoyed. Indeed, in Freudian psychology, the concept of genitality has deeply moral connotations. This, according to Erikson (1964), combines strivings of sexuality and love pointing to 'one of those basic mutualities in which the partner's potency potentialities are activated even as he activates the other's potency and potentialities'. However, as Balint (1959: Chapter 7) pointed out, 'genital love is a fusion of disagreeing elements: genital satisfaction and pre-genital tenderness'. He points out that the reward for bearing the strain of this fusion is the possibility of regressing from time to time to an infantile fantasy of oneness, as happened at times in EATGA workshops, with the fantasy of oneness and of a common language that would be everyone's mother tongue.

It might be objected that the concept of genitality, or the genital character is too reductive. Indeed, as Rieff (1959) pointed out, it was in reaction to Freud's synecdochial use of the word genital – using a part as equivalent to a whole – that Karen Horney used the phrase 'the sincere character', Thomas French 'the integrated character' and Erich Fromm 'the productive orientation'. For Fromm (1956) the orientation is expressed in the realm of feeling by love, 'which is the experience of union with another person, with all men, and with nature, under the condition of retaining one's sense of integrity and independence' (p. 32).

Regression, holding and growth

Beyond the dyad, infantile or amorous, are familial and social situations, in which several or many people coexist. Therapeutic groups, small, median or large (as in therapeutic communities) and workshops are examples with which we are familiar. Even in these, threats to a sense of security and identity can reduce the capacity to allow for the coexistence of simultaneous needs in a mature mutuality. But with adequate holding and common interest, moral growth is possible. I believe that analysis helps to counter the primitive defences and ethical regression that Erikson described, which shut us off from recognising the needs of others. As a patient once said (Brown 1987), 'That's how the group works, it enables you to be *really* selfish, and *really* compassionate, together.'

At a social level, where analysis can only be an indirect influence, I suspect there needs to be an awareness of a social version of what the Balints described as a law-giving father, and of parents whose concerns for each other survive their different interests. The search for God and for social justice can be seen as expressions of those needs.

When it comes to different cultures, whether coexisting relatively peacefully or in open conflict, the danger of regressing from ethics to primitive moralising and 'fundamentalism' is immense. It is so easy to dehumanise the foreigner and the stranger in our midst. We need to develop attitudes and social structures, eventually perhaps at a global level, that embody ethical principles. These might need to incorporate notions of a 'paternal' lawgiver and of parents who both use and overcome their differences. Slanging-matches in Parliament cannot fail to have familial resonances. The newcomer in our midst inevitably echoes the arrival of the unwanted younger child, step-parent or step-sibling (Brunori 1996).

Genitality as a paradigm of transculturality

I propose that we tentatively use the term *transculturality* to describe the ideal relationship between cultures. Analogously to the concept of genitality, this would imply the transcending of culture-bound prejudices and projections. It would acknowledge at least some similarities between different cultures, and some processes which cross over and through them, and so bind them together in a common humanity. The transcending of differences is achieved in the relationship between the sexes in many societies during adolescence and early adulthood. A caricature of differences is fostered by the gender-based subcultures of the latency period, themselves a reflection of the struggle of individuals of both sexes to define their gender identity. Is it the imperative urge of sexuality that provides the motivating energy for this transcending of differences towards mature genitality? Not entirely I think, for this process is often aborted by psychopathology. It is also made more difficult to achieve by those attitudes, customs and myths embedded in the foundation matrix of some cultures which emphasise the inferiority or impurity of women. A gross example is the barbaric practice of infibulation (a destructive form of female circumcision) which deforms the relationship between the sexes as well as the female genitals.

Dick Blackwell (1994), a group analyst working in organisational consultancy and with the Medical Foundation for the Care of Victims of Torture, has commented on my suggestion of a parallel between the vicissitudes of relations between cultures and those of the sexes. Within national cultures relations between classes and those of different colour are also fraught with dehumanising devaluation and projection. We know that these manifestations of primitive narcissistic defence mechanisms are exacerbated in times of economic scarcity and competition, and in the struggle to obtain and maintain self-esteem. Among the notable papers at the Bologna Symposium was one by Farhad Dalal (1997a) proposing that skin colour contributes to the structuring of society and of the psyche in modern Britain. Certainly entrenched labels such as Black and White, and national and other stereotypes, reflect processes which sustain the attitudes that 'otherness' is despicable and threatening. Indeed, in another Bologna paper, Susann Heenen-Wolff (1995) has invoked the idea of the death instinct to explain the depth and ferocity, always potential, of our negative responses to aliens.

However, even if the Death Instinct is an inherent part of human nature, still a controversial issue, the same can be said of the urge to unite in love. It could be argued that humans have a built-in psychological need, not only to join together in love, but also to make sense of the complementary bi-sexuality of the parental couple, and therefore of themselves. And from pre-history in-groups and out-groups also have had complementary relationships, intrinsic to incest taboos and exogamy. Further, human history has not always dealt with aliens and 'otherness' in negative and destructive ways. Instances of mutual enrichment and cultural fertilisation include periods in medieval Spain, and quite recent Bosnia. The shrinking world, falling back into ethnic and cultural enclaves with often disastrous consequences, could be seen to have a psychological need to make sense of its multiculturality.

It therefore remains an open question whether ethical ideals and such a view of transculturality can enter into the world's foundation matrix to a degree that mitigates the effect of individual and group psychopathology. However, group analytic therapy groups are based on such an ethos, so we are justified in asking whether larger groups, institutions and societies are inevitably resistant to them, given enough confrontation and containing.

16

FOULKES'S BASIC LAW OF GROUP DYNAMICS 50 YEARS ON

Abnormality, injustice and the renewal of ethics

Introduction

In 1998 we are celebrating the hundredth anniversary of the birth of Siegmund Heinrich Fuchs (Foulkes). It is a tremendous honour and pleasure to give this centenary lecture and particularly moving to me because it is also a hundred years since my own father was born. In my personal shorthand, F stands for father, Freud and Foulkes! As I came from psychoanalysis to group analysis through Foulkes, his encouraging junior colleagues are in a sense my older brothers. Notable among them are the former Foulkes Lecturers Malcolm Pines, Robin Skynner, Pat de Maré and Lionel Kreeger, some of whom were with me in Foulkes's final group. On 8 July 1976, in the penultimate group session, aged nearly 78, Michael, as his intimates called him, died halfway through an interpretation. It echoed the trailing off in mid-sentence that was a characteristic of his – leaving questions and suggestions hanging in the air to be responded to and developed.

Four years ago several of us attempted to look *forward* from Foulkes's legacy, in a book called *The Psyche and the Social World* (Brown and Zinkin 1994). Here I also want to look *backward*, to where Foulkes came from in writing his first book, *Introduction to Group-Analytic Psychotherapy*, published in 1948 when he was 50.

In that book Foulkes formulated a basic law of group dynamics (Foulkes 1948: 29), that group members collectively constitute the norm from which they individually deviate. It's easy to misunderstand this if we forget the revolutionary nature of Foulkes's vision at a time when individuality and group life were still often seen as antithetical.[1] I'd like to develop some ideas about this revolution.

First, after suggesting it was a creative response by Foulkes to crises in his own life in the turbulent *first* half of the century, I'll link his new vision with the changes that have taken place in the last half century in the physical, biological and social sciences, and quietly in psychoanalysts. These acknowledge the deep connectedness of things and people.[2]

Second, I'll attempt to point to the relevance of the Basic Law to two of my own recent interests, which I suspect were unconsciously influenced by it. One is the way that individuals and groups define what is *normal*, and so deal with what is abnormal, *foreign* or '*other*', illuminated by the work of the European Association for Transcultural Group Analysis. The other interest concerns ideas of *justice* and *fairness*, which have been sharpened for me by involvement in workshops on sibling relationships, organised within the Group-Analytic Society. The title of this chapter deliberately refers to their apparent obverses, abnormality and injustice, as these are issues which contribute to *destructive social and intercultural conflicts and to bringing people into therapy*.

Third, and last, by tracing some of their developmental and evolutionary precursors, I hope to clarify the way in which *ethical relationships* are fostered by engagement in group life. I believe that this process is an important part of the efficacy of analytic group psychotherapy, *and* has wider social implications.

The Basic Law of Group Dynamics

Foulkes used the basic law of group dynamics to describe the healing effect of groups in these words: 'The deepest reason why [these] patients . . . can reinforce each other's normal reactions and wear down and correct each other's neurotic reactions, is that *collectively they constitute the very norm, from which, individually, they deviate*' (Foulkes 1948: 29).

I vividly remember the shock this simple statement created in an audience of students on the Introductory Course of the Institute of Group Analysis. One discerning and vocal student, now a distinguished academic, expressed the discomfort of many with a notion which could imply coercion into uniformity – after all, human susceptibility to coercive suggestion has been well-documented.[3] I think he struck the dual meanings of 'constitute' which in the *Oxford English Dictionary* cluster round two poles: to set or ordain, and to make up or compose. I believe Foulkes leaned to this more dynamic pole.[4]

However, in the same passage Foulkes goes on to explain that each individual is *to a large extent* part of the group he belongs to, and that the collective aspect permeates him to the core. To a *lesser extent* he deviates from the abstract model, standard or norm, *but is a variant of it*. It is this deviation that constitutes individuality, members' psychological fingerprints as it were. In a striking image he proposes a picture of group members submerged in a common pool, with their heads sticking up from the surface.

Foulkes was not promoting uniformity; merely stating that each group has more in common than it at first realises. He wrote, 'It is struck by its differences, which provoke curiosity, hostility and fear. As it proceeds it finds more and more of common ground, and less and less contradiction between individuality and community' (Foulkes 1948: 30). Of course this implies what Foulkes called a 'good' group and its healing power. He blurred over the existence of 'bad' groups, capable for example of coercion and scapegoatism, perhaps for personal reasons I shall touch on in the next section, including leaving Nazi Germany.

There's no doubt that some groups are bad, exploited by pathological leaders, poorly selected and so on. More commonly prospective members fear a group will be bad for *them*. It's when these fears are not realised, or when they are *but are worked through* that the boldness of Foulkes's viewpoint becomes apparent.

Group analysis, with its emphasis on intersubjectivity (Brown and Zinkin 1994) is not easy for some people, such as the severely narcissistic, schizoid and emotionally restricted. Their disregard of others, and fear of emotional encounter, deprives them of an opportunity to engage in reciprocal relationships of mutual empathy and understanding. It's these that normally allow us simultaneously to recognise ourselves *and others*, as feeling and autonomous subjects – not fused or alien objects.

In an analytic group, those with disregard of others or fear of real encounter will provoke challenges from the group. Hurt or frustrated, other group members might know enough about their anxieties to provide empathy and support as well as alternative models of relating. Even in profound psychopathology such sensitive challenges can promote change from tenuous to fuller connectedness, not only with the *self* as in psychoanalysis, but also with *others* (Dolan *et al.* 1997).

Often too frustrating or threatening for a single therapist, such people can be helped in a group over time. They include people with addictions, perversions and psychosomatic states (Brown 1985b, 1989). And, as Estella Weldon (1997) pointed out in her Foulkes Lecture two years ago, even anti-social characters and criminals can be reformed through mutual confrontation and empathy.

As well as helping those in severely disturbed narcissistic and borderline states, groups contribute too in the treatment of schizophrenia (Pines and Schermer 1994; Schermer and Pines 1998), which may be seen as the ultimate turning away from intimacy and reciprocity. The use of inpatient groups for the treatment of schizophrenia has been described as enabling patients with inadequate capacity for symbolising to internalise helping figures (Rey 1994). Without this concrete reminder of living objects, they tend to regress into a dead, lifeless world. In the sense that Foulkes meant it, socialisation is equivalent to normalisation; not uniformity, but humanity. Let me tell you a story from my earliest days in psychiatry.

About 40 years ago I was working in a small psychiatric hospital of some 500 beds. That's important because it meant that staff and patients had opportunities for face-to-face contact. Nightly ward rounds included the chronic wards where I encountered a severely deteriorated schizophrenic. He required periodic ECT to prevent him hurling himself through the nearest window.

Tom had been an art student, so if I saw him shuffling down the corridor I'd arrange to stand in front of one of the reproductions lining the walls. As I hoped, he eventually joined me and we were able to exchange reactions to the pictures. Before I'd heard abut Winnicott, we'd set up a 'transitional space' in which we could relate without too much threat.

The social therapists agreed to set up still-lifes for him to paint, something he'd not done for years. Soon he was able to relate more easily with others in the hospital community, in which we were trying to set up a social programme, certainly before I'd heard of Foulkes.

Then Tom was able to go out to evening classes and finally won a scholarship to attend full time at the local art college, where he became a celebrity. How much he was buoyed up by the belonging and encouragement can be gauged by his relapsing into hallucinations during the first summer vacation, back full time as a hospital patient. But the next summer his relapse was minor, and in the third vacation he sustained his progress and was finally discharged from hospital never to return.

Such mutual influence towards normality and humanity is more difficult when face-to-face contact is avoided in institutions and groups which are too large. Freud (1921) pointed out that mobs, as opposed to organised groups, are prone to spiralling regression and suggestibility, where primitive mechanisms of splitting and projection lead to scapegoating and dehumanisation. Many of you will have experienced the regressive pull of large groups (Kreeger 1975) in courses run by the Institute of Group Analysis. I well remember the dual pressure to remain silent to avoid being ignored or ridiculed, *and* to speak so as not to be annihilated.[5]

As Pat de Maré (De Maré *et al.* 1991) has pointed out, fear of loss of self in large groups can engender hatred; but the energy can be transformed into dialogue if people face each other in a safe setting with containing leadership, particularly in median-sized groups of 18 to 20. In fact Tom had broken down in deeply alienating circumstances. Threat of loss of self and unprocessable hatred might well have precipitated his breakdown. His recovery involved him finding himself in a containing and holding environment in which contact with others was not too threatening, in groups that were not too big.

I now realise it's clarifying to link Foulkes's idea of levels of communication and relationship to the issue of group size – from two to infinity. You'll recall he distinguished successively deeper levels (Foulkes 1964: 114). The larger the group, the more do deeper transpersonal levels predominate.[6] These can be benign and unifying as in pop concerts, or malignant and divisive as in wars and ethnic conflicts. The individual can feel enhanced or annihilated. Let me illustrate with another story.

Last year we were all caught up in a *transpersonal phenomenon* following the death of the Princess of Wales. The atmosphere was such that as an individual one felt that to question Diana's saintliness would have put one at risk of lynching. Within my small analytic groups however, personal connections made the toleration of different views at least expressible and thinkable. In contrast, the television commentator David Dimbleby, bound to be discreet in the huge public context, appeared to be the 'victim' of a Freudian slip – perhaps we should call it a Foulkesian slip. When the cortège passed what he called the 'infamous spot' in Whitehall where King Charles I had been executed, instead, he remarked that this was the place where *Prince* Charles was executed, before quickly correcting his meaningful error! Viewed in terms of Foulkes's basic law, the deviant (Dimbleby's unconscious) represented what the group-as-a-whole couldn't acknowledge (and perhaps his own regicidal Oedipal wishes, and mine?).

Before turning to some biographical facts and conjectures about Foulkes the man, I'd like to point out some recent corrections to his apparent idealisation of groups. They help us to explain the difference between good and bad groups, between those which are facilitating and those which are coercive and destructive. Leading contributors have been Lionel Kreeger (1992), Louis Zinkin (1983) and, most comprehensively, Morris Nitsun (1996). His idea of the 'anti-group' refers to the negative processes constantly shadowing positive processes in group life. Hatred of sharing is one of its most powerful motors, often overlaying memories or fantasies of parents together in the primal scene, or the sight of a sibling at the breast. I believe this hatred and associated anxiety underlie the reluctance of many people to join a group.[7] I shall refer later to the concept of the anti-group as providing a specifically group-analytic perspective on issues of abnormality, injustice *and* the renewal of ethics within and *between* groups.

At an individual level, the intensity of the hatred of sharing came home to me forcibly after a patient I'd had in psychoanalysis for several years reluctantly agreed to join a twice-weekly group with a colleague, while she continued with me for a while in less frequent individual sessions. I felt we'd become stuck in a regressive transference. In our now reduced individual sessions I was able to see that the change-over led to alteration in her relationship, with herself and with others. But at first she told me the group was terrifying – 'It was them or me,' she said, 'I'd not give an inch, or give everything so as not to be found out.' Eventually the group released us from what had become a closed system, and enabled her to resume her development (Brown 1988).

Creative crises in Foulkes's life

Sadly I can make only brief mention of Foulkes's personal life, but Elizabeth Foulkes (1990b) has written a valuable biographical memoir. Foulkes's own 'autobiographical notes' are more an account of his professional development, but in these, Foulkes (1968) describes the creative frenzy in which his first book had been written, culminating in an acute coronary attack.[8]

I believe that in a sense the book marked the completion of Foulkes's own personal transformation.[9] He'd survived 15 years of turmoil, personally triumphing over a developing social system based on hate, prejudice and injustice. He did so partly by leaving Nazi Germany, but also by creating group analysis and testing it in the crucible of the Northfield Military Neurosis Centre, described by Tom Main in the first Foulkes Lecture in 1977 (Main 1977). The definitive history of Northfield has yet to be written. But there is no doubt that Foulkes's creation of group analysis, already begun before Northfield (Foulkes and Lewis 1944), represents a radical view of human relationships.

Talking recently to Elizabeth about the effect on Foulkes of the dramatic and traumatic social changes in his life made me rethink his optimism about groups. My previous impression had been that it was based largely on his secure place as the youngest child by several years of a large bourgeois family. Although Jewish, his family had long been assimilated into German life, and he felt a normal part of it. His eldest brother was named after Richard Wagner, and like his sister and other two brothers, Siegmund himself was named after a character in Wagner operas. Foulkes joined the German army in the First World War at the age of 18.

To repeat some well-known facts, Foulkes studied medicine and neurology in Germany after the First World War before training as a psychiatrist and psychoanalyst in Vienna, where his analyst was Helene Deutsch, and then returned to Frankfurt as director of the Psychoanalytic Clinic. Here he came into contact with leading members of the famous academic Marxist Institute for Social Research, such as Adorno, Horkheimer, Marcuse and Fromm, and met members of the separate University Department of Sociology, headed by Karl Mannheim. Mannheim was assisted by Norbert Elias, who became a life member of the Group-Analytic Society. Sabine Rothe (1989) has given a penetrating picture of the fruitful interchange between sociologists and psychoanalysts that influenced Foulkes.

A special culture had developed in Frankfurt sociology at that time. I feel sure it influenced Foulkes's view of what constitutes a good group. The Elias scholar Stephen Mennell (1989) describes the culture as having shed the authoritarian and hierarchical character then still prevalent in many German universities. After seminars, staff and students continued discussions in cafés rather than bars, because respectable young women – especially if unmarried – would have been out of place there. It was very definitely a mixed circle, very different from other departments where staff and students met only formally, and students often belonged to traditional male societies. They met in *Gasthauser* and mixed little in female company – except when making excursions, as Mennell put it, 'to women of another class'. In contrast, you can see that feminism was stirring in Foulkes's Frankfurt!

After 1933 everything changed for Foulkes. He came to England, requalified in medicine, became a training member of the British Psycho-Analytical Society, divorced his German Jewish wife and married an English gentile. He even anglicised the spelling of his surname. During the Second World War he was an officer in the British Army at Northfield. By this time his sister Senta, named after the personification of redemptive love in Wagner's *Flying Dutchman*, had died in a Nazi concentration camp. Foulkes went on to establish group analysis and, as a consultant at the Maudsley Hospital, was part of the British psychiatric establishment. One could say he adapted but didn't succumb. He maintained his *creative marginality* – a Jew in Germany, a German in England, a psychoanalyst in psychiatry. He integrated and saw the value of many viewpoints.

Now to some less well-known facts. Elizabeth told me that Foulkes didn't personally feel a victim of injustice – he was sad, but preoccupied with practical things. In his autobiographical notes he merely hints at difficulties migrating to what he called 'the country of my choice'. We get a *glimpse* of his insecurity in a sort of 'keep your distance' letter from Ernest Jones. Jones had played a part in his coming to this country, but the letter hints at Foulkes's wish for a closer relationship than Jones wanted.

Foulkes's stoicism, perhaps even denial, seems to have been his way of dealing with earlier traumas that I'd not been aware of previously. He'd learnt that he was an unwanted late child, who when naughty was told by mother that she'd had a difficult confinement with him. She was unable to breastfeed him and employed a wet nurse. Commenting on this he'd say he'd had two mothers, one dark, one blonde. We can wonder whether such split early objects helped his transition and his ability to turn trauma into triumph.

In fact later his main childhood attachment was to a grandmother, whom he visited every day. One of his most powerful memories was of telling her that he'd learnt at school that the Earth went round the sun. Her reply, 'Do you really believe that?!' stayed with him, underpinning Kurt Goldstein's questioning of received ideas when he worked with him as a neurologist in Frankfurt, and reinforcing Foulkes's own courage to do the same.[10]

From grandmother, Goldstein, psychoanalysis and sociology he learnt the value of multiple viewpoints, the integration and transcending of parts into wholes. The dynamic relationship between figure and ground, process and context became part of Foulkes's thinking as he moved towards creating group analysis in Exeter in 1940[11] (Foulkes and Lewis 1944; E. Foulkes 1990).

Parallels to advances in the physical sciences

The emphasis Foulkes put on connectedness and communication as parts of the therapeutic process parallels the view of modern physics.[12] Indeed Andrew Powell (1994) has extended Foulkes's central concept of the *group matrix* by proposing that mind and matter are twin facets of the same *universal matrix*.[13]

We now know from the physical as well as the human sciences that there is no such thing as a non-participant observer. We form part of a matrix in which everything connects. We're a part of patterns of relationships that cross generations to the evolutionary origins of the human species, and across the divides between seemingly different social cultures. Our minds are biologically and socially constructed by the systems in which our individuality is embedded. We are therefore usually unconscious of these influences until we confront other individuals or social systems, in a setting that encourages reflection and communication.

Parallels to advances in psychoanalysis

Foulkes remained a psychoanalyst while developing his radical new vision. However, in an article towards the end of his life (Foulkes 1973: 227) he stated that the psychoanalytic point of view should be seen as a deliberate abstraction, and that the multipersonal hypothesis of mind is nearer to the true nature of events.

But even within psychoanalysis – which tends to blot out the social world – the development of object-relations theories, self psychology and attachment theory have all challenged the old idea of the isolated individual best treated by a blank-screen analyst untouched in the process. There's a developing interest in the intersubjective and relational aspect of psychoanalysis (Dunn 1995; Jones 1997; Kennedy 1998), in which psychic processes are embedded in a relational matrix.

For example, Thomas Ogden's (1994) idea of the 'analytic third', an unconscious intersubjective *construction* of analyst and analysand, is a sort of matrix they create together in the transitional space between them. This is clearly a dyadic form of the group-analytic matrix.[14]

It's interesting to note that Paula Heimann's (1950) breakthrough in recognising the crucial communicative role of countertransference was published just two years after Foulkes's first book. Countertransference in this newer sense refers to what therapists feel in response to how patients treat them, often unconsciously. Psychoanalysts and group analysts now accept that they are deeply involved participant observers in the interpersonal fields or therapeutic matrices in which we immerse ourselves.[15]

One of my favourite stories from pre-clinical student days is of a researcher leaving his laboratory one night, determined to find out what chimpanzees do when he's not there. He locks up and walks noisily down the corridor, then tiptoes back. Bending down to look through the keyhole, he encounters a chimpanzee's eye looking at *him*.

Abnormality

How normal we feel and are judged to be will depend on how we fit into the norms of the systems we emerge from, their values and expectations, from mother–infant dyad, to family, to communities, and from generation to generation. All these systems depend on a degree of conforming to promote a sense of cohesion and shared belonging.[16]

Many people seek help because at some level they feel abnormal. Others fear normality when it's associated in their minds with dullness and submission – the *coercion* referred to by critics of Foulkes's basic law. For both types of person, the prospect of joining a group might seem threatening and contribute to their resistance. Sensitivity to these issues is necessary to facilitate their making a move that can greatly benefit both types.

I recall a young man, the successful but anxious son of a broken marriage. He'd fought against his mother's neediness of him with the result that his attractiveness to women became a constant threat. He avoided long-term commitment and took explicit pleasure in being different from others. After some time in the group, he found someone who was prepared to give *him* up, and was thus able to allow falling in love to turn into reciprocal non-idealised loving.

One day, a woman in the group expressed her wish to be more balanced, not to see work as her life to such a degree that she ruled out having children, and truly loving her doting husband. She'd been father's favourite until, at puberty he couldn't cope with her emerging sexuality. The new father-to-be resonated to this. In a strong voice he said he used to be like that. He never wanted to be normal. Now he could enjoy a growing intimacy with his partner, and the sight of *their* baby on the scan was a huge pleasure to both. It was a moving moment for all the group, accentuated by another father-to-be echoing his experience. Both these men had come to express and work through fears of a hitherto 'alien' destructiveness, towards women in particular. The range of what could be considered normal was thus enlarged for all the group.

What is abnormal depends on where you draw the line, who and what is included within the bounds of acceptability. In modern Britain, old markers are increasingly seen as arbitrary and unjust, e.g. colour, class, religion and sexual orientation. Exclusion on such grounds is now often seen as unjust and unfair.

The work of the European Association for Transcultural Group Analysis has explored the way the struggles between self and other are played out between cultures, between therapists and clients from different cultures, and in individuals and groups that straddle or move between cultures. Just as the individual doesn't really know him or herself without the mirror of others, we don't fully know our own culture until we encounter other cultures. Hence the value of travel. On the other hand, forced migration – as in

Foulkes's case – and the loss of one's mother tongue rank among the great historical traumas for individuals and social groups (Hoffman 1989). We now know that our culture forms a deep non-individualised part of the personality of each of us – part of what Foulkes called the foundation matrix (Brown 1992a, 1992b; Le Roy 1994). To refer back to the basic law, in a transcultural workshop, a new norm is created from which individual *cultures* deviate.

Throughout the history of every society we can discern a struggle between self and other, between what's comfortably familiar and what's strange and foreign. As a colleague in the transcultural field has written: 'La voix étrangère est-elle musique ou bruit?' (Lecourt 1998). Why is foreignness so threatening? We're still struggling with the answer.

For Freud (1921) hatred of the Other was the means by which the ego preserves *itself* from the death instinct. This still controversial concept was humanised by Melanie Klein (1928) who related hatred of the Other, including those who speak foreign languages, to the infant's shock on recognising the sexual facts of life, before it has itself acquired language. Whether or not there is a death instinct, we need to explain the ferocity of the destructive forces provoked by differences.

Many of us prefer to view aggression as secondary to frustrated primary love (Fairbairn 1952; Balint 1965; Winnicott 1975). But can in-group/out-group hatred be reduced to instinct and infancy? I believe that a fuller explanation needs to encompass issues of identification, identity and narcissism, operating at a social as well as at a family level. The phenomena of racism and xenophobic nationalism bear this out only too well (Dalal 1997b). Social factors such as powerlessness, frustration and insecurity need to be taken into the equation, like the effect of Germany's humiliation after the First World War on its subsequent history.

Many individuals and some societies can transcend such tendencies. Throughout a review of texts from early Greek, Hebrew and Christian, to feudal, Renaissance and modern times, Julia Kristeva (1991) demonstrates how universality oscillates with exclusiveness. Often the two attitudes coexist. During the Renaissance, Montaigne's humanism expressed an interest in self *and* in otherness, the exoticness of newly discovered territories and their inhabitants. He recognised the multiplicity of the self and, along with it, respect for the strange and foreign. Montaigne was faced with the opening up of the *geographical* New World, as we are faced with the *informational* New World.

Kristeva's historical survey echoes and complements that of Norbert Elias (1939, 1991b) in relation to the social binding and distribution of aggression, sexuality and habits such as eating and excreting. These can become the reason for hating the foreigner – like disdaining people who eat with their hands – unless we see our own habits in their true developmental and historical context, individual and social.

One of the uncomfortable realities is that though boundaries between the familiar and the strange or foreign can become barriers, and be used to justify destructiveness as in xenophobia or ethnic cleansing, they also provide a partially illusory psychic 'envelope' (Anzieu 1984) that strengthens self-identity and a sense of we-ness, as in 'belonging groups' (Rouchy 1995). These range from football fan clubs and nations to – as we know – schools of psychotherapy. It's when this envelope is thick and rigid that uniformity and group cohesion threaten individuality and the humanity of outsiders – as in totalitarian states and fundamentalist interpretations of religions.[17] Morris Nitsun (1996: 261) has suggested that *polarisation* between isolation and *all-consuming affiliation* is characteristic of the anti-group culture. You'll catch an echo of Earl Hopper's description in his Foulkes Lecture last year, of a fourth basic assumption state of aggregation/massification. It is *between* these poles that meaningful exchange occurs across borders and boundaries, whether in trade or therapy.[18]

Injustice

One day recently a senior group analyst said to me, 'Group analysis is very difficult!' – and went on to describe being berated by a group member for addressing someone else *too soon* after she'd spoken. My colleague had waited what he'd felt a long time to ensure the first member had finished. But *she* had felt it a mere moment, and that she was a victim of cruel injustice.

Doubtless we can all recall such experiences, as victims or as arbitrators. After all, one of the first things we learn to say is 'It's not fair.' Indeed, Eric Rayner (1995a) has reported that such a theme emerged within 10 minutes of the start in over 80 per cent of sessions in his psychoanalytic practice; not just grievances, but also self-blame and injustice to others. In my experience it's even more common in group analysis, where sharing is an integral part of group life.

In psychopathology, wrong-doing and being wronged figure as guilt and persecution. During therapy, forgiving oneself or others – notably parents – are important milestones. And yet the subject of justice has been neglected by psychoanalysts and group analysts.[19] In my view, an important function of the group conductor is to act as a *Monitor of Justice*, within the group and within *ourselves*. We have to use our power justly. This might include apologising for our own mistakes.

A recent wide-ranging study of philosophical theories of justice (Cullen 1992) describes how thinking about justice, from Aristotle to modern times, retains dual significances of morality and legality. Nowadays philosophers distinguish between justice as *entitlement*, as *fairness*, as *equality* and as *impartiality*. Justice in therapy involves all four components. I shall briefly look at each in turn within the group-analytic context.

1. The sense of *entitlement* in patients can be normal, based on affirmation of one's rights, or it can represent a pathological claim for special privileges. An exaggerated sense of entitlement or being *cheated* is based on deep-seated narcissistic wounds (Billow 1997). When a group member feels isolated and unhelped by fellow members or the conductor, the sense of injustice can be *unbearable*. Walking out in outraged response to an experience of withholding of fairness or entitlement is much commoner in group than individual therapy. Usually the member returns during the session or later, providing an opportunity for really creative transformational work by the whole group. I'll give an example.

David came from a strict puritanical background. One day he walked out angrily from a session. He'd previously tended to withdraw in hopeless misery, as though unable to make demands for attention – in retrospect we can see – because he wasn't entitled to it. Such 'selfishness' in the family would have been *proof* of his unworthiness. Towards the end of the session in question, I referred to his silence. David then spoke about a crisis in his relationship with a young woman, and explained in detail about his *partner's* emotional conflicts, her previous marriage and so on. When I expressed concern that he should have a chance to talk about his *own* feelings, as we only had some ten more minutes of the session, *he got up and left the group in a fury*. This, and his absence next time, shocked the group.

When David returned I suggested his angry response could be a chance for us to understand its deeper sources. He responded by talking very movingly of feeling *low on his parents' busy agendas*, of not feeling entitled to any sort of priority as a child and adolescent. This turned out to be highly significant for David, and for many others in the group. Some members wept at unmet longing, others expressed fear of their anger at not getting their needs met.

It was then dramatically illustrated in a dream by a woman with major problems of sibling rivalry. In the dream, the group is being held in a smaller and therefore more crowded room. The dreamer challenges a new member, who then gets up to smoke and sets fire to something in the ashtray. The dreamer tries to stifle it, and at my bidding fetches water, but the smoke causes me to collapse. The dreamer moves to the floor with me, stroking my back. (I think it must be significant that in reality the dreamer's mother had died of chronic respiratory failure. The new member I believe represents the dreamer's not yet fully introduced anger at me.) Another member reported a dream in which, again, a new member joins the group. I lead the group into a different room this time *with 20 people in it* (another expression of being too crowded).

So problems of entitlement and sharing were to the fore for a long time in the group to which David had returned: how to get one's own needs met within a sibship, but also how to free oneself from parents, especially when they are needy and vulnerable.

2. The sense of justice as *fairness* can be seen as having its psychological roots in the earliest interplay of infant and mother, then with father and siblings. The psychoanalyst Enid Balint expressed this very well in her article 'Fair Shares and Mutual Concern' (1972), which preceded most of the recent observational arch on infant development (Stern 1985; Brazelton and Kraemer 1990; Trevarthen 1993).[20]

Balint described two main theories about the origin of concern for others – one related to patriarchal moral law, where fairness is the same as equality and impartiality, the other to the relationship of infant and mother during early demand feeding. Here fairness is *not* the same as equality; any frustration of the infant's greedy self-satisfaction is felt as unfair. Balint noted that the child needs a relationship with a law-giving father, *and to experience the way parents continue to be concerned for each other despite their differences of interest*.[21]

However, instead of considering siblings or peer relationships as such, Balint sees the *group therapy situation* as a way of providing the multiperson relationship that allows a capacity for concern to develop. (I think she was drawing on her experience in Balint groups for general practitioners and others.) Of course sibling transferences are everyday occurrences in group analysis, where we can see how the development of healthy peer relationships require their recognition and resolution, especially when they are destructively negative (Grunebaum and Solomon 1980, 1982, 1987; Brown 1998a).[22]

3. Justice as *equality* in a group transcends preoccupation with how much air-time each member receives. This is common in the early stages of group membership, especially in those with a strong sense of injustice; it moves into recognition of members' equal value.

4. Justice as *impartiality* involves the conductor recognising everyone's equal value. We don't get drawn into taking sides in conflicts, at least not prematurely and dogmatically.

The renewal of ethics[23]

You'll have noted an ethical dimension in much of what I've said so far. It's implicit in Foulkes's basic law of group dynamics, with its assumption of deep connectedness between diverse individuals. Such ideas as social justice and loving your neighbours as yourself are easy to accept when they're not of another culture or colour, 'on the other side of the tracks', or the other side of the world. The more we polarise and project, the more blinkered we become. As in the story of a man entering a pub – was it in Belfast? When asked if he was Catholic or Protestant he replied, 'I'm a Jew.' 'Yes,' was the reply, 'but a Catholic Jew or a Protestant Jew?'

In contrast Shakespeare, as a *pan-European* Englishman, saw good and evil at *home* as well as abroad. Hamlet returns to Denmark in disguise. Feigning madness to cover his knowledge of the crime of his mother and uncle, he'd been exiled to England, there to be killed. The gravedigger jokes that his madness wouldn't be noticed in England, as 'all there are mad'! Shakespeare is clearly gently mocking the clownish gravedigger.[24]

Soon after Freud (1930: 143) dismissed the effectiveness of ethics and morals against raw instinctual desires and the death instinct, asserting that the commandment to love thy neighbour as thyself was impossible to fulfil, Melanie Klein (1933) placed their origin in the centre of our earliest development. For her, the capacity for concern and reparation springs from the infant's recognition that the hated mother is the same person as the loved mother; that is, when the paranoid-schizoid position is superseded by the depressive position. However briefly, we recognise that the destructiveness we project out into the world is our own. Arrival at the depressive position needs to be supported and developed by secure and facilitating parenting, education and social structures.[25]

This achievement in the first year of life is *always* threatened, as we know from working with psychotic and borderline patients, and from viewing the world around us, where manifestations of the anti-group abound, divisive, intolerant and destructive.

But in the process of socialisation, a whole new universe of learning begins (Kohlberg 1981). One of the arguments for pre-school education is that it enables children to learn to live together, to establish the basis for more mature peer relationships and friendships. Here as well as in the family, children's consideration of others can receive contextual support.[26] The same thing happens in an analytic group, where as well as early conflicts, contextual deficiencies that have distorted or stultified peer relationships can be explored and compensated for. To paraphrase Foulkes, it's a form of peer-relationship-training-in-action.

Theoretically we have a long way to go to understand the progressive and constructive as well as the regressive and destructive aspects of human interaction in groups – what we could call the 'pro-group' as opposed to the anti-group. However, we already have *clinical* evidence from group analysis that altruism is not *just* a disguise for rampant selfishness. Echoing Foulkes's optimism, we also have evidence that altruism has *biological* and *neurological* underpinning. Remember the reciprocal nit-picking of monkeys!

I want to touch ever so briefly on evidence about the basis of altruism from evolutionary biology and from the neurology of consciousness; and I shall mention the views of Jurgen Habermas, a modern sociologist with roots in the Frankfurt School that influenced Foulkes during his stay in that city.

1 First, evolution. A recent book entitled *The Origin of Virtue* (Ridley 1996) has brought together a lot of evidence of the survival value of co-operation. It takes a wide-ranging view of the coexistence of selfishness and co-operation in nature as a whole, and in primates and homo sapiens in particular. Post-Darwinian evolutionary knowledge recognises modes of co-operation amounting to 'altruism' as part of effective struggle for survival, more obvious in some species than others, and integral to the social life of primates like ourselves. Part of biological *and* social

evolution is the capacity to distinguish authenticity, not just discern threats.[27]

2 Second, neurology. The evolution of consciousness is linked with the development of speech. Language contributes to what is called 'higher order consciousness' and the development of the sense of self. Consciousness in higher forms requires 'a delicate responsiveness to the needs and intentions of others'. Categorisation into good and bad, same and different, allows for the development of social co-operation (Edelman 1989)

3 Third, morality. Social co-operation is necessary for the development of shared morals and ethics. Habermas has developed a theory of communication he calls 'discourse ethics'. Moral judgements, he claims, are not just social conventions, nor the preference of isolated individuals. They are based on consensus reached in discussion (Outhwaite 1996: 12).

You could rightly say that the evidence I quote is partial and tendentious. But I believe I'm not alone in discerning the emergence of a new consensus, spurred on by the globalisation of economics, telecommunications and the Internet, not to mention the awareness of what a mess we've made of this century in so many ways. It recognises the necessity of mutual concern, and rights linked with responsibilities, to each other, and to the communities and the planet we share. It's expressed in the Gaia principle of the interconnectedness of creation, manifested in the ecology movement (Russell 1982), in interfaith dialogue (Küng 1990) and through feminism. Male emphasis on justice, fairness and equality is being increasingly complemented by a more female approach to morality stressing attachment, responsibility and care (Gilligan 1982).[28]

Interdisciplinary studies seek common ground, such as in a recent book called *The Politics of Attachment* (Kraemer and Roberts 1996), which brings together writers from a range of fields – psychoanalysis, sociology, law and politics – all acknowledging the human need to belong, to be connected. Another sign is the increasing use of mediation to resolve marital and industrial disputes. Another is the development of methods of diplomacy to humanise opponents divided by historical enmity and mutual projection.[29]

After the Thatcher years, society is being reclaimed. Geoff Mulgan, the founder of the Demos think tank, is now a special adviser to the Cabinet. His recent book *Connexity* (Mulgan 1997) emphasises the role of community in both harnessing and liberating the energy of individuals. He has many interesting things to say about parenting and social policy, responsibility and ethics. Foulkes – and Norbert Elias, who contrasted *Homo Apertus* (Open Man) with *Homo Clausus* (Closed Man) – would have known what Mulgan means when he writes: 'The more open self finds it easier to deal with others, to understand their perspectives. fears and aspirations . . . maturing means accepting your incompleteness, your permeability to other people' (1997: 60).

In the first group I quoted from, a young woman who'd been abused by her father repeatedly found herself in abusive relationships with men, trusting too soon and risking too much. The two men in the group who had shown an empathic concern for their pregnant partners impressed her deeply, particularly as they had acknowledged and integrated a streak of destructiveness towards women. As they spoke about their partners in one session, we could sense her disbelief transform into recognition that though men, they were ethically competent.

This recognition, needing an imaginative leap and a change of attitude to the Other is part of what psychoanalysts speak of as 'genitality', the ability to respect and even celebrate gender difference. I've extended this to include an open attitude to cultural differences, calling it *transculturality* (Brown 1995) – a jargonised but concise alternative to saying 'like Michel de Montaigne' whom I described in the section on abnormality, as grounded in his own culture, but stirred by and respectful of others, that highlighted the virtues and deficiencies of his own.

Conclusion

In concluding, I want to emphasise how Foulkes's basic law informs the issues of abnormality, injustice and ethics. It implies that the groups we inhabit, social and family, if good enough, have a capacity to encourage unity in diversity, to the advantage of individuals and the group-as-a-whole. Respect for differences within a wider common interest and humanity provides the basis for an ethic that overcomes exclusion and injustice. Given enough free speech and dialogue, groups have a wisdom and power that can lead to the fall of all sorts of totalitarian regimes, internal and external (Brown 1982, 1986) – like the underground newspapers in Soviet Russia.

But we must be alert to the bad group, the mean-spirited anti-group. What I call the *values of group analysis* can be seen as being constant tension with their opposites. We'll never exist only on the left side of the table (I invite you to add to the list).

Likewise, the therapeutic group from which individuals deviate is *never ideal*. It is what the individual member and the group-as-a-whole can make *of the good and the bad* that determines the therapeutic process – the strangeness of others, the struggle with fairness, and the development of a capacity for concern for others in the process of defining and developing oneself (Brown 1987a). The move from sole preoccupation with our old problems and their origins to facing the new problem of relating more fully and fairly with a diverse group of others becomes the group norm.[30,31] Thus the group-as-a-whole promotes and regulates the commonality and diversity of its members, in accordance with Foulkes's basic law.

An ex-submarine commander summed it up well. Previously hiding his own vulnerability and needs behind an impenetrable practicality and helpfulness to others, he commented before he left, 'That's how the group works! It enables you to be really selfish and really compassionate, together' (Brown 1988). I would add, *not one at the expense of the other*.

Let Foulkes have the last word. The German refugee who had recreated himself and created group analysis in Britain from a variety of perspectives, in 1948 explained the particular potency of psychotherapy in a group like this: '[the patient] can find himself in others and others in himself, and in this way free himself from old prejudices, as it were, and develop a more mature, creatively adaptable character' (Foulkes 1948: 26). In this centenary year, close to the new millennium, we could extend this to the relationship of cultures within a global community, and so on. It further underlines Foulkes's prescience 50 years ago, and our continuing and growing debt to him.

Acknowledgements

I am extremely grateful to Elizabeth Foulkes for her generosity with reminiscences and historical material, to Dick Blackwell and Dorothy Brown for their very helpful comments, and to June Ansell for her customary skill and patience.

Notes

1 However, over a hundred years ago the sociologist Durkheim (1984/1893) asked: 'How does it come about that the individual, whilst becoming more autonomous, depends ever more closely upon society?' He went on to relate this 'organic solidarity' to the division of labour.

2 Another characteristic of 'Foulkes in action' as a group conductor was his frequent use of the words 'deep' and 'deeper' to point to the less conscious elements in the individual and the group mind, and their connectedness.

3 Experimental social psychology has demonstrated that group norms develop in perceiving illusory movement of a point of light (Sherif 1936). An individual will misperceive the length of a line when deliberately deceived by fellow group members (Asch 1952). Uncharacteristic sadistic behaviour can be induced (Milgram 1964). The power of totalitarian regimes and 'total institutions' does not need more experimental evidence.

4 It became clearer to me in conversation with Jaak Le Roy after the lecture that the *creation* of the norms by group members, *including the conductor*, is of the essence of group analysis.

5 I believe that if one can hold this tension, it is likely that when one *does* speak, one acts as a spokesperson for the group-as-a-whole, voicing something that *has* to be said for the transpersonal entity.

6 *Everyday* relationships are unconsciously influenced by *transference* reminders of figures from the past. Deeper *projective* levels involve others seeming to contain unwanted aspects of the self, even being provoked into doing so in projective identification. Finally at the *primordial* level boundaries of the self are blurred and permeated by the unconscious transpersonal influence of a shared culture.

7 Lionel Kreeger in his Foulkes Lecture six years ago drew attention to the role in group life of *envy* and its pre-emption. Earlier, Louis Zinkin had challenged the

benign view of mirroring described by Foulkes and developed by Pines (1982) with his concept of *malignant mirroring* (Zinkin 1983). Morris Nitsun (1991, 1996) has focused on the destructive forces in groups, the anti-group, and their therapeutic potential. They can lead to scapegoating, groups breaking up, or individuals leaving prematurely; but duly acknowledged they can be levers for change.

8 'It gave me acute coronary trouble . . . working day and night, smoking incessantly (not like me otherwise). Some people said to me: "This is not a book, it is an experience which changes one's outlook." This is what it was meant to be' (1968: 204). His second coronary attack brought his life to an end some thirty years later.

9 Through studies of the lives of Freud, Jung, Max Weber and others, Peter Homans (1989) has related the ability to mourn losses – personal, political, religious, etc. – to psychological discovery; a deeper sense of self leads to new forms of meaning.

10 Kurt Goldstein, working with brain injuries, was influenced by Gestalt psychology. Foulkes's idea of the group matrix (Foulkes 1964: 292) – the hypothetical web of communication and relationships in a group – has its origins in Gestalt ideas about the dynamic relation of parts and wholes, and also in Elias's concept of configuration. In this, each individual is a process bound by more or less fluid ties of interdependence (Denning 1997).

11 SHF worked in Exeter, Devon before joining the Army. His car had broken down near a sensitive military establishment; the suspicious authorities unable to detain him as an 'enemy alien' (he already had British citizenship) ordered him out of London.

12 He believed that the origin of neurosis is *between* people, in what can't be expressed, in appropriate responses withheld or distorted. Only secondarily are such failures internalised and continued in new conflicts, in difficulties in relationship based on transference distortions and mistrust. Therapy involves unblocking communication in a facilitating environment.

13 Post-Newtonian developments in physics point to an emerging paradigm that recognises the fundamental interconnectedness of everything. Scientists tend to see the world as a dynamic web and rather than describing particles use matrices to represent change and transformation (Capra 1982; Read 1997). In the new science, influences are felt in the absence of force signals, correlations develop spontaneously and patterns emerge from within. Quantum and chaos theory focus on new patterns that emerge when parts combine to form wholes (Marshall and Zohar 1997), which could be a metaphor for what happens when an individual joins an analytic group.

14 The communicational aspect of projective identification is part of this trend in psychoanalysis. So is recognition of the effect of the analyst's personality, including his or her unconscious propensities. Robert Langs' (1973) work on the bipersonal field, and Hans Loewald's (1970) view of analyst–patient interaction as providing a 'psychic field' for the development of the patient can both be seen as dyadic (two body) variants of group analysis.

15 Foulkes's prescience in 1948 is attested to by such subsequent changes in psychoanalysis, in family and marital theory and practice (Skynner 1987; Behr 1994), and work within therapeutic communities (Whiteley 1994). In turn, group analysis has creatively absorbed object-relations theory, self psychology and attachment theory (e.g. Glenn 1987; de Zulueta 1993; Marrone 1994, 1998; Maratos 1996; Harwood and Pines 1998), and has applied Winnicott's concept of 'holding' and Bion's of 'containing' to the function of the group-analytic matrix (James 1994).

16 Dalal (1998) describes four main reasons why we behave in broadly similar ways: (1) biological programming; (2) the greater efficiency of a cohesive group; (3) the

sense of belonging bestowed by conformism; (4) shared structures of thought amounting to a 'social unconscious' lead us to think alike.

17 At the deepest level they may evoke early memory traces of the womb (Elliott 1994). They can be used defensively in what Earl Hopper (1997) has described as a Fourth Basic Assumption state – massification/aggregation. Such defences preclude the coexistence of differentiation and communication, which are the essence of group analysis. Without boundaries and differentiation, beneficial exchange cannot take place (Zinkin 1994), nor can fruitful dialogue occur (Schlapobersky 1994). These are needed for a group to move from mere cohesion – sticking together – to more mature and coherent relating to each other despite differences (Pines 1994, 1997). Indeed Bente Thygessen (1992) has made a cogent case for *diversity* acting as a therapeutic factor.

18 Exclusive and excluding groups are afraid of the diversity which is the essence of Foulkes's Basic Law. Only with a degree of openness and heterogeneity can groups enrich themselves, and individuals find themselves more fully through the mirror of others. As Dick Blackwell (1994) has put it, each group member is an observer with a view that may correspond to or differ from that of others. This promotes individuality and diversity in the group, a diversity of which they are all afraid. Typically (as a group analyst) he adds that the therapist may be equally afraid.

19 In *Civilization and its Discontents*, Freud (1930) stated that the first requisite of civilisation is that of justice. On the other hand, we now know that social injustice and strife can be the price paid for social defences against primitive neurotic anxieties such as wrapping ourselves in our psychic envelopes. They can lead to unconscious collusion in the suffering of others (Jaques 1970). Justice needs to be comprehensive and all-including within any society. The International Court of Justice and the United Nations Declaration of Human Rights aim to include all humanity.

20 We now know that the tiny infant – even the foetus – is extremely sensitive to sensory stimuli. Within hours of birth the movements and sounds of others, especially mother, are responded to, leading to 'proto-conversations', particularly face-to-face interplay and turn-taking. These are facilitated by mother tuning-in and expressing herself to the infant emotionally and verbally. The infant's sense of self emerges from its sense of being recognised and responded to by familiar mirroring (Emde *et al.* 1991; Gergely and Watson 1996).

21 Of course this begs the question of single-parent families and the controversial issue of same-sex parents. What is important is that the developmental setting should be fair and just for everyone in it.

22 See Special Section in the September 1998 edition of *Group Analysis: Papers from the Sib-Links Workshop*, edited by Luisa Brunori and Gerald Wooster.

23 Since completing this paper I rediscovered one by Mullan (1987) describing group therapy as an ethical way to change people psychologically; in the process they become more virtuous, but therapist paternalism weakens their moral agency and autonomy. Likewise, in a recent examination of the ethics of psychoanalysis, Hinshelwood (1997) states that its fostering of individual autonomy and integration is threatened by the potentially coercive power of the analyst. Hence the virtue of Foulkes's preferred backseat role as conductor not leader, perhaps as Husemann (1997) has suggested, for historical reasons. If we forget it, patients can tell us – like the one who told me, in so many words, to shut up!

24 Both stories underline the developmental importance of triangulation (Wooster 1983). Mother and infant need relationships with others such as father, siblings or at least a social world to permit separation and individuation.

25 Many psychoanalysts and sociologists interested in the psychosocial sphere have

used these Kleinian concepts (Jaques 1970; Alford 1989; Menzies Lyth 1989; Rustin 1991). But we can learn from wider psychological, sociological, biological and philosophical perspectives (Wilson 1993), and the multiple intersubjective viewpoints offered by group analysis touched on here.

26 Kohlberg has developed his work on moral development over many years. He sees reversibility as at the heart of the Golden Rule of ethics: 'Put yourself in everyone else's place', or 'moral musical chairs' (1981: 197). It has recently been shown experimentally that pre-school children can improve their acknowledgement of both sides of moral dilemmas by being asked a simple question acting as a 'contextual support' (Oppenheim *et al.* 1997). Such phenomena occur in what Vygotsky (1978) called 'the zone of proximal development' – the distance between actual and potential development 'as determined by independent problem-solving and the level of potential development as determined through problem-solving under adult guidance or in collaboration with more capable peers'. Loewald (1970) noted something similar in psychoanalysis, in which the reciprocal responsiveness of analyst and analysand allows the latter's development to a higher level of organisation; group analysis also uses these 'more capable peers'.

27 Ridley even proposes the existence of an 'exchange organ' in the human brain, which enables us to exploit reciprocity, trade favours and reap the benefits of social living (1996: 131). This could be seen as counter to Dawkins' 'selfish gene' thinking (Dawkins 1976), and a new gloss on Foulkes's conviction of man's social nature.

28 Particularly when considering social and transcultural problems, I have found it useful to follow Erikson's distinction between morality and ethics (Erikson 1964). Morals are more primitive and imposed by threats, ethics more mature, based on ideals, rational assent and a promise of self-realisation. Erikson conceived of an 'epigenetic' progression – each stage carrying traces of earlier ones, like onion skins: childhood morality based on fear, through adolescent ideas of universal good often expressed in ideological terms, to adult ethical powers.

29 A special issue of *Group Analysis* (21, 1, 1988) was devoted to articles on the theme of mediation. Harnessing the potential of irreconcilable opponents talking together privately and informally is the basic of Track II Diplomacy (Volkan *et al.* 1991). It led to the Dayton Accord, the ailing Oslo agreement and is being attempted in Northern Ireland. Robert Rapoport (1997) died completing a book *Families, Children and the Quest for a Global Ethic*; he ends by emphasising the educational role of families collaborating with teachers – the rights of children are to incorporate gender equity, valuing diversity, and cultivation of communication skills, negotiation and peaceful conking resolution. Informal collaboration has been developed in business management techniques aimed at problem-solving and innovation (Hargrove 1998).

30 This is an aspect of what Caroline Garland (1982) called 'taking the non-problem seriously'. The values of group analysis are also expressed through members commenting, e.g. on others' honesty, courage or generosity – and in noting their progress with pleasure.

31 By this I mean the Golden Rule of 'do to others what you would want done to you' versus self-righteous condemnation of others.

17

PAIRING BION AND FOULKES

Towards a metapsychosociology?

Half-jokingly I once suggested (Brown 1985a: 216) that rather than hope Bion and Foulkes would pair posthumously, we should work to integrate their contributions. I had argued that Bion's idea about basic assumption states reflects the negative processes in groups, the dark side of a group's capacity to work together creatively and that they are more likely to predominate in certain conditions. These include the way they are conducted and the organisational culture. Examples of the former include a remote and mystifying style and talking only to the group-as-a-whole; of the latter, settings which discourage free communication and shared responsibility, which Foulkes believed were essential for healthy growth and development. Bion emphasised the difficulties in the relationship between individual and group, Foulkes the inextricability and creativity of the relationship. Thus Foulkes talked to the group and to individuals, holding that group interpretations inevitably address most members, and that individual interpretations are saying something to all.

Bion described the problem of psychoanalysis as 'Growth and its harmonious resolution in the relationship between the container and the contained, repeated in individual, pair and finally group (intra- and extra-psychically)' (Bion 1970: 15–16). Now, more than ever, I am convinced that the work of Foulkes and his followers helps us to illuminate and resolve that problem. If we work towards integrating the ideas of Bion and Foulkes, we could arrive at a metapsychosociology. A lot of the spadework has already been done. I wish to use some of it.

Freud developed his metapsychology to conceptualise the vicissitudes of instinctual drives within the individual, culminating in the so-called structural theory of a personality structured into ego, superego and id (Freud 1923); each part a subsystem of the whole. Similarly a metapsychosociology would need to visualise a series of systems and subsystems. These could embrace several elements (De Maré 1972): (a) *structure*, incorporating the group beyond the individual isolate; (b) *processes* such as a development of a sense of belonging, identification, and differentiation from others. These would have to include both positive and negative precedes, in the sense that they are or are not compatible with both self-respect and respect for others; and (c) content such as values, good/bad, simplicity/complexity; uniformity/diversity. These would include the value accorded to 'individualism' and to group-belonging and participation. Bion summed this up in his idea of humans being group animals at war with their ghoulishness (Bion 1961). Foulkes's contrasting idea is that groups provide the matrix out of which individuality emerges (Foulkes 1973). In Freud's metapsychology the superego is, as it were, the Trojan horse in which the social breaches the individual. A Foulkesian metapsychology will allow for the influence of the social at all levels of individual and group interaction.

Beyond the vicissitudes of individual development, the stuff of our everyday clinical work, such a theory could help us to account for the impact on groups of individuals of social trauma, victims of conflict and oppression, as well as the subtler blockages to co-operative work epitomised by the basic assumptions. To do this we need to be aware of the operation of the social unconscious as well as the individual unconscious and the way the context influences what goes on within it.

I have begun to think again about Bion and his un-worked-out non-relationship with Foulkes, helped by the thinking of a new generation of group analysts, notably Morris Nitsun (1996) and Farhad Dalal (1998), both of whom are to a degree critical of Foulkes. In addition I want to bring in the systemic approach of Agazarian, and group relations thinkers influenced by Bion (Turquet 1974, Lawrence 2000). These have been further illuminated by Earl Hopper's attempts to link psychoanalysis, group analysis and sociology (Hopper 1997), and by the work of others who have applied group analytic ideas to organisational consultancy. They have helped me to integrate both my experience of working as a clinician, and participation in the work of the European Association for Transcultural Group Analysis. This has inevitably involved thinking about transcultural and intercultural phenomena; respectively focusing on similarities and communication across cultures, and differences and failures of communication. The crucial significance of boundaries is illustrated by work on the body image, briefly reported here as a metaphor for group identification, holding and containing. It is explored using the concepts of bi-logic (Matte-Blanco 1975, 1988) and the vicissitudes of intersubjectivity (Brown 1994).

1 Morris Nitsun

Morris Nitsun (1996) challenges Foulkes's excessive optimism about therapeutic groups, and recognises that groups as well as individuals can be the source of aggression and destructiveness. In developing his concept of the anti-group, the ever-present potential for destructiveness shadowing creative group processes ('the pro-group') he suggests that basic assumption groups are manifestations of anti-group processes (p. 66): '[The] basic assumptions undermine the capacity of the group to achieve its purpose. The group is preserved – or there is an attempt to do so – but at the expense of personal and group development.'

Nitsun cautiously but powerfully extends the concept of the anti-group to 'natural groups' – to families and to organisations, and to social cultures. What he calls 'the indivisible link between individual and group, person and culture' involves different levels of the organisational whole in a complex way. He uses a mirroring analogy in which the anti-group is a prism in which the psyche and the social world 'act as containers for each other, mutually reflecting each other in an ongoing cycle' (Nitsun 1996: 268). Unlike Dalal (1998) he starts with an intra-psychic phenomenon – failure of the environmental mother to provide a context in which to acquire a creative relationship to self and other – to group relationships in family and social groups. He does however go on to consider social failures to care for people suffering scarcity and basic requirements for life and dignity.

In his conclusions (Nitsun 1996: 286), he proposes three integrated perspectives: the dialectics, ecology, and aesthetics of groups.

(a) Dialectics refers to a continuous cycle of mutual creation and negation, in a sense of Foulkes *and* Bion, construction *and* destruction. The group is never one thing, defined and static, 'it becomes what it is in the interplay of different modes of experience'. Nitsun is wrong though, I think, to counterpoint anti-group basic assumption states with being stuck in cohesive idealisation of the group; that is not Foulkesian, it is better seen as basic assumption one-ness (Turquet) or massification/aggregation (Hopper), which are discussed later.

(b) Ecology refers to the ecological viewpoint brought to wide attention by Bateson (1972). It draws on principles of how human systems such as groups are formed and maintained by the communication of information, including the interaction of ideas. Durkin (1981), Blackwell (1994) and Agazarian and Gantt (2000) have developed these systemic ideas. Boundary issues are vital to any systemic approach, e.g. whether boundaries are permeable or impermeable. Interestingly Nitsun prefers the term ecological to systemic 'as it generates more directly a vision of the group in its multiple contexts as it struggles towards its destiny as a living system' (Nitsun 1996: 289).

    A well-functioning therapeutic group can become increasingly flexible and inclusive, so long as the pro-group predominates and comes to dialectical terms with the anti-group.

(c) Aesthetics relates to the way in which the group is experienced as a creation integrated from the fragments unfolding at the time into coherent patterns within the (dialectical) flux in the (ecological) holding environment. I think Nitsun is right when he suggests that both group members and therapists achieve aesthetic satisfaction from the transformational

> potential of the group which can lead to moments of insight, wisdom and beauty.

This creative view of group functioning, in which the group creates itself, contrasts with that of Anzieu (1984) whose work on training groups emphasises the *illusory* nature of groups but links naturally with Winnicott's idea about creative play within transitional space (Winnicott 1971b). This is, as it were, the *Anlage* of the cultural products of society. It will be noted that this implies a centrifugal process, starting in the space between baby and mother, progressing outward to the space between wider and wider networks of people. It also implies that the individual comes first. This is directly challenged by Farhad Dalal, who emphasises the priority of the group, and the centripetal forces of influence. I turn now to Dalal's contribution without agreeing that either direction of influence can be seen as primary.

2 Farhad Dalal

Farhad Dalal's criticism of Foulkes is in some ways more radical than that of Nitsun. He makes a case for Foulkes having had a failure of nerve in the face of his own radicalism, anxious not to endanger his professional identity as a psychoanalyst. According to Dalal's reading of Freud and Foulkes the latter drew back from the full recognition of his awareness of the social world penetrating and moulding not only the ego and superego, but the id, the supposed seat of innate instinct (Dalal 1998: 46). It is the deepest levels of communication that have the widest transpersonal influences which permeate groups and societies to a degree that comprises what he calls the social unconscious (Foulkes 1964: 52). In contrast with psychoanalysts such as Winnicott, who considered healthy individuals make healthy groups, Foulkes said that whether or not individuals are healthy depends on the state of the group to which they belong; health and disturbance are a function of a 'balance in the total field of interaction' (Foulkes and Anthony 1957: 54). Anyone working with families or groups today would surely agree with this. Dalal however criticises Foulkes, and most group analysts, for sticking to Freud's theory and prioritising the mother–infant paradigm in formulating 'deep' interpretations.

What Dalal approvingly calls radical as opposed to orthodox Foulkes, breaking free from individualism, draws more on the work of the sociologist Norbert Elias (rather than Freud). But Foulkes was half-hearted about it, accepting Elias's idea that individual mind and personality are formed by the social nexus in which they develop, but ignoring the facts of social power relationships which Elias emphasised.

Dalal highlights the differences in our understanding of the relationship between the so-called internal world and the so-called external world, particularly in terms of which has priority. The philosophical and clinical arguments are perhaps endless and irresolvable. For example, Cohn (1996) has argued from a basis in existential phenomenology that Foulkes recognised the intersubjective basis of mind, quoting his statement: 'I do not think that the mind is basically inside the person as an individual . . . The mind that is usually called intrapsychic is a property of the group' (Foulkes 1990b: 277). In the same issue of *Group Analysis*, Diamond (1996) attacks my interpretation of intersubjectivity (Brown 1994) as too restricted to a psychoanalytic viewpoint. Countering her criticisms of my interpretation of clinical material enabled me to clarify, at least for myself, that it was the cut-off 'autistic' elements, caused by intolerable pain and anxiety during individuals' development, that led to psychopathology (Brown 1996). This withdrawal is aided by the fact that people have their own bodies which become sanctuaries and projection screens, just as 'belonging groups' do in social life. (I refer to the body image further on.) The situations of safety or suffering can become an infinite series in the unconscious (see references to bi-logic later on).

Foulkes's emphasis on communication, articulated increasingly in the therapeutic process, involves translating unthought and unspoken processes into symbols, including words, and extending them from the 'internal' awareness into dialogue with others – whether an individual therapist or a group; that is, from 'internal' into 'external' space. According to Elias, symbols (language, knowledge and thought) are directed towards control of the social and natural world in which a person is located (Elias 1991a: 77). In place of narrow sociological theories which view the individual as infinitely plastic, more sophisticated ones such as those of Elias (1991b), Vygotsky (1978), Mead (1934) and Burkitt (1991) present a picture of mutual engagement and transformation of the internal and external worlds, much nearer to the group-analytic view.

Dalal points out that even Winnicott, by placing the transitional space between mother and infant in which 'me' and 'not-me' are originally negotiated, cuts short a potentially wider perspective on self and other in the wider society by seeing the influence as one-way; i.e. avoiding seeing culture as penetrating the mother–infant relationship. One example of this is the effect of the infant's gender. Foulkes on the other hand, for example, saw the Oedipus complex not solely as a stage in the child's development, but as preceding even the birth of the baby, and as influenced by social attitudes towards gender and authority (Brown and Zinkin 1994: 3ff).

Dalal points to the radicalism of Fairbairn as being greater than Winnicott's, by giving the interpersonal, the 'external', priority over the intrapersonal, the 'internal'. He saw the libido as object-seeking rather than pleasure-seeking, with aims to relieve innate tensions, and the infant as constructing its internal object world – containing both libidinal and anti-libidinal objects – as a result of failures and frustrations in relation to external objects. Yet Fairbairn disappoints Dalal in his seeming disregard of the social world. In contrast Foulkes recognised that the social world permeates the individual, but Dalal criticises him for failing to extend his theory about what takes place *inside* a group (important for group therapy) to account for what takes place *between* groups (which would take us to a wider theory of the sort I am trying to adumbrate).

One of Dalal's master strokes is to recruit the thinking of the increasingly influential psychoanalyst Ignacio Matte-Blanco (Matte-Blanco 1975, 1988; Rayner 1995b). The theory of bi-logic describes two different systems of logic operating in the mind: *asymmetrical*, in which things are categorised as different from each other, either/or; and *symmetrical*, in which all objects are identical. The former is the world of rationality and 'secondary process thinking', the latter of poetry and dreams and 'primary process thinking', in which there is no necessity to split and differentiate, no negation. Asymmetrical logic differentiates, while symmetrical logic homogenises to an infinity in which all differentiation is lost. According to Matte-Blanco both forms of logic coexist. Thus the psychoanalytic view that individuals exist in groups, and the view that groups exist inside individuals, are complementary. The complexity of this coexistence is clarified, Dalal asserts (1998: 217), by comparing the flowering or unfolding model of development, with its roots in psychoanalysis, to the 'cybernetic' idea of fields of influence, of mirroring and coherence (Pines 1998), and corrective feedback loops to which Nitsun was also referring.

Dalal (1998: 226) points to the fact that at different times Foulkes acknowledged that both the individual *and* the group are abstractions. But he did not join up these realisations. To have done so, in Dalal's opinion, would have led to a radical post-structuralist theory that is both exciting and frightening. To get a perspective we have progressively to stand outside the context we are inside in order to scan it, to enter another context, ad infinitum. He would rescue us by reminding us of the power structures in the world that decide who has power and who not, who is included in favoured categories and who excluded, in short, who is 'us' and who 'them'.

3 Yvonne Agazarian

Yvonne Agazarian has been developing her theory for nearly 40 years (Agazarian and Gantt 2000). One of her earliest published papers (Agazarian 1962) was on *role* as an isomorphic bridge in the relationship between the individual and the group. This links with G. H. Mead's earlier sociological work, but was systematically presented 20 years later in her theory of the 'visible and invisible group' (Agazarian and Peters 1981) in which she differentiated the several ways in which the individual and group systems interact as seen from different perspectives: (1) The *person perspective* 'explains individual behaviour in terms of genetic inheritance, developmental history and environmental influences'. (2) The *member role perspective* 'explains individual behaviour in terms of how the person unwittingly coaches the group to respond to him in ways that replicate and bind past conflicts'. (3) The *group-as-a-whole perspective* explains gross group behaviour in terms of group composition, developmental history and environmental influences'. (4) The *group role perspective* explains group behaviour in terms of the group as a whole delegating one or more of its members to perform group roles that bind, contain or express group conflicts. 'Invisible group theory' explains individual dynamics in terms of a discrete individual system and separates it from the equally discrete group system which explains group dynamics. As Agazarian (1983) explicates, the individual system has two subsystems – person and member; and the group system has two subsystems – group role and group as a whole. 'All three systems are in hierarchical relationship. Their structure and function are, through their principle of isomorphy, related.'

This complex but careful description integrates systems theory and Lewinian field theory. Its clarity is far from most therapists' experience, unless perhaps they have been through Agazarian's vivid training seminars. However, her thinking sheds light on some of the problems highlighted by Dalal and links with some of Matte-Blanco's ideas mentioned above. For example, Agazarian distinguishes between *stereotype* and *functional* subgroups: the former forming around similarities and striking differences, the latter also forming around similarities but *integrating* differences. Unlike most group analysts, who characteristically lead from behind, she sees the task of the therapist to promote actively the 'right' sort of subgroup formation.

For Agazarian every system exists in the environment of the system above it, and is the environment for the system below it. This hierarchy is 'contextualised' as *the observing self-system* discriminates and integrates information, developing the ability to experience itself both as a person-as-a-whole with membership in many internal subgroups, but also as a member of the group as a whole and its subgroups (Agazarian and Gantt 2000: 239).

Much of Agazarian's work is rigorously intellectual, as in the method she describes as SAVI (system for analysing verbal interaction), later her systems-centred practice. But concluding her recent book (Agazarian and Gantt 2000: 254) she claims that her approach has contributed 'an understanding that it is not the human dynamics themselves that contribute to the success or failure in therapy, but the development of a context in which they can be addressed and explored rather than acted out'. In this Agazarian is very group-analytic in the Foulkesian sense.

The active role that Agazarian takes in therapy to promote the 'right' sort of subgroup formation could be seen as similar to the promotion of enabling, as opposed to restrictive, group solutions to group focal conflicts, described by Whitaker and Lieberman (1964). Her awareness of the narcissistic trauma that can be inflicted by group-as-a-whole interpretations in training (T) groups conducted on the Tavistock model led her to 'rescuing' individuals through eye contact, as though to affirm their continued existence for her. She proposed that Bion's basic assumptions are 'core emotional response states that serve the group much as ego defence mechanisms serve the individual' (Agazarian and Gantt 2000: 83). She was influenced by the theory of group development in T group events described by Bennis and Shepherd (1956), involving two initial phases: (1) dominated by issues of power and control in which the group attempts to seduce the leader to a 'good protector role' to defend it against chaos (BaD); and (2) dominated by competitiveness, which when frustrated leads to a fight-flight Ba culture manifested in inter-member scapegoating, but finally coalesces into a 'barometric event' – a ritualised attack on the leader. When successful this leads to the location of 'evil' in the 'bad' leader and 'good' in the group, thus freeing the group from its struggle with the leader for power and control, and allowing it to turn to issues of intimacy. You will note the similarity of thinking to that of Winnicott when he described 'the use-of-an-object', mentioned below.

4 Fourth and fifth basic assumptions: Turquet, Lawrence and Hopper

In discussing the contributions of Nitsun and Dalal I have focused on the two-way relationship between the individual and group, extended to society, then with the help of Agazarian have begun to allow for the effect of intermediate groupings and subgroupings. This brings us to a body of knowledge and theory that has been mainly the preserve of specialists in group dynamics consulting to organisations in industry, commerce and public institutions. It has been promoted especially by the Tavistock Institute of Human Relationships and the Grubb Institute in the UK, and the A. K. Rice Institute in the USA. One method of working has been through group relations workshops, the so-called Leicester Conferences, in which the work task is the examination of relationships within and between groups of participants within the total situation of the conference. Another application is consultation to organisations in trouble. The fact that the interests of the organisation and those of the individuals in it can be in conflict, for example, over methods and hours of work and levels of pay, is obvious, and so is the powerful effect on the functioning of the total organisation of whether or not workers at all levels are satisfied and motivated.

It is significant, I think, that this way of studying group processes can be very stressful for some individual company members. Agazarian's method of making eye contact described above differentiates her from the more detached style of some conductors who model themselves on Bion and the 'pure' Tavistock method. Kleinian psychoanalysts have contributed massively in this field (e.g. Menzies 1961; Jaques 1974) and the influence of Bion's work continues to predominate. This has resulted in a preoccupation with primitive 'psychotic' anxieties – fear of annihilation and persecutory attack –

and defences against them. One could argue that, as with Bion's method of conducting small groups (Brown 1985a: 216–17) the way the staff of group relations workshops carry out their roles can also promote the anxieties they study. This is not to say that studying the worst possible outcome is not valuable in reaching towards healthy models of organisational life.

As Lawrence (2000: 126) has pointed out, the theme of 'order' has always been present in the Tavistock conferences through emphasis on leadership, responsibility authority organisation and the 'politics of relatedness'. This is studied in the 'psychoanalytic' exploration of possible transference and countertransference feelings between the managerial and consultant staff of the conference and its membership. For example, the staff will often appear as a privileged subgroup in the conference, at the same time destructive, persecuting, protecting and benign. The assumption is that such 'fantasies' are just that, but there is no doubt that such experiences occur in any conference when power is arrogated by staff. They could however be augmented by the style and method of leadership. Ideally, working through such transference feelings enables the membership to take responsibility for learning from such experiences.

These extensions to Bion's theory of basic assumption states, I believe, help to humanise it by recognising the complex ways by which individuals keep afloat in groups and find nourishment in them, even put roots down in them. Pierre Turquet introduced the basic assumption of oneness (BaO) in which 'members seek to join in a powerful union with an omnipotent force, unobtainably high, to surrender self for passive participation and thereby feel existence, well-being and wholeness' (Turquet 1974: 357). In this state the individual is lost in oceanic feelings of unity – as in crowds of football supporters – or in oneness personified in a single person – as in 'salvationist inclusion' achieved by following a cult religious leader. Writing of his experiences in the large group in Leicester Conferences, Turquet (1975) traces the individual's 'conversion' from being a disconnected singleton to an individual member (IM) by establishing relationships with other singletons. He or she then has to struggle against being taken over as a membership individual (MI) in the large group in which group membership may be felt to counter self-definition and needs. This threat is greatest when membership of a large group is equated with the singleton's own destructive feelings. Turquet points to transitional states, between singleton, IM and Ml and back again. Certainly this accords with my own experience in large groups held in the Group-Analytic Society and Institute of Group Analysis, which some people find so threatening they drop out while others enjoy the exhilaration of the transformations. The latter are probably more secure personalities or, at least having survived such experiences before, feel less threatened.

Gordon Lawrence has introduced the complementary concept of a basic assumption's 'me-ness' (Lawrence *et al.* 1966), starting with Turquet's idea of the singleton, and which Lawrence sees as increasingly dominant in a world of increasing individualism and consumerism. This precedes Turquet's analysis of the progression of the individual through the life of the group 'because the individual does not want to have relations'. Instead of moving towards intersubjectivity in which the sentience of others is acknowledged in a mutual 'we-ness', the 'I' becomes an object to itself, a 'me'. BaM represents an attack on the possibility of learning from relating to others. The group is not allowed to exist and achieve its primary task.

BaO and BaM represent extreme states hindering the function of self-reflecting work groups that parallel the double nature of the individual as an ego and part of a 'we-go' (Klein 1976). They are integrated, seen as twin opponents of both unbearable suffering and of creative relating, in Earl Hopper's idea of a basic assumption of massification/aggregation (Hopper 1997, 2003). He developed this in the course of exploring, over many years, the interface between his first professional identity as a sociologist with his later practice as a group analyst and psychoanalyst, particularly with severely traumatised and/or personality disordered individuals.

Hopper's concept of a BaM/A seems particularly relevant in understanding what he calls 'the patterns of incohesion and traumatic experience in the unconscious life of groups'. Cohesion, Hopper states, refers to the *appearance* of unity of feeling and purpose enabling people to work together in harmony, and is not based only on patterns of communication (as it would be in a 'coherent' group). There is an optimal degree of cohesion for different phases of group development; too little interferes with decision and action, too much inhibits individual creativity and can lead to over-idealisation of the group, scapegoating and denigration of other groups. The degree of cohesion is influenced by the therapist or leader. Pines (1981) has argued that a mature group aims for coherence rather than cohesion, the difference being the amount of diversity that can be creatively integrated within the group and its component members. I think the important thing is how people can co-operate and belong, along with others, to an identifiable group, while at the same time being true to themselves and their *own* component parts.

Whereas Turquet saw BaO as a regressive group response to multiple stimuli and response bombardment, Hopper sees Incohesion: Aggregation-/Massification (I:A/M) as occurring in a group of traumatised people who have encapsulated intrapsychic oscillations between fission and fragmentation, fusion and confusion. Those who developed contact-shunning 'crustacean' defences will tend to personify states of *aggregation*; those whose defences involve merger-hunger 'amoeboid' processes, will tend to personify states of *massification*. The former Hopper equates (Hopper 1997: 459) with Turquet's singletons, the latter with his membership individuals, leaving Turquet's individual members (IM) as those with an optimal degree of cohesion for working in groups. (These two categories of Hopper are reflected in work I did on body image many decades ago, and to which I shall refer later.)

Hopper's thinking recognised the deep levels of pain and fragmentation that underlie such group phenomena, akin to Bion's ideas about basic assumptions and the Kleinian tendency to present the underlying anxieties as psychotic. Work in group relations workshops would indicate that they arise in 'average' groups of 'average professionals' and therefore they arise from all levels of health and pathology. My own experience in therapy groups (Brown 1985a) is that basic assumption phenomena are common transient features of well-functioning group-analytic groups with very mixed levels of pathology.

5 Group-analytic organisation consultancy

Following Robin Skynner (1989), in the last few years several colleagues have applied group-analytic concepts to organisational consultancy. Rifkind (1995), working with staff groups dealing with HIV infection, has highlighted boundary and 'dynamic administration' issues in promoting staff's 'emotional literacy' and hence their ability to contain the huge emotional disturbance evoked by this work. She describes the staff group as a microcosm of the wider community setting, able to attend Janus-faced to their own internal processes and what is happening outside.

Nitsun (1998a, 1998b) develops Foulkes's concept of *mirroring* in consultation, aiming to strengthen boundary differentiation by clarifying dysfunctional mirroring, in groups and individuals, to increase their capacity to adapt to the organisational task. He traces isomorphic mirroring through the concentric systems from the wider environment to what he calls 'the organisational psyche' with its shared fantasies and unconscious attributions [note, not the individual psyche]. Nitsun uses Foulkes's ideas of *levels* of group functioning (current, transference, projective and primordial), the group *matrix*, the inseparability of internal and external relationships, figure-and-ground, and the crucial role of *communication*; but he also introduces his own concept of the anti-group in relation to organisational pathology (which we have already seen Nitsun equates with Bion's basic assumption states).

Wilke (1998) describes Oedipal and sibling dynamics in groups occurring especially at times of rapid change, and defending against the inability to mourn and feel remorse. Imposed organisational change, he holds, reproduces early infantile anxieties to do with 'separation of me and not-me' and the need to move into the early phase of Oedipal conflict; but at the same time puts it in terms of social psychology: 'An organisation of this type is characterised by high levels of anxiety about boundary issues, role strain and normative expectations.' (This double way of thinking implies isomorphism between the theoretical systems of individual and social psychology which may or may not be justifiable; we will need to think about this further.)

Rance (1998) in keeping with Foulkes's emphasis on network (nexus, 'plexus,' etc. at different points in his writing) uses systems theory and psychoanalytic theory, as well as Foulkes's basic idea of the social origins of personality Rance develops the idea of staff consultation as a *conversation*, often extending over several months.

Like Wilke and Nitsun, Blackwell (1998) recognises the potential chaos in organisations undergoing change, but sees the creative potential of managing the anxiety stirred up by instability in the system. As he puts it, following Foulkes, a group analytic approach provides a model for counteracting regressive tendencies by promoting *communication* and *dialogue*. This helps to avoid the twin dangers of rigidity and chaos, especially when reflexivity in 'the bounded instability' of the matrix can include humour and playfulness.

However, Spero (1999), a group analyst who works with Harold Bridger (a colleague of both Bion and Foulkes at Northfield), quotes Foulkes's warning to those working in the organisational context not to go too far into underlying meaning or private personal motivation, i.e. to differentiate clinical and non-clinical work, therapy and consultation. For Spero an important function of the consultant is to keep the organisation in mind, along with its task and members' roles, reflecting at the same time on the tensions created by the task in both individuals and groups.

This *holding* and *containing* of very difficult countertransference feelings – also emphasised by Wilke in his way of working as a consultant – reflect Colin James's (1984, 1994) integration of Winnicott's and Bion's complementary but distinct concepts. Both can be seen to operate within the group-analytic matrix, and occur (or do not) in all group phenomena, from the mother–infant dyad to society.

Social construction (Campbell 2000) offers a unifying view of organisational consultants and of the individual self which is consistent with Foulkesian group analysis. The organisation is seen as socially constructed continuously, daily, even momentarily, by individuals interacting; it is continuously changing and reinventing itself, like the dynamic matrix in group-analytic therapy (Campbell 2000: 28). The individual self, likewise, is constructed in the interaction between the self and others (p. 16). This view is entirely consistent, for example, with Foulkes's basic law of group dynamics (Foulkes 1948; Brown 1998b) that the group *constitutes* (i.e. creates) the norm from which individuals deviate. But it has to maintain its boundaries and contain its diversity despite difference and emergent tensions.

6 Transcultural work

I shall now draw on experiences studied by the European Association for Transcultural Group Analysis (EATGA), which relate to the sort of massive trauma and disruption to which Hopper refers. The history of Europe, especially in the last century, is one of oscillation between forced attempts at imperial massification and struggles to unpick larger masses into smaller groupings, both of which have involved destructive wars, wholesale dislocation and exile of populations, and mass exterminations, not to mention the continuation of social divides in power and discrimination. It would not be surprising then if rational co-operation between individuals and between groups and nations tends to be hampered by oscillation between the fears of massification and aggregation. Current disputes about European integration could be seen as a demonstration of Hopper's basic assumption.

The work of the intercultural workshops organised over the last two decades by the EATGA have demonstrated how, with goodwill and professional interest often stemming from a personal history touched by past European trauma – much of the destructiveness can be contained and reflected on in ways that diminish scapegoating and stereotyping. Through alternating small and large groups, people from different cultures are confronted by how much they have in common. Intermediate-sized groups, between the size of a nuclear family and a large social group, have allowed exploration of issues to do with differences of language, religion, and nationality and the effect of migration. Historical antagonists recognise the mutuality of their suffering inhumanity; 'You are the enemy I killed my friend' as the First World War poet Wilfred Owen wrote before he himself was killed.

The depth at which cultural and national identity and conflicts are incorporated in each individual's personality is part of what Foulkes (1975) meant by the foundation matrix, which included shared myths, values and standards. In the EATGA this is often referred to as the non-individualised part of the personality (Le Roy 1994). Kaës (1987) pointed to four major psychic functions of culture: (1) maintaining the individually undifferentiated basis of psychic structures needed to belong to a social whole, a 'we-go'; (2) ensuring a set of common defences; (3) providing points for identification and differentiation which guarantee the continuity of distinctions between the sexes and generations; (4) constituting an area of psychic transformation by providing signifiers, representations, and the means for organising psychic reality.

My own observations, during the first workshop in Maastricht (Brown 1987b) is that there is a parallel in small and large group settings which can be related to movement between the (Kleinian) paranoid-schizoid and depressive positions. One way the small and large groups differed was in the relative linguistic homogeneity of the small groups, so that frustration, confusion and fear of annihilation, or at least non-recognition, were commonest in the large groups. (One manifestation was the non-provision of a German-speaking small group, and the apparent embargo on German in the large group.) Themes and developments reflected each other, though small groups were explicitly more personal, large groups more cultural. Issues of identity were prominent in both, but the former dealt more with the history of individual struggles with ambivalently cathected parental objects, while moving towards individuation and intimacy; the latter with cultural history, language and identity. The fear of non-recognition and annihilation gave way gradually in both settings as the paranoid-schizoid was succeeded by the depressive position, and basic assumption phenomena were replaced by differentiation, reconciliation and mutual concern. This was not without crisis and struggle, especially powerful in the large group, evident, for example, in the confrontation between Jews and Germans in the subsequent workshop in Heidelberg (Brown 1992a). Such powerful and explosive phenomena are more likely in large groups, where it is much easier not to hear or see individuals, and to resonate to cultural history, myths and stereotypes. This is augmented by the 'psychic envelopes' (Anzieu 1984, 1990), illusory notions of nation and race, with their attendant mythology. These make it much more difficult to attain the empathic mutual identification that is necessary for reconciliation and mutual concern. This requires genuine encounters, real confrontation and encounter – not the pseudo-confrontation that is based on paranoid projection (Brown 1988).

Rouchy (1995) has contributed to our appreciation of 'secondary belonging groups' such as educational, occupational and recreational groups, beyond the primary family, as completing the cultural interiorisation begun in the family, perhaps permitting individuation and object relating that were not sufficiently attained there, and 'concretising the grasp on space and time'.

7 Boundaries and barriers – the analogy with the body image

As Louis Zinkin (1994) argued, boundaries between systems mediate a balance between centrifugal and centripetal processes. Exchange, vital in psychotherapy, economics and all living systems, implies permeable boundaries. One of our conclusions in *The Psyche and the Social World* (Brown and Zinkin 1994) was: 'Boundaries between individuals are to varying degrees permeable. The more rigid and seemingly impermeable the boundaries – that is, the more they become barriers – the greater the use of projection and projective identification to supplement them, and obtain an exclusive identification based on 'myths of purity and homogeneity, rather than plurality.'

The need for clear, even rigid and impermeable boundaries around oneself and 'one's own kind' is largely a measure of insecurity and fear of inner fragility. The analogy of the body image may be instructive. We all have an unconscious kinaesthetic and proprioceptive model of the body that influences the sense of ourselves in the world (Schilder 1935; Scott 1948) both in health and disease, and extend it beyond our physical boundaries, e.g. to our cars (Brown 1959b). Fisher and Cleveland (1958) developed a way of studying the body image by means of the projective Rorschach ink blot test in a wide range of psychosomatic and psychiatric conditions, deriving barrier (B) and penetration (P) scores which can be rated as ranging from high to low. B scores were high in people suffering from 'body boundary disorders' (e.g. skin and musculo-skeletal) compared with those suffering from internal (e.g. gastrointestinal) disorders. P scores were high in fragile schizophrenics. Many years ago I used this test to study the susceptibility of chemical workers to develop contact dermatitis (Brown and Young 1965). We discovered that psychological orientation towards either introversion or extraversion (differentiating between social and thinking I/E, especially when these were discordant) interacted statistically with other traits such as ego-strength, anxiety threshold, hunger for tactile contact, and degree of rigidity and intolerance of ambiguity. Summarising these findings (Brown 1997) it appeared that if subjects were social introverts but thinking extraverts (i.e. impulsive rather than reflective) they had lower ego strengths and anxiety threshold and more hunger for tactile contact; if they were social extraverts (but reflective and perhaps ruminative) they tended to be emotionally constricted, rigid and intolerant of ambiguity.

In his book *The Group and the Unconscious*, Didier Anzieu (1984) describes groups as suffering from not having a body, and having to imagine one by developing an imaginary 'envelope' or ego-skin (as do individuals). Metaphors of the group as a 'body' with individual 'members' capable of 'esprit de corps' bear this out. Based on work in short-term training groups, Anzieu describes the image of the group body as a 'pseudo-organised principle' corresponding to a 'nostalgic dream of symbiosis between members' (Anzieu 1984: 241), echoing Turquet's BaO or Hopper's Ba. A more dynamic approach could be offered by the application of attachment theory (Marrone 1994, 1998) to the human need to belong from infancy to the multiplicity of identifications and real belonging groups that make up a human's lifespan. One can imagine a series of organising metaphors from womb (Elliot 1994) to global universality.

8 Concluding questions and speculations

Is it meaningful to draw an analogy between the body image and models we make concerning the inside and outside of the individual in relation to his or her family, the family in relation to others, and the various secondary groups with which we identify, and nations, etc.? I suspect it might help us to see the *complexity* of developmental negotiations, for example, by enabling us to allow for variations in basic security within each system, the degree to which basic needs are met, and the predominant values and attitudes to others. These would involve a capacity for centrifugal as well as centripetal empathy, for flexibility and inclusiveness. There does seem to be a relationship between the security and satisfaction experienced in a system and the values it develops towards others.

Do the apparent differences between 'optimistic' Foulkes and 'pessimistic' Bion relate first to the values of the conductor/therapist/chairman/leader, and second to 'where the group is at' in terms of the security, satisfaction of needs and the flexibility of the group and the individuals comprising it?

I believe that a crucial difference is Foulkes's view of persons and groups as open systems in dialectical relationship to one another.

A comprehensive 'metapsychosociology' would integrate the mutual interaction and interpenetration of psyches and social worlds, at all levels, conscious and unconscious. I suspect that a key role in this integration could be played by the concepts of bi-logic and mathematical set theory developed by the psychoanalyst Ignacio Matte-Blanco (1975, 1988), particularly in relation to what Foulkes (1964) called the social unconscious. These concepts involve the coexistence of two modes of thinking, asymmetrical and symmetrical, which on the one hand discriminate and classify and follow the principles of 'secondary process' logic (things exist in specific time and space); and on the other hand follow the 'primary process' logic described by Freud (1915) as characteristic of the unconscious – without contradiction and negation and manifested in displacement, condensation and symbolisation. The unconscious is timeless and spatially infinite. Inside and outside coexist and are interchangeable – as we see in dreams and psychosis. Boundaries and barriers dissolve. A first step in applying Matte-Blanco's thinking to group analysis has been taken by Wilson (1997), and Dalal, as mentioned earlier, has extended its use into social psychology and a deeper understanding of the social unconscious. He has used bi-logic to throw light on relationships between groups of 'us' and 'them'. These can have devastating consequences when feeling gets cut off from thinking, and stereotyping is associated with putting groups and/or populations into the same degraded or demonic category (Dalal 2002).

Matte-Blanco (1988) offers a new perspective on processes like projection and identification. He relates them to what he calls 'despatialisation'. Foulkes's thinking of the social world as simultaneously inside and outside us (here as well as there) would be described in bi-logic terms as a Simmasi – simultaneously asymmetrical/symmetrical structure. In relation to time, Volkan (2001) has described as 'time collapse' the process by which 'chosen traumas' are reactivated at times of conflict in the form of historical national myths, such as the 1389 AD Battle of Kosovo in the Balkans, or the Sack of Jerusalem in 70 AD, and the Crusades in the Middle East. In bi-logic this could be an Alassi – alternately asymmetrical/symmetrical structure.

It is well known that Foulkes emphasised communication in his theory and practice, and that he recognised it as occurring at several levels: (1) in everyday communication; (2) through transference; (3) through projection and bodily processes; and (4) at the primordial level of the 'collective unconscious'. These levels, as they descend, are decreasingly individual and conscious. They move from the *personal*, as narrowly defined, to the *interpersonal*, to the *transpersonal*. But as Puget (1991) puts it, they interact in the dialectics of inner, interpersonal and social worlds.

Bion's concept of container-contained, the emergence of thought from primitive bodily sensations as a response to frustration, of conceptions and preconceptions, and the destructiveness of psychotic processes through attacks on linking and knowing can all be brought to bear on these dialectics. Basic assumption states in themselves reflect a one-way process, from the individually disavowed to the jointly enacted.

I shall return to the structures, processes and contexts required for a metapsychosociology mentioned at the beginning. In teaching I have used Figure 17.1 to illustrate the *structural* relationship of individuals and groups. It indicates that an individual is born into a family in a society and carries both within him or herself, as well as being within them. The individual contains groups and therefore is, in a sense, a group; and takes these into the group and society in which it makes its home, or seeks therapy; these in turn, more or less contain the individuals constituting them. *Processes* by which people and groups develop involve 'psychoanalytic processes' such as introjection, identification and projection, but also interaction, intersubjectivity, dialogue, mutual construction and transformation, which are more the realm of group analysis, and of Winnicott (1971b), Ogden (1994) and of self psychology (Harwood and Pines 1998). It is here that Foulkes's deeper level of communication and relationship are relevant, and Matte-Blanco's bi-logic is needed to understand the constant ready availability of pigeonholing, stereotyping and prejudice, but also their dissolution in waves of similarity (Rayner 1995b). The *contents* of our cultures, values and ideologies *flow from* and *feed into* the processes which sustain the structures we create and have created for us. Structures, processes and contents interact. When we talk about mental structures, we are referring to dynamic structures: individuals and groups in complex dynamic interaction.

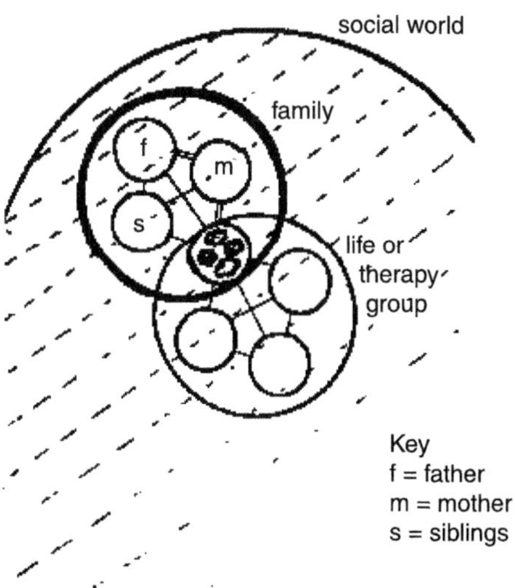

Figure 17.1 External and internal worlds.

Stacey (2001), a group analyst who teaches management studies and complexity theory, has drawn attention to the international basis of social events in which unpredictable crises can develop seemingly spontaneously through self-organising patterns. As he puts it, we form the social in patterns of continuity which *at the same time*, paradoxically, give rise to transformations. At a micro-level this is a good description of what happens during spontaneous interaction in group-analytic therapy. Stacey states that mind requires that the maker of a gesture has the capacity to evoke, in the self, the response generated in the other(s). Accepting the attitude of others towards 'me' leads to a private dialogue between 'I' and 'me' (the subject and object). He claims that the individual mind involves conversation with self; the social mind a conversation with others. They coexist. You will see that complexity theory is consonant with Foulkes's idea of free-floating conversation, communication at all levels, resonance, condenser phenomena and universality. Making and apprehending similarities and connections – in bi-logic terms – involves symmetrisation. Reaching a limit and erecting a boundary involves asymmetrisation. Transformation in therapy entails redrawing boundaries. The dynamic ebb and flow needs sufficient trust in the system for risks to be taken, and the necessary element of play in 'transitional space' (in Winnicott's terms) to allow transformation to occur.

How difficult and complex these processes can be has been highlighted by Nitsun and Dalal, and by Agazarian in her analysis of different ways in which individuals use and are used by groups. The intersubjective ground, as is pointed out by existential phenomenologists such as Cohn and Diamond, is nearer to the symmetrical relationships of bi-logic; this is challenged by a sort of pseudo-individualism which Foulkes described as autistic, and by groups (such as totalitarian societies) that constrain and oppress rather than contain; such groups do not allow the development of transformation and maintain the mistrust and hate to others.

Behind this are the contents of the group, particularly the values of the group and social system, unconsciously active in what Foulkes called the 'foundation matrix'. Bion wrote about man being a group animal at war with his ghoulishness, and the struggle of the individual to relate to the group being as fraught as the infant's with the breast. In contrast Foulkes viewed the group as the matrix of individuality. These are two seemingly disparate views; unless one sees each as valid in certain circumstances – e.g. when the breast is experienced as predominantly bad or good, or we are talking about a 'good' or a 'bad' group. But the group-analytic view offers a set of values that I have described as in constant conflict with their opposites (Table 17.1).

These I believe are supported by much recent neurological, biological and sociological evidence (Brown 1998b). They are part of a substantial philosophical stand represented by Axel Honnuth (1995), who emphasises the struggle for the establishment of relations of mutual recognition as a precondition for self-realisation. As he puts it: 'It is individuals' claim to the

Table 17.1 The values of group analysis

The values of group analysis		
homo apertus	v.	homo clausus
Inclusiveness	v.	Exclusiveness
Fairness	v.	Entitlement
Consensus norms	v.	Imposed norms
Ethics	v.	Moralism[1]
Democracy	v.	Authoritarianism
Religious dialogue	v.	Fundamentalism
Universalism	v.	Nationalism
Pro-group	v.	Anti-group
–		–
Etc.		Etc.

intersubjective recognition of their identity that is built into social life from the very beginning as a moral tension, transcends the level of social progress institutionalised thus far, and so gradually leads – via the negative part of recurring stages of conflict – to a state of communicatively lived freedom' (Honnuth 1995: 5).

If we begin to discern meaningful patterns of dynamic structures, processes and values that influence the balance of creative and destructive processes within individuals and groups, and between individuals and groups – and thus influence psychological and social pathology and health – we shall have the makings of a useful metapsychosociology. Working with the contributions of Bion and Foulkes, and their discrepancies, will have helped us towards what will be a dynamic international model in which vicissitudes of relatedness play a key part (in contrast to the vicissitudes of instinctual drives in Freud's metapsychology). As implied by Figure 17.1, it will allow for the development from one-person to two-person psychology (as in the mother–infant and psychoanalytic dyads) to three-person psychology (a triangulation epitomised by the Oedipus complex), to four-body psychology (and thus sibling rivalry as suggested by Rickman (1957), to multi-person psychology as in groups. It will at the same time allow for a contrary current, as social influences impinge on individual ontogeny. I have already proposed a spiral movement in good therapy groups from psychological confinement within individual and family ('the inner world') to a fuller intersubjectivity with others (Brown 1994); in a 'bad group' this could be reversed.

1 By this I mean the golden rule of 'Do to others what you would want done to you' versus self-righteous condemnation of others.

The model will reflect the establishment of identities, individual and social, and thus of differences and boundaries, which in some circumstances can be transcended in an ongoing creation and re-creation of meaningful existence. The situation of power and authority, and the role of context in forming meaning will be acknowledged. So will the influence of group size – small, large or median (De Maré *et al.* 1991) – and whether dialogue and discourse are possible (Brown 1982: Schlapobersky 1994). Finally it will allow for the possibility of group function being based on defensive illusions (as in basic assumption states) or on coherent co-operation despite conflict, anxiety and pain, We might need a series of inter-related models and viewpoints. These could include (echoing the structure of this chapter):

1 Nitsun's model of a dialectic between destructive and constructive forces in groups of individuals that can lead to transformation.
2 Dalal's rebalancing of individual and group to allow for the presence of the social 'even' in the mother–infant dyad, and his attempt to use bi-logic to explain intergroup dynamics e.g. stereotyping.
3 Agazarian's model of different types of relationship between individuals and groups, and how they use each other.
4 Extensions of basic assumption theory by Turquet, Lawrence and Hopper that relate to the deep anxieties aroused in some circumstances when people are combined in groups.
5 We need to account for the role of culture and personality, and for trans-cultural and intercultural phenomena, including social trauma. The social unconscious – Foulkes's deepest layers of transpersonal communication – could include the bi-logical symmetrisation of basic assumption states.
6 We need to develop clearer and more dynamic models for the formation and functions of boundaries – literal and metaphorical – within interacting systems, such as those sketched in Figure 17.1. Attachment theory might be useful in showing up the security-seeking need to belong, aided by complexity theory with its focus on emergent patterns that display both continuity and potential for transformation.

By taking equal account of positive and negative processes in groups, of association and dissociation, we might be clearer in our understanding of the view of Elias (1991b) – who influenced Foulkes – that the individual is a level of the group (even Homo Clausus, the 'we-less I') and of the way harmful group processes (e.g. Ba states) arise when the component individuals feel ignored or disenfranchised, or collectively want to avoid facing up to something. We are into the area of sociology. But what about the body, the area of biology? Can we develop a truly comprehensive bio-psycho-sociology? If so, we could begin to integrate social psychology – which Freud could only speculate about in essays such as 'Totem and Taboo', 'Group Psychology and the Analysis of the Ego', 'The Future of an Illusion', and 'Civilisation and its Discontents' – with deeper understanding of the struggle between social order and chaos, between 'ego' and 'we-go', and the individual physical consequences of stress and social trauma.

Freud's metapsychology (Freud 1915) was an attempt to provide a theory of psychological processes in the absence – at that time – of an adequate physical substrate. Now, the burgeoning of neuropsychology offers such a substrate with its application to infant development within the mother–infant dyad, attachment theory and affect regulation via the right brain and limbic system (e.g. Schore 1994; Taylor *et al.* 1997).

The neurobiological approach could complement a metapsychology, and give it a bodily biological base. Indeed in a recent interview Schore (2001) states his belief that groups and cultures offer affect-regulating self-object functions – a self psychology concept – acting as external psychobiological regulators of human internal states. Cultures, Schore holds, acting through their prescribed child-rearing practices, imprint on the earliest members of society those affects that can be socially expressed face to face. Almost echoing Foulkes, he adds that this determines what affects are conscious and what unconscious and/or expressed physically. Bion would say the latter involves physical 'beta' rather than mental 'alpha' functions in individuals, and predisposes to basic assumption states in groups. At this point, beyond metapsychosociology, we could say that if Bion and Foulkes are not twinned (thankfully), their thinking is intertwined.

18

BION AND FOULKES

Basic assumptions and beyond

Introduction

Wilfred Bion is justly famed in the world of group therapy for his studies of groups in the years 1948 to 1957. Although subsequently he did not work with groups himself, these papers, which were brought together in 1961 in the book *Experiences in Groups* (Bion 1961) continue to stimulate and worry those of us who do.

Bion took groups very seriously. His ideas are challenging, and some, which I shall come to at the end of this chapter, profoundly helpful. It is my wish here to contribute something towards threshing the chaff of Bion's contribution from the corn. For some of his ideas are, I think, ultimately inadequate and misleading as a basis for therapy, particularly the unmodified concept of basic assumptions which is dealt with in the main body of the chapter, after the Introduction.

Bion asserted that these primitive states of mind tend to dominate groups and interfere with their declared task. He related the emotional attitudes organised in these states to unconscious basic assumptions of dependence, fight–flight, or pairing. At different times a group will behave as though satisfaction, safety and the future require respectively that the group depends on a succouring leader, fights or flees from a common enemy, or waits for some pair to create together the wherewithal for the group's salvation. Few of us have not been grateful to him for helping us to understand something of why our institutions and committees get stuck. Dependence on the chairman, blaming the absent saboteurs, or hope that a fruitless discussion between two will provide a perfect answer for all, can often alert us to the need to do some work ourselves or sink further into collusive evasion of reality.

Yet, in contrast to those studying group dynamics in training and research settings (Bennis and Shepherd 1956), many therapists find that attempts to use the concept in a clinical setting encounter serious problems, theoretical and practical. This is perhaps particularly so for those of us working on group-analytic lines originally developed by S. H. Foulkes. (Foulkes 1948, 1964, 1975; Pines 1978). We rarely speak about basic assumption states or use them as guides in our work. Why is this, when seemingly related phenomena can be observed in our groups at times? An attempt to answer this question and to differentiate and reconcile the two approaches may throw light on both of them.

Before examining the concept in more detail, it may be helpful to look at several of Bion's related ideas, some unexceptionable, some confusing, following roughly their development in his book to the point where they culminate in the idea of basic assumptions.

He wrote early on that 'the group is essential to the fulfilment of a man's mental life – quite as essential to that as it is to the more obvious activities of economics and war' (Bion 1961: 53). He went on to demonstrate his view of the interpenetration of individual and group in putting forward the scheme that 'the group can be regarded as an interplay between individual needs, group mentality, and culture' (1961: 55). What did he mean by group mentality and culture?

Bion conceived of *group mentality* as 'the pool to which anonymous contributions are made' (i.e. contributions disavowed by individual group members) 'and through which impulses and desires implicit in these contributions are gratified' (1961: 50). To become part of the group mentality any individual's contribution has to enlist that of others. Bion seemed to expect that group mentality would be opposed to the avowed aims of the individual members of the group. Moreover, he appeared to imply (1961: 103) that the level of deep interaction between members of a group is what he called 'protomental', corresponding to a developmental stage in the infant before differentiation of body and mind, i.e. in the preverbal first few months. This is the level of functioning in which Bion went on to locate basic assumption phenomena.

How he conceived of *group culture* is less clear. On the whole, the term seems to signify the group atmosphere and the way members relate to each other, including the therapist. However, at some points in his writing, it seems to merge with the idea of group mentality. At other points, group mentality and culture seem to differ in that the former concerns 'bad' and unconscious processes, the latter 'good' and more conscious ones (Bion 1961: 60). Indeed Bion wrote:

> My attempt to simplify, by means of the concepts I have adumbrated, will prove to be very misleading unless the reader bears in mind that the group situation is mostly perplexed and confused; operations of what I have called the group mentality, or of the group culture, only occasionally emerge in any striking clear way.
>
> (Bion 1961: 57)

In my view Bion's major errors may have been, first, considering 'group mentality' as composed only of disavowed aspects of individual members – a sort of pool of projective identification – and secondly, separating so sharply consciousness and unconsciousness as manifested in individual and group. Indeed, Bion himself stated that he did not find the three concepts of 'group mentality', 'group culture' and 'individual' useful in practice (Bion 1961: 61), though what he came to call basic assumption states were described as happening when the group culture was dominated by states of group mentality which interfered with its explicit task. He now saw group behaviour as involving three sets of conflict: (a) in the individual, between wishes to belong and to be independent of the group, (b) between individual and group, when aims of group and at least some memory seem discordant, and (c) between the explicit task of the group and its 'basic assumption tendencies'. In an analytic group, conflicts (a) and (b) can indeed be discerned. But it would be misleadingly simplistic to imply that all the resistance to analytic work can be attributed to the group's 'basic assumption tendencies', or that bringing them into the open by interpreting them would itself ensure the dissolution of resistance. In the final section of the chapter I shall propose that a more practical theoretical framework is provided by Foulkes's concept of the 'group matrix' and his view of therapy as involving the promotion in it of communication at all levels. It is based on a greater appreciation of the positive as well as the negative consequences of group membership. It recognises the interpersonal basis of individuality, conscious and unconscious, external and internal, from mother–infant dyad, to family group and beyond. It is summed up in Foulkes's idea of the group as the matrix of the individual's mental life.

Bion's first paper in *Experiences in Groups*, written during World War II with John Rickman on the basis of their short spell of work in the rehabilitation wing of a military neurosis hospital (where they were succeeded by Foulkes), attempted to define the qualities associated with 'good group spirit'; that is, the positive aspects of group culture. They found these to include (a) a common purpose; (b) common recognition of group boundaries in relation to larger units or groups; (c) capacity to absorb new members and relinquish old ones without fear of the group disintegrating; (d) freedom from rigid internal subgroups; (e) recognition of the value of each individual for his contribution; and (f) capacity to face discontent and cope with it in the group. At the end of this first paper, fresh and modern though written 40 years ago, Bion and Rickman assert that 'there is a useful future in the study of the interplay of individual and social psychology, viewed as equally important interacting elements' (Bion 1961: 26). They also rightly pointed out that 'psychology and psychopathology have focused attention on the individual often to the exclusion of the social field of which he is a part', but in his subsequent work on groups, Bion seems to have over-reacted against this tendency.

Although the rest of the book struggles with fascinating complexities, it appears to dwell on the negative aspects of group functioning and to offer a one-sided view of the interplay between individual and social psychology as we see it in therapeutic groups, a view that can be misleading both theoretically and in practice. Bion stated his belief that groups are essential to the fulfilment of mental life yet, paradoxically for a psychoanalyst and unlike Foulkes, he seemed to be in danger of losing sight of the individual in his attempt to discern that which was characteristic of groups. Focus on individual dynamics and the subtlety of the network of interaction in the group was sacrificed in favour of grasping another layer of phenomena.

It seems to me that this overemphasis on the group, to the neglect of the individuals who had come to therapy for their own pressing individual needs, combined with a therapeutic stance derived from a particular form of *individual* psychoanalysis – formal and hieratic – may explain the prominence of frustration as a characteristic of the groups Bion reports on in his book. He attributes the frustration and the consequent resentment in part to the nature of any group to deny some desires, e.g. the wish for privacy, in satisfying others, such as the wish for company. This is indisputable, but it is not so easy to follow his proposition that most resentment is caused through 'expression in a group of impulses which individuals wish to satisfy anonymously, and the frustration produced in the individual by the consequences to himself that follow from that satisfaction' (Bion 1961: 54). He suggests that the power of the group to fulfil the needs of the individual is challenged by the group mentality, and that the group meets this challenge by the elaboration of a characteristic group culture. Though this seems to belong to a different level of group dynamic from that of Ezriel's 'required, avoided and calamitous relationships', or of Whitaker and Lieberman's focal conflict theory (1964) involving 'disturbing and reactive motives and restrictive and facilitating solution' (Sherwood 1964) his emphasis on the negative and defensive aspects of group culture is noteworthy. In terms of Ezriel's ideas (Ezriel 1952), such a culture would be dominated by required relationships; in terms of focal conflict theory by reactive motives and restrictive solutions. Working through these are everyday group tasks.

So rather than their being inevitable and major features of groups, alternative or additional explanations of the degree of frustration and resentment he observed are Bion's unwitting promotion of a group culture that neglected the individual, and his simultaneous implicit devaluation of the group's potential to foster individual fulfilment. It is true that Bion granted that the group is potentially capable of gratifying some of the individual's needs, excluding those that can be obtained in solitude or in family life, but by concentrating on those manifestations of group mentality he dubbed as basic assumptions, the bulk of his book does not allow for the positive and facilitating aspects of groups, therapeutic or other. Thus it might be that some ambivalence to groups as well as his style of working may have contributed to the prominence of the phenomena he described. I never saw Bion working in groups, but have observed groups conducted by therapists influenced by him. This suggests to me that his attitude and style in the group may well have been remote and oracular, as he himself seems to have recognised. Writing about a particular group session he states: 'Before the patient began to alarm the group my interpretations might have been oracular pronouncements for the ceremonious silence with which they were received' (Bion 1961: 56). Ultimately the very different sorts of individuals Bion and Foulkes were must have influenced the way they conducted groups, and therefore the way the groups developed, and their own influence on the world of psychotherapy. Perhaps they could provocatively be termed shaman and anti-shaman.

Let me turn in more detail to the manifestations of group mentality that Bion is most widely known for, the *basic assumptions*. (a) First I shall describe them briefly; (b) then attempt to link them with individual as well as group psychology; and (c) try to integrate them with the Foulkesian group-analytic view which I believe does greater justice to the interplay of individual and group life. Finally, (d) I shall attempt to answer the question posed earlier, why is it that group analysts rarely invoke and use the concept of basic assumptions, and offer some thoughts about the light the Bionian and Foulkesian models throw on each other.

Brief description of basic assumptions

Bion described basic assumptions as primitive states of mind which are generated automatically when people combine in a group. These states are inevitable because of the dilemma created by the dual pulls of man's individuality and of his 'groupishness'; as Bion put it: 'The individual is a group animal at war, not simply with the group, but with himself for being a group animal and with those aspects of his personality that constitute his groupishness' (Bion 1961: 131). They develop instantaneously and involuntarily as a result of the individual's possession of a hypothetical 'valency' springing from a primitive protomental system existing in early infancy before body and mind were differentiated (Bion 1961: 153). The fantasies and emotional drives associated with these basic assumptions unconsciously dominate a group's behaviour in a way that is apt to interfere with its explicit work task and so prevent understanding and development. In the case of a therapy group, the basic assumption organisation interferes with exploration by the group of the feelings and problems of individuals in it. Appropriate leaders are drawn in by the basic assumption states, by no means necessarily the formally designated leader, and can be inside or outside the group, a person, a book of laws or history.

While leaving open the question of how many basic assumption states there might be, Bion named three: *dependence* (expecting solutions to be bestowed by the therapist/leader); *fight/flight* (fleeing from or engaging in battle with adversaries, particularly outside the group); and *pairing* (encouraging or hoping for a coupling of individuals which could lead to the birth of a person or idea that would provide salvation). As the philosopher of science Michael Sherwood (1964) has pointed out, basic assumptions seem not to be observed phenomena or even empirical propositions, but either a priori premises or descriptive labels. What is basic to each form of organisation is an emotional state – respectively of dependency and awe; or of hostility and fear; or of optimism and hopefulness. The 'as if' basic assumption follows from this and is an attempt to explain it in the absence of its overt expression, even when the group may be acting on it.

The three basic assumption states, Bion suggested, are institutionalised respectively in the church, the army and aristocracy. In these 'specialised work groups' (1961: 156) the basic assumption states tend to foster their work task; respectively to organise dependency on a deity, to defend the realm, and to ensure the next generation of superior leaders. In other groups the basic assumptions tend to interfere only with explicit work tasks with which they are discordant. However, it is difficult to follow Bion's bald assertion that there is a sharp distinction between the reality adjustment of basic assumption and work group states. It is also difficult to accept that basic assumption states do not coexist at times rather they 'inevitably' alternate, as he states. Indeed at one point (1961: 64) he states: 'A group which shows itself intolerant of activities that are not forms of fight–flight, will nevertheless tolerate the formation of pairs. Reproduction is recognised with fight–flight in the preservation of a group.'

Individual and/or group

As will be seen in the next section, Bion came to use Kleinian ideas about primitive mental mechanisms and the early infantile stage of the Oedipus complex in individual development to explain the basic assumption states. However, he started trying to restrict his view of what went on in groups to the group context alone, as though 'individual' and 'group' are not mutually interacting systems. Nevertheless it is not difficult to relate his ideas about basic assumptions to concepts originating in other psychoanalytic theories as stated elsewhere (Brown and Pedder 1979). The relation between basic assumption and work groups implies (Bion 1961: 99) an analogy to that between primary and secondary process thinking. Further it is possible to imagine the three basic assumptions of dependence, fight–flight and pairing as linked by fantasy systems associated with the oral–dependent, separation–individuation and Oedipal stages of individual development. In terms of the erotogenic zones of early psychoanalytic instinct theory these would be related to oral, anal and phallic stages of development. However, like group analysis, modern psychoanalytic thinking is more concerned with the vicissitudes of the emerging self and 'object relationships' and with motivational systems rather than instincts. As George Klein (1976) put it:

> The essential clinical propositions concerning motivation have nothing to do with reducing a hypothetical tension; they are inferences of directional gradients in behaviour, and of the object relations involved in these directions. They describe relationships needed and sought out, consciously or unconsciously, and how they are fulfilled through real and conceptual encounters, symbol and action. The key factors then, in the psychoanalytic clinical view of motivation are relational requirements, encounters, crises, dilemmas, resolutions and achievements – not a hypothetical 'tension reduction'.

The individual is part of a group from earliest infancy – initially a group of two, the mother–infant dyad, then a group of three or more as the existence of father and siblings have to be accommodated – later a series of overlapping family and social groups. These coexist in external reality and the developing individual's internal world.

The caricature (Melanie) Kleinian interpretation tends to reduce all psychological processes to their supposed most primitive infantile origins. It is apt to see the infant in the adult, not the person struggling to develop from infant to toddler to schoolchild to adolescent and onwards. Anna Freud's developmental lines and Erikson's psychosocial stages are reductively telescoped into what many would see as an over-simplified scheme. Despite the fact that Kleinian analysts such as Jaques (1955) and Menzies (1960) have illuminated the more primitive anxieties and defences active in institutions, it remains true that most Kleinian analysts tend to view man's social existence through eyes which do not look beyond the crib (even if the reality of the crib is allowed). The reality of the individual's changing context is minimised or denied by them. This contrasts with the view of others, including group analysts, that fantasy and external reality dance together and that individuals seek to be true to themselves and part of groups larger than themselves. As George Klein wrote (1976): 'Two components of selfhood must be recognised: a centrifugal assertion of personal autonomy, and a centripetal requirement for being an integrated and needed part of a larger, more encompassing entity or social unit. The reconciliation of this dual requirement as a condition for integrated selfhood itself creates one of the most basic sources of potential conflict.'

In a sense though, this is what Bion meant; but his decision to avoid viewing basic assumptions within the context of individual development blinds him in one of his two eyes, for man is both an individual *and* a social being. Bion's decision accords with his emphasis on treating the group rather than the individuals in it. It also reflects his Kleinian id-psychology, with its seemingly sharp distinction between primary and secondary thinking. Because of this we read a lot in Bion's writings about 'basic assumption groups', and relatively little or virtually nothing about the psychological processes involved in the work of the 'work group', which we ourselves might describe in terms of enabling individuals to discern and overcome the blocks to their continuing search for autonomy and relatedness. Rather less than 10 per cent of the book concerns itself with work group functions (notably Bion 1961: 98–113, 143–6), and in fact says next to nothing about them. Instead Bion writes about the relationship between work group and basic assumption functions, the supposed origin of the latter in a protomental level of development, and speculation about their relation to psychosomatic illness and economics.

Bion seems to imply that if the group is told when it is not working, it will know how to and get on with it. But psychotherapy is a form of education in the fullest sense of the word. A good teacher would not be satisfied with only telling his pupils to get on with it; he needs to sustain the working process and in a sense embody it as Foulkes did. Ezriel, the other main influence to the Tavistock Clinic approach to group psychotherapy, as described by Heath and Bacal (1972) at least includes 'because . . .' clauses with his interpretations. His interpretations of the required, avoided and calamitous relationships with the transference figure of the conductor suggest to individuals why they may be behaving and experiencing in a certain way. Yet, as Heath and Bacal remark, restricting interpretations to the 'here and now', and expecting individuals to make the link with their current life outside and with their past 'presupposes capacities that possibly not all patients have'. (Robin Skynner's (1979) ideas about the importance of modelling as well as of interpretations in therapy, especially for more deprived, non-verbal or chaotic people, are clearly relevant to this problem.) One might add that the Tavistock approach – unlike that of group analysis, which encourages analysis by the group – because it emphasises interpretation by the therapist, would seem to foster 'static assumption dependence' and excite feelings of frustration. These factors may have contributed to the disappointing results found by Malan and his colleagues (1976) in their study of outcome of group psychotherapy conducted at the Tavistock Clinic, contrasting with the much better results described by Barbara Dick (1975), who used a technique based on group analytic methods. The few in the Tavistock series who did particularly well were people who had had previous individual therapy. That is, they might be presumed to have learned already how to apply psychodynamic ideas to their own personal problems, and thus to be less confused and frustrated by a technique that seems to ignore them.

A Foulkesian interpretation

The fact that a concept, on its own, is a poor basis for effective therapy, does not invalidate it. How can the idea of basic assumptions be integrated into a more useful scheme such as Foulkesian group analysis?

We would probably all agree that, as in a family, the reality of belonging to a therapeutic group demands that we face up to jealousy, envy and a considerable degree of frustration of dyadic dependency wishes. It also requires us to play an active role in our own salvation, and eventually to eschew the defence of blaming external agencies, including siblings and parents. Within the group matrix, both reality and fantasies can be discerned, talked about and eventually understood. What fantasies underlie basic assumptions? In his final chapter Bion himself suggests that the basic assumption theory may be inadequate: 'I have drawn attention already to the fact that these three states of mind have resemblances to each other that would lead me to suppose that they may not be fundamental phenomena, but rather expressions of, or reactions against, some state more worthy of being regarded as primary' (Bion 1961: 162–3).

He goes on to trace the basic assumption states to defences against or reactions to psychotic anxieties, and mechanisms of splitting and projective identification springing from an extremely early and primitive primal scene (1961: 164). I believe that the primal scene is the archetypal provoker of feelings of exclusion. If the reality of belonging to a group does involve facing up to jealousy, envy and the frustration of dyadic dependency, it is not surprising that primitive fantasies and anxieties of this type are stirred up in an analytic group. If these are regarded as related to the narcissistically painful recognition by the child of separateness from mother and of the real relationship between parents, then defences against recognition of the primitive Oedipal situation can involve any of the (at least) three basic assumptions. Pain, experienced by the self as a result of frustration or disillusion, evokes rage and fantasies of punishment and destruction associated with paranoid or depressive anxieties. Following, but modifying, Bion's view of the importance of the 'primal scene' in basic assumption states, one might propose something like the following:

1 In the 'basic assumption dependence' there is regression into the state of 'merging' of the early mother–child nursing dyad, in which there is no room for the reality of an intruding father or sibling – it is denied. According to Mahler *et al.* (1975) the psychological birth of the infant takes place in the second or third year of life, as he emerges from the symbiotic phase into a phase of separation and individuation. (This involves successive sub-phases: (a) differentiation and development of the body image; (b) practising of autonomous functions; (c) a rapprochement crisis in which attention is redirected to mother; finally, (d) consolidation of individuality and beginning of constancy of objects and the self.) It is in the space created by the realisation of separateness that the Oedipal triad comes to be recognised and internalised, and the capacity to cope with the Oedipal crisis laid down. This emergence into the family network marks, one could say, the beginning of the social birth of the infant (Figure 18.1).
2 In the 'basic assumption fight–flight', an intruding threat is challenged or fled from. There is no time for maternal succouring, but equally

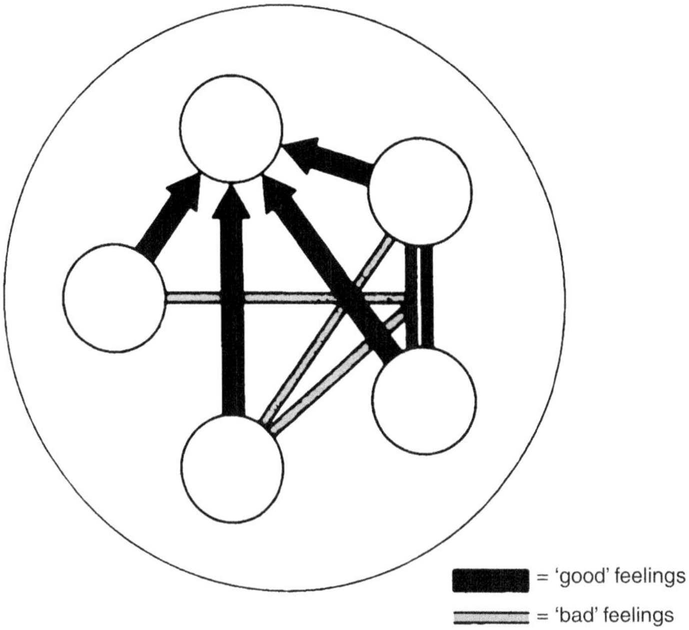

Figure 18.1 BA dependence

none for the fear of parents nor for passive contemplation of their sexuality or 'favouritism' towards siblings. It is as though an apparent identity of interests blurs differences in the group; separation and individuation are avoided within the group, but emphasised in at least some crucial external relationships. Ambivalence within the group is avoided through excessive use of projection. In massive social manifestations of the basic assumption, such as war and political upheaval, the reality of external threats can overshadow the reality of internal fantasy (Figure 18.2).

3 In the 'basic assumption pairing', the sexual theme is most nearly explicit, but passive contemplation is maintained through idealisation, in which a mood of hopefulness prevents the emergence of destructive rage. This characteristic of the 'basic assumption pairing' contrasts with more mature renunciation and resolution of Oedipal rivalry through identification. As pointed out by the sociologist Talcott Parsons (1964): 'The parents' erotic solidarity thereby forces him to a higher level of value-internalisation than that governing *any* dyadic relationship within the family and prepares him, in his latency period and in subsequent orientations outside his family to internalise still higher-level patterns of value.' Revolutionary zeal could be viewed as a reaction to the fruitfulness of tradition, linked with the idea of parental fruitfulness; we

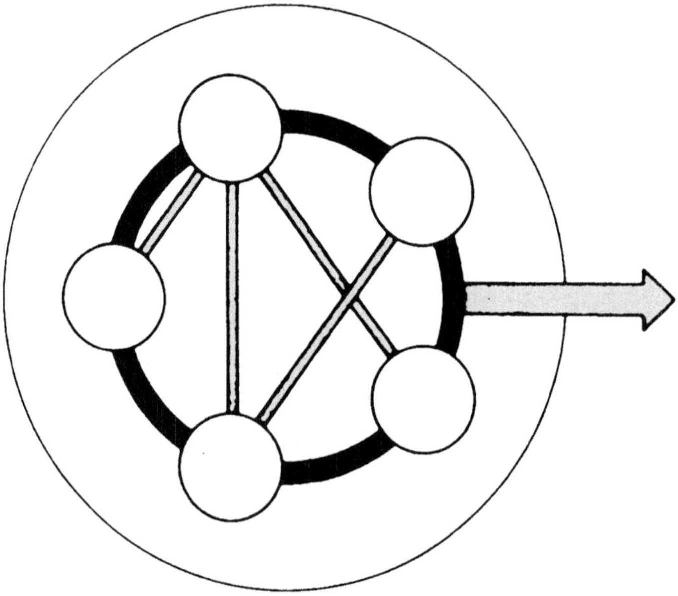

Figure 18.2 BA fight/flight

often come back to traditional values when we in turn are challenged by the fruitfulness of our own children. Equally, blind traditionalism may be a manifestation of 'basic assumption pairing' (Figure 18.3).

A composite hypothesis based on these ideas would be as follows: the group dominated by a basic assumption is one which avoids reality testing of those elements in it which embody creative strength and self-reliance, as well as of those involving hatred and despair. In the dependency group strength resides in the leader, in the fight–flight group badness resides in the outside enemy, and in the pairing group rage and despair are kept at bay only by hopeful illusion. In the dependency group, there is no chance for integration of the group's own strengths because of 'depressive anxiety', with fear of destructive feelings. In the fight–flight group, adoption of the 'paranoid position' avoids testing out the essential ambivalence of relationships. In the pairing group, assertive feelings cannot be mobilised in a way that makes the defeat of rage and despair less dependent upon hopeful illusion. Perhaps pairing is an intermediate state, defensive against both depressive and persecutory anxieties (in the Kleinian sense). I shall give examples of each type of basic assumption group encountered in group-analytic practice, and hope to illustrate some of this hypothesis with clinical material.

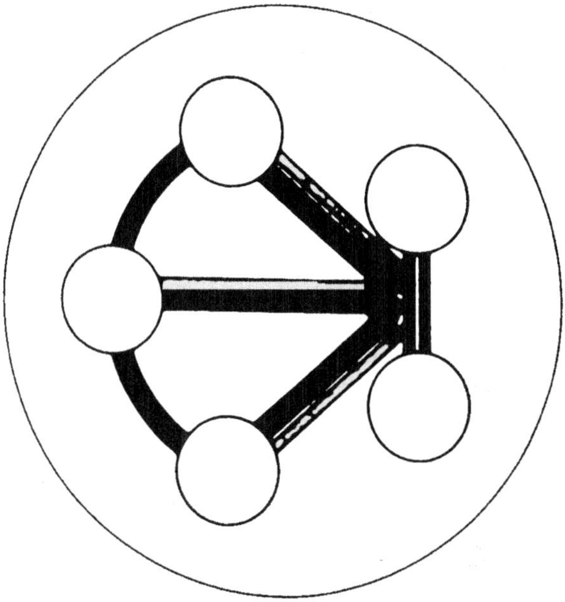

Figure 18.3 BA pairing

'Basic assumption dependency' group

An underlying shared attitude of dependence on the conductor is usual in the initial stages of all groups. The group analyst accepts this, but does not encourage it, so that the group members feel safe enough, in due course, to turn away from him in disappointment towards a more active involvement with other group members. Dependence is more characteristic of some individuals and groups, especially in regressed states. It has to be allowed but also, eventually, challenged and worked through, as in this example.

A pre-break session in a group of hospital outpatients, all originally referred because of psychosomatic disorders, was dominated by a mood of sullen isolation which left activity to the two co-therapists. It could be viewed as a group dominated by the 'basic assumption dependence'. This appeared to be confirmed, following a comment by one of the therapists that members seemed to be avoiding feelings about differences between them as well as about what they have in common at this time, by J admitting to disturbing feelings of jealousy which she had become increasingly aware of recently. She asked for 'offerings' to explain their origin. This patient had originally complained of extreme lassitude which overlay an impenetrable repression of sexuality and of jealous resentment within the family, and which had begun to lift as she came to realise her jealousy and envy in relation to a brother born when she was four. L and M began to talk of their hatred of each other because of things said on a previous occasion. R described how she had recently asserted herself by finishing with an unsatisfactory boyfriend, and no longer needed the group which she felt to be unresponsive and dead like a brick wall. M revealed that he had experienced pain in the stomach following the last session, in which he had attacked L for expressing indifference to him; he had replied that he would therefore never care for her. R responded by saying that she had felt the same sort of pain when trying to hold things together with her boyfriend, and also at the age of four when she had seen her mother feeding her newly arrived infant sister. L, a compulsive eater, reported a bad week, cut off from feelings. She had had a nightmare of being with a young godchild who was (in the dream) a diabetic like herself. She had to give her insulin, but 'accidentally' gave her the same dose as she has herself, i.e. a massive overdose. Commenting on it, L said the godchild was herself; she neglected herself by taking risks with her own diabetes control. Moreover, turning aggression on herself could be linked with the birth of a sibling shortly after she was weaned at the late age of two.

The group finished with a recognition of each person's avoidance of strength out of a fear of omnipotent destructiveness, leading – until it was faced – to a regression to an undifferentiated state. When it was faced, L was able to see a little more clearly that she avoided her own strength because of her fear of murderous jealousy, and M because of his fear that if he were to be an unqualified success in his life, this could lead to envious attacks by others. Finally, recognition of their shared rage at the therapists for leaving them, and their fear of the consequences of its expression, allowed them to repeat their resolve to have a session together during the break as they had discussed previously, and then decide they did not need to. Disavowed destructive sibling and Oedipal rivalry no longer blocked the path to co-operation, nor did they need to rely on 'manic' denial and 'acting out'.

Comment

In retrospect it seemed that denying the reality of bad feelings towards siblings and parents (fellow patients and therapists in the group) cut members off from the support and solidarity with the 'good enough siblings and parents' in the group, and prevented their moving through ambivalence towards freer interchange and interaction with each other at a non-transference level. (The history of this slow-open group was marked by a striking difficulty in welcoming newcomers.) Both their comments about the avoidance of differences and similarities in the group, and the therapists' style of not behaving like 'brick walls', seemed to promote therapeutic change. This involved the ability of the group to face differentiation and the fear of their own strength, so that defensive weakness could be transcended. Feelings about transference relationships in the group – towards the therapists and each other – came to be expressed and explored rather than somatised, displaced or turned on the self as formerly.

'Basic assumption fight–flight' group

This phenomenon has been vividly evident at times in groups composed both of patients in private practice and of students in an associated training institute having their training group analysis. The mixture usually works well, to the mutual benefit of both sets of group members, despite the envy of each for the supposed advantages enjoyed by the other. For example, trainees may envy the patients their freedom from the 'expectation' to be healthy and mature, and their chance to be a 'real' patient; patients may envy trainees their supposed greater health and special relationship with the therapist, etc. The institute or particular supervisors and teachers may be reacted to as an intruding and even persecuting superego, awesome and vengeful parents or part-objects.

Following a summer break, during which I had made a few changes in the furnishings of the room we met in, these were not reacted to overtly, even the large, rather flamboyant 'double' couch. What did emerge was the hidden rage that one trainee had felt for some months over an apparent leakage of confidentiality. Some group material had seemingly come to the notice of his female supervisor, implying that we were talking together behind his back. Strong feelings were mobilised in the group about the intruding and unfair relationship I had with the institute as a whole, which became, as it were, a scapegoat. The members of the group seemed united in indignation against it.

It was not until the next session that the changes in the room came into focus, with fantasies of my being different, and of the pictures (the same as had always been there) having been painted by my wife. Much Oedipal material emerged, with expression of impotent rage at the primal scene. A patient who had despised the paintings in the room as dull and obsessional, and was sure they had been painted or chosen by my wife or, if not, by me, came to express powerful disappointment in her sensual and erotic strivings towards her deserting father. Contrasting with the unthinkableness, for some, of sexual activity with father was the excited enjoyment of a man who openly maintained an erotic intimacy with his teenage daughters. The group managed to contain these discrepancies, and allowed space for thinking to representatives of each extreme position.

Comment

The scapegoating of the institute, with the group led in basic assumption fight–flight by the seething trainee, could be seen as displacement, allowing avoidance of ambivalence in relation to the conductor, who had 'failed' them in the break and, by changing the room in their absence, provoked primal scene fantasies. The trainees and non-trainees were united in their sense of injustice. It was not necessary to draw the group's attention to the basic assumption, or even the scapegoating. The Oedipal theme and ambivalence emerged spontaneously in many forms, contributed to by several members, and involving for many their relationship with the conductor. Jealous rivalry and ambivalence towards the conductor were now containable within the group.

'Basic assumption pairing' group

Pairing is often observed in groups. Collusion by the rest of the group is obviously necessary, and any resentment may be left to the conductor's countertransference, e.g. a feeling of being excluded.

The session to be described was the fourth after a short holiday break, seven months after the start of the group. Issues of jealousy had come out in the first session after the break, and in the session before the one concentrated on here a good deal of covert hostility to the oldest woman patient. (She is a professional who had had a lot of physical ill-health and at times in the group she was imagined as having a special relationship with me.) One of the older male patients was away.

At the beginning of the session in question, he returned, explaining that he had had a bad attack of colic. Anxious enquiry was then made about the health of the oldest woman, and she spoke movingly of her own infuriatingly offhand treatment at the hands of the specialists. As these two members revealed themselves as suffering, burdened by bad parental introjects and guilt, they struck up a pairing relationship. The rest listened apparently passively but unresentfully as they intimately shared feelings about their very similar family backgrounds.

It was only after I had pointed this out to the group, *and* asked about the two *most* silent members, that the underlying material emerged. This was about destructive projections and introjections. One of the silent members said he had been waiting and sulking. He recalled, when three or so, attempting to detain his mother after she had tucked him in for the night; when she insisted on rejoining father in the parental bedroom, he momentarily hallucinated her to be a giant beetle. This resonated. The other most silent member said she felt *herself* to be a beetle, especially in relation to a group member who she thought must see her as a beetle. It emerged that she specially liked him, but he was having to leave the group in a few months' time. He, in turn, responded with a rush of energy that dissipated the sleepiness he had been feeling. Linking this with the profound sense of loss and guilt over the early death of his father, he told how he empathised with the hero of Kafka's story 'Metamorphosis'.

In the following session very powerful material emerged. The beetle-hallucinator revealed he had felt intense jealous rage at being excluded. This focused on the imagined relationship between the oldest woman and me, but brought alive 'autistic' non-specific feelings of despair and painful exclusion as a child, and his passive attempts to get either of his parents to engage with him. Now, in the group, he became sadistic and scathing towards each of the others in turn. Later material from some of the women related to wishes for merging, and pain and rage at the loss of perfect 'permanent' love. An interpretation made sense to many that they were reacting to the premature shattering of the experience of symbiosis, and the fear of ambivalence and autonomy.

Comment

These powerful feelings had been kept covered by the 'group defence' of pairing. This seemed to be relatively superficial, but had to be brought to the group's notice before it dissolved to allow exploration and sharing at a much deeper level. Perhaps this is because of the intensity and primitiveness of the feelings and fantasies which seemed to involve both depressive and persecutory anxieties. One wonders if it required some indication from the conductor that he could approach and contain these before the rest of the group could follow suit.

It will be noticed that there is much overlap in the clinical material just quoted from three different groups illustrating each of the three basic assumptions. This confirms Bion's modest statement in his concluding chapter (Bion 1961: 165–6):

> There is much to suggest that these supposed 'basic assumptions' cannot be regarded as distinct states of mind. By that I do not mean to claim that they are 'basic' explanations which between them explain all conduct in the group . . . but that each state, even when it is possible to differentiate it with reasonable certainty from the other two, has about it a quality that suggests it may in some way be the dual or reciprocal of one of the other two, or perhaps simply another view of what one had thought to be a different basic assumption . . . It may be difficult to see because the presenting emotional tone is so different. Anxiety, fear, hate, love, all, as I have said, exist in each basic assumption group. The modification that feelings suffer in combination in the respective basic assumption group may arise became the 'cement', so to speak, that joined them to each other is guilt and depression in the dependent group, Messianic hope in the pairing group, anger and hate in the fight–flight group.

Bion and Foulkes: an integration

Finally, let us return to the questions raised at the beginning of this chapter. Why are basic assumption states seldom commented on in group-analytic groups? And what light does this throw on the nature of the group-analytic approach to groups as opposed to that of Bion?

The apparent absence or unobtrusiveness of basic assumption states in groups conducted on group-analytic lines is probably due to two things: first, the encouragement of spontaneous interaction and communication at *many levels*, which discourages their development; second, the role of group analyst, which is not that of a sphinx-like therapist. It aims at a flexible attitude which conveys both an analytic and a democratic spirit, through modelling as well as by interpretation. My impression would be that the mere interpretation of basic assumptions could perpetuate them and not lead to group work on the basis of mutuality and joint endeavour. In fact, as stated earlier, it is striking how Bion failed in his writing to state what work a psychotherapeutic group should do. Following Foulkes, we would see it as developing members' autonomy and relatedness, with themselves and within the group, fostered by working towards ever more articulate forms of communication and communion. This involves relating in all senses of the word: making oneself understood and trying to understand the communications of others, seeing yourself in and through others and discovering them in and through yourself, recognising both similarities and differences, and respecting and enjoying both. Though members are in the same boat, they are so for different reasons. Perhaps particularly in slow-open groups, individual members not only switch into and contribute to the group culture, they also to varying degrees hold back from it, consciously or unconsciously, for reasons of their own (Bion's 'anonymous contributions'). They are at different points of individual development and group involvement. If this is not recognised, the individual is likely to feel coerced and depersonalised by an emphasis on group phenomena. (Training group experiences of the Leicester Conference type, Rice 1965, are perhaps less harmful as they involve 'normal' people in short-term closed groups and do not aim at helping individuals except in a limited work-centred way.)

What light do group analytic concepts throw on Bion's formulations? The two-dimensional nature of Bion's scheme is highlighted by Foulkes's multidimensional view of the therapeutic task as one of *widening and deepening communication at many levels*: (a) the level of current adult relationships (or 'working alliance'); (b) the level of *individual* transference relationships; (c) the level of projected and shared feelings and fantasies, often from early preverbal stages of development (prior to separation and individuation from symbiotic merging); (d) a primordial level of archetypal universal images. 'It will be seen that these levels range from the more conscious objective "everyday" relationships to increasingly subjective and unconscious fantasy relationships; from more to less clearly differentiated and individual relationships (Brown and Pedder 1979: 129). Bion's relative neglect of the group's ego functions and its work task, and his failure to discuss where and how it is achieved, are made good by Foulkes's central concept of the *matrix* as the place in which group communications are made, distortions are corrected and group culture develops. It is in the matrix that interpersonal problems come to be located and where the individual can question his boundaries and re-establish his identity.

Foulkes deemed the matrix as 'the hypothetical web of communication and relationship in a group. It is the common shared ground which ultimately determines the meaning and significance of all events and upon which all communication and interpretations, verbal and non-verbal, rest' (Foulkes 1964: 292). He likened the relationship of manifest and latent content of communications to that between manifest and latent dream thoughts, and stressed that the 'group matrix is the operational basis of all relationships and communications. Inside this network the individual is conceived as a nodal point. The individual, in other words, is not conceived as a closed but as an open system' (Foulkes 1964: 118). In the matrix, group processes are transpersonal. Psychological processes are seen as taking place in the matrix, 'while at the same time involving the various individuals in different specific ways and constellations. Just as the individual's mind is a complex of interacting processes (personal matrix), mental processes interact in the concert of the group (group matrix). These processes relate to each other in manifold ways and on a variety of different levels (Foulkes 1975: 130). Foulkes went on to explain that he saw it as the therapist's task to remain equally attentive to what was happening in the individuals and in the group.

Foulkes's concept of *resonance*, through which group members react to what occurs at different levels of consciousness and regression, *according to their needs and preoccupations*, seems an essential ingredient of group work; in order to co-operate in discovering their autonomy, individuals need freedom to discover themselves at their own pace. (In contrast, having always to accommodate oneself to a group interpretation of basic assumptions must be like being coerced into a Procrustean Great Bed of Ware. It forces a false choice between the polarities of schizoid isolation or false self compliance.) After all, Foulkes always stressed the treatment of the individual; 'the individual is being treated in the context of the group with the active participation of the group' (Foulkes and Anthony 1973). Group analysis is 'psychotherapy *by* the group, *of* the group, including its conductor' (Foulkes 1975: 3).

Thus Bion and Foulkes put forward very different pictures of individuals interacting in groups. Bion's seems two-dimensional – individuals are either alienated or falsely co-operative, the group is either working on some superficial or imposed task or is avoiding genuine encounter. This is perhaps a caricature, and it could be argued that simplification is necessary to explain a new and fundamental idea. And no one could sustain a general criticism of Bion's views as simple, in any sense of the word. In contrast, Foulkes's picture is multidimensional, complex, and at first glance could be judged as woolly and lacking the bite of paradox and pessimism. But he did not underestimate the difficulty of analytic work and the powerful resistances it has to encounter, both individual and group. However, he believed in and fostered the group's own therapeutic and analytic power. Figures 18.4 and 18.5 attempt to illustrate the two different pictures, projected from the conventional circular cross-section.

Ultimately the choice of approach must depend on their explanatory and predictive value in the clinical setting and on their therapeutic usefulness. This must include their ability to deal with basic assumption phenomena. If these do exist – and I believe that something corresponding to them can be observed in all types of groups, and can seriously obstruct work in groups operating badly at a deep level – the analytic task is to recognise them in order to help the group to transcend them. In practice, pointing them out is rarely necessary. Concentration on them seems less desirable than understanding and working through the resistances to acknowledging and communicating the underlying conflicts and anxieties within relationships in the group matrix. These are manifested in and through the *individuals* in the group, as well as the group as a whole. Individuals speak for the group and the group for individuals. Individuals personify aspects and attitudes of the group, often initially disavowed by others, and represent

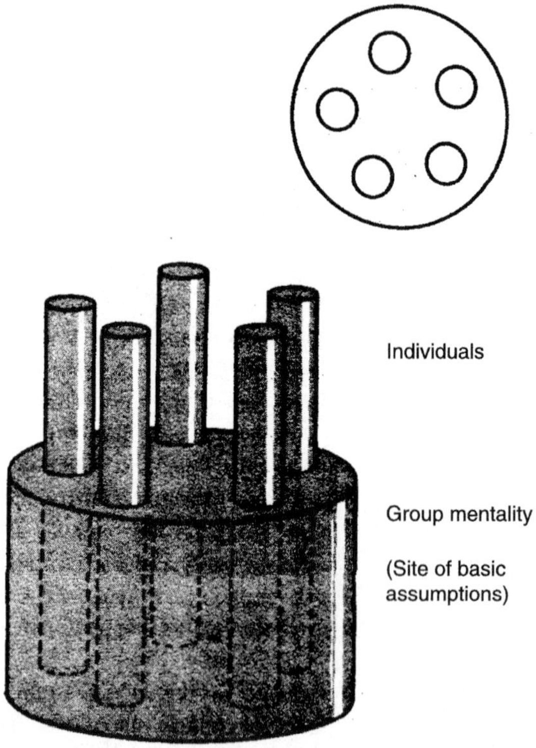

Figure 18.4

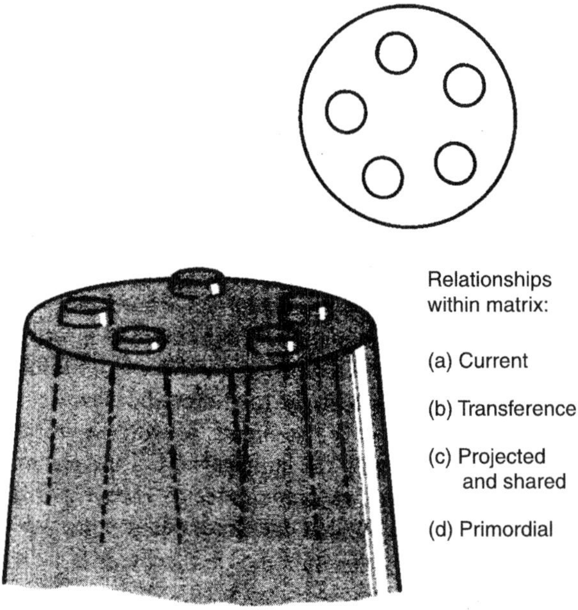

Figure 18.5

polarities which may later become reconciled within individuals and the group as a whole.

Perhaps we have, in their constant attention to the individuals within the context of the group, the main explanation of why basic assumption states are seldom seen and commented on by group analysts. Foulkes understood the need for balance in man's paradoxical struggle for both individuality and belonging. His background in psychoanalysis and interest in social forces brought new meaning to Gestalt observations of the interaction between figure and ground. The analytic group allows individual and group to discover that their complementarity is at least as real as the opposition stressed by Bion.

From this viewpoint we can wholeheartedly agree with Bion's statement in his summarising chapter, 'Group Dynamics: A Review', that 'the adult must establish contact with the emotional life of the group in which he lives', and with his subsequent rider that his task would appear to be as formidable to the adult as the relationship with the breast appears to be to the infant, and the failure to meet the demands of this task is revealed in his regression' (Bion 1961: 141). I think it is likely that this rider applies particularly to those who have failed to cope adequately with experiences at the breast, or with the entry into social life which involves coping with the impingement of the parents' relationship and of siblings. What we cannot accept, except as a paradox, is Bion's subsequent assertion that the group does not exist in reality. He states:

> The belief that a group exists, as distinct from an aggregate of individuals, is an essential part of this regression, as are also the characteristics with which the supposed group is endowed by the individual. Substance is given to the fantasy that the group exists by the fact that the regression involves the individual in a loss of his 'individual distinctiveness', indistinguishable from depersonalisation, and therefore obscures observation that the aggregation is of individuals.
>
> (Bion 1961: 142)

Such may be the nature of regression in the supposed basic assumption states, but I have no doubt that regression also takes place in groups in a way that is not so psychotic. Individuals can regress, as can groups as a whole, in an 'as-if' way that keeps in touch with the reality of the group and of other members in it. They can be experienced as womb, breast, mother, others in the family, aspects of the self, part-objects, etc., without their real existence, at another level, being lost touch with. The statement that implies that the group does not really exist only makes sense at the level that, for a baby, its mother does not exist as a separate person, and therefore the 'group of two' does not exist. Even a group of strangers meeting for therapy for the first time exists. Bion's assertion that the group is a delusion is like insisting that transference is *always* psychotic, never neurotic or even normal. This view could accord with that of Ada Abraham (1973), who has powerfully challenged the notion put forward by Bion, Jaques and Menzies that the conscious or unconscious fantasy systems connecting group members are psychotic phenomena. She points out that this level of communication occurs in normal groups, including those functioning well. As she states, fantasy activity may endorse as well as disturb group development, and promote healthy processes such as cohesion. Normal groups are not just work groups, their role is not the destruction of fantasy relationships, but a change in their quality and their free communication. 'This is achieved by forming a communicative system in which the individual feels free and learns how to move back and forth fluidly between the conscious and unconscious aspects.'

Beyond basic assumptions

To summarise my main argument in this chapter, Bion's view of a sharp dichotomy between basic assumption states and work group functioning provokes both theoretical and practical objections. On the theoretical side, these states may owe their existence in large part to the conditions imposed on the group by Bion himself, resembling hierarchical institutional structures; and they are inferred from a viewpoint which is far from clear, but is based on a Kleinian approach to mental functioning that is preoccupied with primitive processes to the relative neglect of more mature ego functions. Hence Bion neglects the work group functions of an analytic group; he sees them as opposed by the more primitive functions, not developing out of them and gradually superseding them. This leads to the *practical* objection that the recognition of basic assumption states can only be a sign that analytic work is called for. If they predominate over work group functioning or a group keeps getting stuck in a basic assumption state, it might be right to deduce that the group and its conductor are struggling unsuccessfully against resistance. But the clinical examples given earlier suggest that the resolution of such resistance does not require that the basic assumption states be a focus of therapeutic intervention. And in the simple form in which they were described by Bion, they do not guide us in our therapeutic work. They might be more helpful if we can relate them to more dynamic relationships such as that proposed here and operating in the group both within individuals and between them.

Basic assumptions apart, several of Bion's other ideas are of great value in understanding what goes on in any therapy situation, individual or group. Colin James (James 1981) has recently drawn attention to the value in group therapy of Bion's ideas on thinking, projective identification and the relationship of container and contained. These concern the genesis of thought in infancy from the raw data (β-elements) of primitive, undifferentiated somato-psyche ('protomental') experience; the development of frustration tolerance as a consequence of mother's receptivity to projective identification without inappropriate impulse discharge (retaliation, panic, etc.); and her capacity to contain, and so feed back to the child her perception of his experiences in a more tolerable and less persecutory form. These ideas throw light on the group's developing capacity to think, communicate and tolerate frustration; as a result, these capacities grow in individual members who have become more accepting and understanding of themselves and others. Unlike the basic assumptions, these ideas can be seen to be constantly at play in psychotherapy, and are entirely compatible with the group analytic approach of S. H. Foulkes. As Bion wrote in a later book, *Attention and Interpretation* (Bion 1970): 'The psycho-analytic problem is the problem of growth and its harmonious resolution in the relationship between the container and the contained, repeated in individual pair, and finally group (intra and extra psychically).'

We may need to digest and replace Bion's original concept of basic assumptions – grasp what it contains and modify what is distorting in it – if we are to integrate fruitfully the practical contributions of Bion and Foulkes. We could relax in the hope that Bion and Foulkes will do this themselves in posthumous pairing or start to work on it ourselves.

I would therefore like to finish with some preliminary propositions. Crystallising from the materials I have presented is the notion that unmodified basic assumptions result in groups from avoidance of genuine personal encounter, so that difficult feelings in relationships are disavowed. They are therefore more likely in settings where personal contact is forbidden, inappropriate or best avoided – e.g. committees, large groups, and work situations where disturbed or fragile personalities have to coexist or be supported; and I suspect, therapy groups run on strictly Bionian lines. A leader, an enemy, or a Utopian idea may seem the best solution to all problems.

But in settings which promote genuine contact, such as well-functioning therapeutic groups and the positive phases in therapeutic communities (they too, of course, can operate on basic assumption principles), the facing up to problems and differences, and the expression of feelings however awkward, prevent the emergence or persistence of basic assumptions, at least those discordant with the main purpose of the group. Our task as group analysts is not to promote them in order to study them, but to see that they do not manifest themselves or persist.

We could ask whether basic assumptions are the same, or used in the same way, in different group settings. The hypothesis I have put forward, that basic assumptions can be viewed as group defences against primal scene fantasies and anxieties, might be seen as supported by the clinical examples I gave earlier. However, the function, form and underlying content traced there may be connected with the nature of the group-analytic setting, in which intimacy is both sought and feared; intimacy involving openness and contact between people in the field of vision of other people (Foulkes's 'Model of Three').

It could be that in work groups with other tasks, e.g. committees, or in large institutions and wider social groups, basic assumptions more often offer a way of keeping a group together in the face of chaos and feared loss of control and individuality. And the individual in these settings is perhaps not threatened so much by primitive jealousy and feelings of exclusion as by loss of power and autonomy. He is tempted to withdraw – to fall asleep in committees or opt out of communal life – unless he contributes to the idea of primacy of the group's work task, or a basic assumption more or less concordant with it. My impression is that basic assumption phenomena are more common in these larger, less psychotherapeutic settings; that of dependency particularly so where members are selected for dependency, e.g. psychiatric units, where people go for help, or in states where individuals are reduced to feelings of hopelessness and helplessness; those of fight–flight and pairing in political parties and scientific and psychotherapeutic societies in search of power, Utopian solutions and ultimate answers. One would doubt that primal scene fantasies are the best guide to what is going on here, rather than some more socially and culturally determined variant dealing with the issues of authority and faith, like the myths of Prometheus ('forethought') and Pandora (wife of Epimetheus – 'afterthought'), the Garden of

Eden, the Tower of Babel, or the Crucifixion, Resurrection and Second Coming; myths which may be squeezed into infantile interpretations, but which are more resonant within particular social contexts. Relationships exemplified by such myths may have more relevance than the 'primal scene' to our understanding of social institutions such as church, army and aristocracy – and political ideals and forms such as Marxism and monetarism and the various interpretations of democracy.

This way of thinking could contribute to a 'metasociology' that I believe we need to complement and balance, on the other side of object relations theory, psychoanalytic one-body 'metapsychology'. We could then integrate our clinical experience, wider analytic understanding, and the contributions of social psychology within a more complete view of Man in relation to society and culture. This would include the effect on personal and social development of different social structures and contexts (and vice versa), analogous to but transcending mother's holding and containing. Bion's ideas about basic assumptions, like Foulkes's concept of the matrix, may turn out to be early attempts to establish such a 'metasociology'.

This chapter is a development of ideas originally proposed in 'Some reflections on Bion's basic assumptions from a group-analytic viewpoint', *Group Analysis, International Panel and Correspondence* 12, 3, 1979: 204–10.

REFERENCES

Abelin, E. L. (1980) Triangulation. The role of the father and the origin of core gender identity during the rapprochement sub-phase, in S. Bach. J. A. Barland and F. Lax (eds) *Rapprochement*, New York: Jason Aronson.

Abraham, A. (1973) A model for exploring intra- and inter-individual process in groups, *International Journal of Group Psychotherapy* 23: 3–22.

Adler, G. and Myerson, P. G. (eds) (1973) *Confrontation in Psychotherapy*, New York: Science House.

Agazarian, Y. M. (1962) Unpublished paper referred to in Agazarian and Gantt (2000).

Agazarian, Y. M. (1983) Some advantages of applying multi-dimensional thinking to the teaching practice and outcomes of group psychotherapy, *International Journal of Group Psychotherapy* 33, 2: 243–247.

Agazarian, Y. M. and Gantt, S. P. (2000) *Autobiography of a Theory: Developing a Theory of Living Human Systems and of Systems-centred Practice*, London: Jessica Kingsley Publishers.

Agazarian, Y. and Peters, R. (1981) *The Visible and Invisible Group*, London: Routledge.

Agger, E. M. (1988) Psychoanalytic perspectives on sibling relationships, *Psychoanalytic Inquiry* 8, 1: 130.

Ahlin, G. (1985) On thinking about the group matrix, *Group Analysis* 18: 111–119.

Alexander, F. (1975) *Psychoanalysis and Psychotherapy*, London: George Allen and Unwin.

Alexander, F. and French, T. M. (1946) *Psychoanalytic Psychotherapy*, New York: Ronald Press.

Alford, C. F. (1989) *Melanie Klein and Critical Social Theory*, New Haven, CT: Yale University Press.

Allen, J. (2003) *Bulletin of the Menninger Clinic* 67: 91–112.

Allerhand, M. E. and Gough, H. G. (1950) Personality factors in neurodermatitis: A preliminary study, *Psychosomatic Medicine* 12: 386.

Ammon, G. (1974) *Psychoanalyse und Psychosomatic*, Munich: Piper.

Ancona, L. (1987) Une source de la communication transpersonelle: La transculture, *Revue de Psychothérapie Psychanalytique de Groupe* 9: 10–14.

Anzieu, D. (1984) *The Group and the Unconscious*, London: Routledge and Kegan Paul.

Anzieu, D. (1989) *The Skin Ego*. New Haven, CT: Yale University Press.
Anzieu, D. (ed.) (1990) *Psychic Envelopes*, trans. D. Briggs, London: Karnac.
Asch, A. (1952) *Social Psychology*, Englewood Cliffs, NJ: Prentice Hall.
Atwood, G. E. and Stolorow, R. D. (1984) *Structures of Subjectivity*, Hillside, NJ: Analytic Press.
Balint, A. and Balint, M. (1939) On transference and counter-transference, *International Journal of Psycho-Analysis* 20: 223–230.
Balint, E. (1968) Remarks on Freud's metaphors about the 'mirror' and the 'receiver'. *Comprehensive Psychiatry* 9: 344–348.
Balint, E. (1972) Fair shares and mutual concern, *International Journal of Psycho-Analysis* 53: 61–65.
Balint, E. (1993) *Before I was I*, London: Free Association Books.
Balint, M. (1950) Thrills and regressions, in M. Balint *Object and Subject*, London: Hogarth Press.
Balint, M. (1957) *The Doctor, His Patient and the Illness*, London: Pitman.
Balint, M. (1965) *Primary Love and Psychoanalytic Technique*, London: Tavistock Publications.
Balint, M. (1968) *The Basic Fault: Therapeutic Aspects of Regression*, London: Tavistock.
Balint, M. and Balint, E. (1961) *Psychotherapeutic Techniques in Medicine*, London: Tavistock Publications.
Bartalanffy, L. Von (1968) *General System Theory*, New York: Braziller.
Bateman, A. and Fonagy, P. (2004) *Journal of Personality Disorder* 18: 35–50.
Bateson, G. (1972) *Steps to an Ecology of Mind*, New York: Chandler.
Becker, S. W. (1931) Eczema: Fundamental practical considerations, *Journal of the American Medical Association* 97: 983.
Behr, H. (1994) Families and group analysis, in D. G. Brown and L. M. Zinkin (eds) *The Psyche and the Social World. Developments in Group Analytic Theory*, London: Routledge.
Bennis, W. G. and Shepherd, H. A. (1956) A theory of group development, in J. J. Gibbard, R. D. Hartman and G. S. Mann (eds) *Analysis of Groups*, San Francisco: Jossey-Bass.
Benvenuto, B. and Kennedy, R. (1986) *The Works of Jacques Lacan*, London: Free Association Books.
Bick, E. (1968) The experience of the skin in early object relations, *International Journal of Psycho-Analysis* 49: 484–486.
Billow, R. M. (1997) Entitlement and counterentitlement in group therapy, *International Journal of Group Psychotherapy* 47, 4: 459–474.
Bion, W. R. (1959) *Experiences in Groups*, London: Tavistock.
Bion, W. R. (1961) *Experiences in Groups*, London: Tavistock Publications.
Bion, W. R. (1962) *Learning from Experience*, London: Heinemann.
Bion, W. R. (1967) *Second Thoughts*, New York: Jason Aronson.
Bion, W. R. (1970) *Attention and Interpretation*, London: Tavistock Publications.
Blackwell, D. (1994) The psyche and the system, in D. G. Brown and L. M. Zinkin (eds) *The Psyche and the Social World. Developments in Group Analytic Theory*, London: Routledge.
Blackwell, D. (1998) Bounded instability, group analysis and the matrix: organizations under stress, *Group Analysis* 31, 4: 532–546.

Blaisdell, J. H. (1932) Mental allergy. Report of a case of seborrhoeic eczema with recurrences dependent on the emotional background, *Arch Dermatol Syph* 25: 204.

Bollas, C. (1987) *The Shadow of the Object: Psychoanalysis of the Unthought Known*, London: Free Association Books.

Bowlby, J. (1969) *Attachment and Loss, Vol. 1: Attachment*, London: Hogarth Press and Institute of Psycho-Analysis.

Brazelton, T. and Kraemer, B. (1990) *The Earliest Relationship: Parents, Infants and the Drama of Early Attachment*, London: Karnac.

Brocq, L. and Jacquet, L. (1981) Notes pour server à l'histoire des neurodermites. Du lichen circumscriptus des anciens auteurs, ou lichen simplex de M. le Dr. E. Vidal, *Ann Dermatol Syphiligr* 2: 193.

Brodman, K., Erdmann, A. J., Lorgel, I., Wolff, H. G. and Broadbent, T. H. (1949) The Cornell Medical Index – an adjunct to medical interview, *Journal of the American Medical Association* 140: 530.

Brown, D. G. (1959a) Psychosomatic correlates in contact dermatitis: A pilot study, *Journal of Psychosomatic Research* 4: 132–139.

Brown, D. G. (1959b) The relevance of body image to neurosis, *British Journal of Medical Psychology* 32: 249–260.

Brown, D. G. (1965) Body image and susceptibility to contact dermatitis, *British Journal of Medical Psychology* 38: 261.

Brown, D. G. (1970) A study of the significance of psychological symptoms in eczema, MD thesis, University of Leeds.

Brown, D. G. (1972) Stress as a precipitant factor of eczema, *Journal of Psychosomatic Research* 16: 321.

Brown, D. G. (1976a) Listening to eczema, in H. Maxwell (ed.) *Integrated Medicine*, Bristol: Wright.

Brown, D. G. (1976b) Emotional disturbances in eczema: A study of symptom reporting behaviour, *Journal of Psychosomatic Research* 11: 27–40.

Brown, D. G. (1977) Drowsiness in the counter-transference, *International Review of Psycho-Analysis* 4: 481–492.

Brown. D. G. (1979) Some reflections on Bion's basic assumptions from a group-analytic viewpoint, *Group Analysis* 12: 204–210.

Brown, D. G. (1982) Text, context and texture: free speech in the service of health and healing, *Group Analysis* 15: 207–218.

Brown, D. G. (1985a) Bion and Foulkes: basic assumptions and beyond, in M. Pines (ed.) *Bion and Group Psychotherapy*, London: Routledge.

Brown, D. G. (1985b) The psychosoma and the group, *Group Analysis* 18: 93–101.

Brown, D. G. (1986) Dialogue for change, *Group Analysis* 19, 1: 25–34.

Brown, D. G. (1987a) Change in the group-analytic setting, *Psychoanalytic Psychotherapy* 3, 1: 53–60.

Brown, D. G. (1987b) Context, content and process: interrelationships between small and large groups in a transcultural workshop, *Group Analysis* 20, 3: 237–248.

Brown, D. G. (1988) Confrontation in the group analytic matrix: towards a classification, *Group* 12: 191–197.

Brown, D. G. (1989) A contribution to the understanding of psychosomatic processes in groups, *British Journal of Psychotherapy* 6: 5–9.

Brown, D. G. (1991) Assessment and selection for groups, in J. and P. M. Roberts (eds) *The Practice of Group Analysis*, London: Tavistock/Routledge.

Brown, D. G. (1992a) Transcultural group analysis I: different views of Maastricht and Heidelberg, *Group Analysis* 25, 1: 87–96.

Brown, D. G. (1992b) Transcultural group analysis II: use and abuse of cultural differences: analysis and ethics, *Group Analysis* 25, 1: 97–105.

Brown, D. G. (1994) Self-development through subjective interaction: A fresh look at 'ego training in action', in D. G. Brown and L. M. Zinkin (eds) *The Psyche and the Social World: Developments in Group Analytic Theory*, London: Routledge.

Brown, D. G. (1995) Group analysis, transculturality and ethics, *British Journal of Psychotherapy* 12: 170–177.

Brown, D. G. (1996) Discussion on article by Nicola Diamond, *Group Analysis* 29, 3: 317–320.

Brown, D. G. (1997) The royal road to the mysterious leap: the psychosoma and the analytic process, *Australian Journal of Psychotherapy* 16: 11–26.

Brown, D. G. (1998a) Fair shares and mutual concern: the role of sibling relationships, *Group Analysis* 31, 3: 315–326.

Brown, D. G. (1998b) Foulkes's basic law of group dynamics 50 years on: abnormality. injustice and the renewal of ethics. 22nd S. H. Foulkes Annual Lecture, *Group Analysis* 31, 4: 391–419.

Brown, D. G. (2003) Pairing Bion and Foulkes: Towards a metapsychosociology?, in M. and L. R. Pines (eds) *Building on Bion. Roots: Origins and Context of Bion's Contributions to Theory and Practice*, London: Jessica Kingsley Publishers.

Brown, D. G. and Bettley, F. R. (1971) Psychiatric treatment of eczema: A controlled trial, *British Medical Journal* 1: 729.

Brown, D. G. and Kalucy, R. S. (1975) Correlation of neurophysiological and personality data in sleep scratching, *Proceedings of the Royal Society of Medicine* 68: 530–532.

Brown, D. G. and Pedder, J. (1979) *Introduction to Psychotherapy: An Outline of Psychodynamic Principles and Practice*, London: Tavistock Publications.

Brown, D. G. and Young, A. (1965a) The effect of extraversion on susceptibility to disease: A validatory study on contact dermatitis, *Journal of Psychosomatic Research* 8: 421–429.

Brown, D. G. and Young, A. J. (1965b) Body image and susceptibility to contact dermatitis, *British Journal of Medical Psychology* 38: 261–267.

Brown, D. G. and Zinkin, L. M. (eds) (1994) *The Psyche and the Social World: Developments in Group Analytic Theory*, London: Routledge.

Brown, G. W. (1972) Life events and psychiatric illness, *Journal of Psychosomatic Research* 16: 311.

Brunori, L. (1996) The entry of a 'newcomer' into a psychotherapy group, *Group Analysis*.

Brunstig, L. A. (1936) Atopic dermatitis (disseminated neurodermatitis) of young adults. Analysis of precipitating factors in 101 cases and report of 10 cases associated with juvenile cataract *Arch Dermatol Syph* 34: 935.

Buber, M. (1970) *I and Thou*, trans. W. Kaufmann, Edinburgh: T. and T. Clarke.

Burkitt, I. (1991) *Social Selves. Theories of the Social Formation of Personality*, London: Sage.

Campbell, D. (2000) *The Socially Constructed Organization*, London: Karnac Books.

Canetti, E. (1986) *The Human Province*, trans. J. Neugroschel, London: Picador.

Capra, F. (1982) *The Turning Point: Science, Society and the Rising Culture*, London: Flamingo.

Casement, P. (1985) *On Learning from the Patient*, London: Tavistock.

Clarkin, J. F. and F. A. J. (1982) Selection criteria for brief psychotherapy, *American Journal of Psychotherapy* 36: 166–180.

Cleveland, S. E. and Fisher, S. (1956) Psychological factors in the neurodermatoses, *Psychosomatic Medicine* 18: 209.

Cohen, J. and Kinston, W. (1984) Regression theory: a new look at the cornerstone, *International Journal of Psycho-Analysis* 65: 411–422.

Cohen, M. and Cohen, B. (1952) Countertransference and anxiety, *Psychiatry* 15: 231–243.

Cohn, H. W. (1991) Matrix and intersubjectivity: Phenomenological aspects of group analysis, paper read to European Symposium of the Group Analytic Society (London), Oxford, 1990; published in German in *Gruppenanalyse* (Heidelberg) 2: 41–49.

Cohn, H. W. (1996) The philosophy of S. H. Foulkes: existential-phenomenological aspects of group analysis, *Group Analysis* 29, 3: 287–302.

Colonna, A. B. and Newman, L. (eds) (1983) The psychoanalytic literature on siblings, *Psychoanalytic Study of the Child* 38: 277–292.

Cooley, C. H. (1968) *Human Nature and the Social Order*, New York: Schocken.

Cullen, B. (1992) Philosophical theories of justice, in K. R. Scherer (ed.) *Justice: Interdisciplinary Perspectives*, Cambridge: Cambridge University Press.

Dalal, F. (1997a) Transcultural perspectives on psychodynamic psychotherapy: addressing internal and external realities, *Group Analysis* 30: 203–215.

Dalal, F. (1997b) The colour question in psychoanalysis, *Journal of Social Work Practice* 11, 2: 103–114.

Dalal, F. (1998) *Taking the Group Seriously: Towards a Post-Foulkesian Group Analytic Theory*, London: Jessica Kingsley Publishers.

Dalal, F. (2002) *Race, Colour and the Processes of Racialization*, Hove and New York: Brunner-Routledge.

Dawkins, R. (1976) *The Selfish Gene*, Oxford: Oxford University Press.

Dazord, A., Gerin, P., Seulin, C., Duclos, A. and Amar, A. (1997) Day-treatment evaluation: therapeutic outcome after a treatment in a day-treatment center: another look at the 'outcome equivalence paradox', *Psychotherapy Research* 7: 57–70.

Dean, E. S. (1957) Drowsiness as a symptom of countertransference, *Psychoanalytic Quarterly* 26: 246–247.

De Maré, P. (1972) *Perspectives in Group Psychotherapy*, London: Allen and Unwin.

De Maré, P. B. and Piper, R. (1984) *The Median Group*,

De Maré, P., Piper, R. and Thompson, S. (1991) *Koinonia: From Hate, through Dialogue, to Culture in the Large Group*, London: Karnac.

De Zulueta, F. (1993) *From Pain to Violence: The Traumatic Roots of Destructiveness*, London: Whurr.

Denning, E. (1997) Sport in the quest for excitement: Norbert Elias's contribution to the sociology of sport, *Group Analysis* 30, 4: 477–487.

Diamond, N. (1996) Can we speak of internal and external reality?, *Group Analysis* 29, 3: 303–317.

Dick, B. M. (1975) A ten-year study of out-patient analytic group therapy, *British Journal of Psychiatry* 127: 365–375.

Dickes, S. R. (1965) The defensive function of an altered state of consciousness: A hypnoid state, *Journal of the American Psychoanalytic Association* 13: 356–403.

Dilthey, W. (1961/1926) *Meaning in History*, ed. H. Rickman, London: Allen and Unwin.

Dolan, B., Warren, F. and Norton, K. (1997) Changes in borderline symptoms one year after therapeutic community treatment for severe personality disorder, *British Journal of Psychiatry* 171: 274–279.

Dunn, J. (1995) Intersubjectivity in psychoanalysis: a critical review, *International Journal of Psycho-Analysis* 76: 723–738.

Durkheim, E. (1893) *The Division of Labour in Society*, trans. W. Halls, London: Macmillan.

Durkin, J. (ed.) (1981) *Living Groups: Group Psychotherapy and General Systems Theory*, New York: Brunner/Mazel.

Durkin, H. (1982) Change in group psychotherapy: therapy and practice: a system approach, *International Journal of Group Psychotherapy* 32: 431–438.

Edelman, G. (1989) *The Remembered Present: A Biological Theory of Consciousness*, New York: Basic Books.

Eigen, M. (1983) Dual union or undifferentiation? A critique of Marion Milner's view of the sense of psychic creativeness, *International Review of Psycho-Analysis* 10: 415–428.

Elias, N. (1978/1939) *The Civilizing Process*, Oxford: Blackwell.

Elias, N. (1991a) *The Society of Individuals*, Oxford: Blackwell.

Elias, N. (1991b) *The Symbol Theory*, London: Sage.

Elliott, B. (1994) The womb and gender identity, in D. G. Brown and L. M. Zinkin (eds) *The Psyche and the Social World: Developments in Group Analytic Theory*. London: Routledge.

Emde, R., Biringen, Z., Clyman, R. and Oppenheim, D. (1991) The moral self. Affective core and procedural knowledge, *Developmental Review* 11: 251–270.

Engel, G. L. (1962) *Psychological Development in Health and Disease*, Philadelphia and London: Saunders.

Erikson, E. H. (1964) *Insight and Responsibility*, London: Faber and Faber.

Erikson, E. (1965) *Childhood and Society*, London: Penguin.

Eysenck, H. J. and Eysenck, S. B. G. (1964) *Manual of the Eysenck Personality Inventory*, London: London University Press.

Ezriel, H. (1952) Notes on psycho-analytic group therapy 11: interpretations and research, *Psychiatry* 15: 119–126.

Ezriel, H. (1973) Psychoanalytic group psychotherapy, in L. R. Wolberg and E. K. Schwartz (eds) *Group Therapy 1973: An Overview*, New York: Intercontinental Medical Book Corp, pp. 183–210.

Fairbairn, W. R. D. (1952) *Psychoanalytic Studies of the Personality*, London: Routledge/Tavistock.

Ferenczi, S. (1914) On falling asleep during analysis. I, in S. Ferenczi *Further Contributions to the Theory and Practice of Psycho-Analysis*, London: Hogarth Press.

Finesinger, J. E. and Greenhill, M. H. (1942) Neurotic symptoms and emotional factors in atopic dermatitis, *Arch Dermatol Syph* 46: 187.

Fisher, S. and Cleveland, S. E. (1958) *Body Image and Personality*, Princeton, NJ: Van Norstrand.

Fiske, C. E. and Obermayer, M. E. (1954) Personality and emotional factors in chronic disseminated neurodermatitis, *Arch Dermatol Syph* 70: 261.

Fonagy, P., Target, M., Gergely, G., Allen, J. G. and Bateman, A. W. (2003) The developmental roots of borderline personality disorder in early attachment relationships, *Psychoanalytic Inquiry* 23, 11: 412–459.

Fonagy, P., Target, M., Gergely, G. and Jurist, E. L. (2002) *Affect Regulation, Mentalization, and the Development of Self*, London: Other Press.

Fonseca, A. F. da (1963) Affective equivalents, *British Journal of Psychiatry* 109: 464.

Foulkes, E. (1990) S. H. Foulkes: a brief memoir, in E. Foulkes (ed.) *Selected Papers of S. H. Foulkes: Psychoanalysis and Group Analysis*, London: Karnac.

Foulkes, E. (1994) Personal communication.

Foulkes, E. T. (1989) Further observations from Maastricht, *Group Analysis* 20, 3: 249–250.

Foulkes, S. H. (1948) *Introduction to Group-Analytic Psychotherapy*, London: Heinemann.

Foulkes, S. H. (1964) *Therapeutic Group Analysis*, London: Allen and Unwin.

Foulkes, S. H. (1968) Some autobiographical notes (parts I and II), *Group Analysis* 1: 117–205.

Foulkes, S. H. (1973) *The Group as Matrix of the Individual's Mental Life in Group Therapy*, eds E. Wolberg and E. K. Schwartz, New York: Stratton.

Foulkes, S. H. (1975) *Group-Analytic Psychotherapy*, London: Gordon and Breach.

Foulkes, S. H. (1990a) Oedipus conflict and regression, in E. Foulkes (ed.) *Selected Papers of S. H. Foulkes: Psychoanalysis and Group Analysis*, London: Karnac.

Foulkes, S. H. (1990b) *Selected Papers: Psychoanalysis and Group Analysis*, London: Karnac.

Foulkes, S. H. and Anthony, E. J. (1973) *Group Psychotherapy: The Psychoanalytic Approach*, Harmondsworth: Penguin.

Foulkes, S. H. and Lewis, E. (1944) Group analysis: studies in the treatment of groups on psycho-analytical lines, *British Journal of Medical Psychology* 20: 175–184.

Freud, A. (1936) *The Ego and the Mechanisms of Defense*, London: Hogarth Press.

Freud, A. (1965) *Normality and Pathology in Childhood*, New York: International Universities Press.

Freud, S. (1894) The neuro-psychoses of defence (*SE* 3), London: Hogarth Press.

Freud, S. (1900) *The Interpretation of Dreams* (*SE* 4), London: Hogarth Press.

Freud, S. (1910) The future prospects of psycho-analytic therapy (*SE* 11), London: Hogarth Press.

Freud, S. (1912) Recommendations to physicians practising psycho-analysis (*SE* 12), London: Hogarth Press.

Freud, S. (1915) *The Unconscious* (*SE* 14), London: Hogarth Press.

Freud, S. (1916) *Introductory Lectures on Psychoanalysis* (*SE* 15), London: Hogarth Press.

Freud, S. (1921) *Group Psychology and the Analysis of the Ego* (*SE* 18), London: Hogarth Press.

Freud, S. (1922) *Some Neurotic Mechanisms in Jealousy, Paranoia and Homosexuality* (*SE* 18), London: Hogarth Press.

Freud, S. (1923) *The Ego and the Id* (*SE* 19), London: Hogarth Press.

Freud, S. (1930) *Civilization and its Discontents* (*SE*), London: Hogarth Press.

Fromm, E. (1991) *The Sane Society*, London: Routledge.

Fry, J. (1972) Twenty-one years of general practice – changing patterns, *Journal of the Royal College of General Practitioners* 22: 521.

Garland, C. (1982) Group analysis: taking the non-problem seriously, *Group Analysis* 15: 4–14.

Gergely, G. and Watson, J. S. (1996) The social biofeedback model of parental affect-mirroring, *International Journal of Psycho-Analysis* 17: 1181–1212.

Gilligan, C. (1982) *In a Different Voice: Psychological Theory and Women's Development*, Cambridge, MA: Harvard University Press.

Gilligan, C., Ward, J. V. and Taylor, J. (1988) *Mapping the Moral Domain*, Cambridge, MA: Harvard University Press.

Glenn, L. (1987) Attachment theory and group analysis, *Group Analysis* 20, 2: 109–117.

Glover, E. (1931) The therapeutic effect of inexact interpretations, *International Journal of Psycho-Analysis* 12: 397.

Gordon, R. (1991) Intersubjectivity and the efficacy of group psychotherapy, *Group Analysis* 24: 41–51.

Graham, D. T. and Wolf, S. (1953) The relation of eczema to attitude and to vascular reactions of the human skin, *Journal of Laboratory and Clinical Medicine* 42: 238.

Graham, I. (1988) The sibling object and its transferences: alternate organizer of the middlefield, *Psychoanalytic Inquiry* 8, 1: 88–107.

Green, A. (1974) Absent meaning and double representation, *International Journal of Psycho-Analysis*.

Green, A. (1975) The analyst, symbolisation and absence in the analytic setting, *International Journal of Psycho-Analysis* 56: 1–22.

Greenberg, J. R. and Mitchell, S. A. (1985) *Object Relations in Psychoanalytic Theory*, Cambridge, MA: Harvard University Press.

Greenson, R. R. (1967) *The Technique and Practice of Psychoanalysis*, London: Hogarth Press.

Grinberg, L. and Grinberg, R. (1989) *Psychoanalytic Perspectives on Migration and Exile*, trans. N. Festinger, New Haven, CT: Yale University Press.

Groen, J. J. (1957) Psychosomatic disturbance as a form of substituted behaviour, *Journal of Psychosomatic Research* 2: 85.

Grunebaum, H. and Solomon, L. (1980) Towards a peer theory of group psychotherapy I: on the developmental significance of peers and play, *International Journal of Group Psychotherapy* 30: 23–49.

Grunebaum, H. and Solomon, L. (1982) Towards a theory of peer relationships II: on the stages of social development and their relationship to group psychotherapy, *International Journal of Group Psychotherapy* 32: 283–307.

Grunebaum, H. and Solomon, L. (1987) Peer relationships, self-esteem and the self, *International Journal of Group Psychotherapy* 37: 475–513.

Guilford, J. P. (1940) *An Inventory of Factors STDCR*. Beverly Hill, CA: Sheridan.

Guttmacher, J. A. and Birk, L. (1971) Group therapy: what specific advantages?, *Comprehensive Psychiatry* 12: 546–556.

Hargrove, R. (1998) *Mastering the Art of Creative Collaboration*, New York: Business Week Books.

Harlow, H. F. and Zimmerman, R. R. (1958) The development of affectional responses in infant monkeys, *Proceeds of the American Philosophical Society* 102: 501.

Harrison, T. (2000) *Bion, Rickman, Foulkes and the Northfield Experiment*, London: Jessica Kingsley Publishers.
Hartmann, H. (1958) *Ego Psychology and the Problem of Adaptation*, New York: International Universities Press.
Harwood, I. and Pines, M. (1998) *Intersubjectivity and Self-Psychological Pathways to Human Understanding*, London: Jessica Kingsley Publishers.
Heath, E. S. and Bacal, H. A. (1972) A method of group psychotherapy at the Tavistock Clinic, in C. J. Kaplan and H. S. Sager (eds) *Progress in Group and Family Therapy*, New York: Brunner/Mazel.
Heenen-Wolff, S. (1995) Identity of the death instinct: aspects of transcultural research, *Group Analysis* 28: 159–165.
Heimann, P. (1950) On countertransference, *International Journal of Psycho-Analysis* 31: 81–84.
Herron, J. T. (1965) Neurodermatitis, *Medical Journal of Australia* 1: 421.
Hill, O. (1977) The psychological management of psychosomatic diseases, *British Journal of Psychiatry* 131: 113–126.
Hinshelwood, R. D. (1997) *Therapy or Coercion?*, London: Karnac.
Hoffman, E. (1989) *Lost in Translation*, London: Minerva.
Homans, P. (1989) *The Ability to Mourn: Disillusionment and the Social Origin of Psychoanalysis*, Chicago: University of Chicago Press.
Honnuth, A. (1995) *The Struggle for Recognition: The Moral Grammar of Social Conflict*, Cambridge: Polity Press.
Hope-Price, G. (1982) Sibling rivalry and the therapy group. Unpublished.
Hopper, E. (1997) Traumatic experience in the unconscious life of the group: a fourth basic assumption, *Group Analysis* 30, 4: 439–470.
Hopper, E. (2003) *Traumatic Experience in the Unconscious Life of Groups*, London: Jessica Kingsley Publishers.
Horwitz, L. (1977) A group centred approach to group psychotherapy, *International Journal of Group Psychotherapy* 27: 423–439.
Husemann, K. (1987) Transcultural problems in individual and group analysis, *Revue de Psychothérapie Psychanalytique de Groupe* 9: 65–76.
Husemann, K. (1997) Discussion on paper by Raymond Battegay and Ali Tarik, *Group Analysis* 30, 2: 228–232.
Ingram, J. T. (1933) The personality of the skin, *Lancet* 1: 889.
Jacobson, E. (1964) *The Self and the Object World*, New York: International Universities Press.
James, D. C. (1981) W. R. Bion's contribution to the field of group therapy, in E. Wolberg (ed.) *Group and Family Therapy, An Overview*, New York: Brunner/Mazel.
James, D. C. (1984) Bion's 'containing' and Winnicott's 'holding' in the context of the group matrix, *International Journal of Group Psychotherapy* 34: 201–213.
James, D. C. (1994) Holding and containing in the group and society, in D. G. Brown and L. M. Zinkin (eds) *The Psyche and the Social World: Developments in Group Analytic Theory*, London: Routledge.
Janssen, P. and Wienen, G. (1995) Group analysis with ulcerative colitis and regional ileitis: The discovery of the scream, *Group Analysis* 28: 87–96.
Jaques, E. (1970) *Work, Creativity and Social Justice*, London: Heinemann.
Jaques, E. (1974) Social systems as a defence against persecutory and depressive

anxiety, in J. J. Hartman, R. D. Mann and G. S. Gibbons (eds) *Analysis of Groups*, San Francisco: Jossey-Bass.
Jones, E. (1956) *Sigmund Freud: Life and Work*, Vol. 1, London: Hogarth Press.
Jones, E. E. (1997) Modes of therapeutic action, *International Journal of Psycho-Analysis* 78: 1135–1150.
Kaës, R. (1987) La troisième différence, *Revue de Psychothérapie Psychanalytique de Groupe* 9–10: 5–30.
Kaës, R., Anzieu, D., Bejarano, A., Gorik, R. and Scaglia, H. (1975) *Le désir de former et la formation du savoir*, Paris: Dunod.
Kennedy, R. (1998) *The Elusive Human Subject: A Psychoanalytic Theory of Subject Relations*, London: Free Association Books.
Kepecs, J. G. and Robin, M. (1950) Life situations, emotions and atopic dermatitis, *Proceedings of the Association for Research into Nervous and Mental Disorders* 29: 1010.
Kernberg, O. F. (1965) Notes on countertransference, *Journal of the American Psychoanalytic Association* 13, 38–56.
Kernberg, O. F. (1975) *Borderline Conditions and Pathological Narcissism*, New York: Jason Aronson.
Kernberg, O. F. (1976) *Object Relations Theory and Clinical Psychoanalysis*, New York: Jason Aronson.
Khan, M. M. R. (1960) Regression and integration in the analytic setting, in M. M. R. Khan *The Privacy of the Self*, London: Hogarth Press.
Khan, M. M. R. (1974) Silence as communication, in M. Khan *The Privacy of the Self*. London: Hogarth Press.
Khan, M. M. R. (1977) Secret as potential space, in M. and K. I. S. Tonnesmann (eds) *Psychoanalysis and the Changing Society. Festschrift in Honour of Paula Heimann*, London: Hogarth Press.
Kinder, D. (1989) Sibling rivalry and the analysis group. Unpublished.
Klain, E. (1986) Confrontation and acting-out in group analysis, *Group Analysis* 19: 153–166.
Klauber, J. (1987) *Illusion and Spontaneity in Psychoanalysis*, London: Free Association Books.
Klauder, J. V. (1925) The cutaneous neuroses. With particular reference to psychotherapy, *Journal of the American Psychanalytic Association* 85: 1983.
Klein, G. S. (1976) *Psychoanalytic Theory*, New York: International Universities Press.
Klein, M. (1975/1928) Early stages of the Oedipus conflict, in *Love, Guilt and Reparation and Other Works 1921–1945*, London: Hogarth Press.
Klein, M. (1975/1933) The early development of conscience in the child, in *Love, Guilt and Reparation and Other Works 1921–1945*, London: Hogarth Press.
Klein, M. (1975/1935) Contribution to the psychogenesis of manic-depressive states, in *Love, Guilt and Reparation and Other Works 1921–1945*, London: Hogarth Press.
Klein, M. (1975) *Love, Guilt and Reparation and Other Works 1921–1945*, London: Hogarth Press.
Knauss, W. (1985) The treatment of psychosomatic illnesses in group-analytic psychotherapy, *Group Analysis* 18: 177–190.
Kohlberg, L. (1981) *The Philosophy of Personal Development: Moral Stages and the Idea of Justice*, New York: Harper and Row.

Kohut, H. (1971) *The Analysis of the Self*, New York: International Universities Press.

Kohut, H. (1977) *The Restoration of the Self*, New York: International Universities Press.

Kohut, H. and Wolf, E. S. (1978) The disorders of the self and their treatment, *International Journal of Psycho-Analysis* 59: 413–426.

König, K. (1986) Unpublished paper read at 9th Congress of the International Association of Group Psychotherapy.

Kraemer, S. and Roberts, E. (eds) (1996) *The Politics of Attachment: Towards a Secure Society*, London: Free Association Books.

Kreeger, L. (ed.) (1975) *The Large Group: Dynamics and Therapy*, London: Constable.

Kreeger, L. C. (1992) Envy pre-emption in small and large groups. 16th S. H. Foulkes Annual Lecture, *Group Analysis* 25, 4: 391–408.

Kristeva, J. (1991) *Strangers to Ourselves*, trans. L. S. Roudiez, New York: Columbia University Press.

Küng, H. (1990) *Global Responsibility: In Search of a New World Ethic*, London: SCH Press.

Lacan, J. (1966) *Ecrits: A Selection*, trans. A. Sheridan, London: Tavistock Publications.

Langs, R. (1973) The patient's view of the therapist: reality or fantasy?, *International Journal of Psychoanalytic Psychotherapy* 2: 411–431.

Langs, R. J. (1978) *The Listening Process*, New York: Jason Aronson.

Langs, R. (1979) The interactional dimension of countertransference, in L. Epstein and A. H. Finer (eds) *Countertransference: The Therapist's Contribution to the Therapeutic Situation*, Northvale, NJ: Jason Aronson.

Larkin, M. (1991) Some ethical issues in feminist oriental therapeutic groups for women, *International Journal of Group Psychotherapy* 41: 199–215.

Lawrence, W. G. (2000) *Tongued with Fire: Groups in Experience*, London: Karnac.

Lawrence, W. G., Bain, A. and Gould, L. J. (1996) The fifth basic assumption, *Free Associations* 6, 37: 28–55.

Laxenaire, M. (1983) Group analytic psychotherapy according to Foulkes and psychoanalysis according to Lacan, in M. Pines (ed.) *The Evolution of Group Analysis*, London: Routledge and Kegan Paul.

Leary, T. (1956) *Interpersonal Diagnosis of Personality: A Functional Theory and Methodology for Personality Evaluation*, New York: Ronald Press.

Lecourt, E. (1998) La musique, lien transitionnel entre les cultures et ses applications thérapeutique, in R. Kaës (ed.) *Différence Culturelle et Souffrances de l'Identité*, Paris: Dunod.

Leigh, D. (1968) Management of psychosomatic disorder, *British Medical Journal* 4: 753.

Le Roy, J. (1987a) The cultural structuring of the personality and intercultural relationships, *Group Analysis* 20, 2: 147–153.

Le Roy, J. (1987b) Processus dans un seminaire transculturel d'analyse de groupe, *Revue de Psychothérapie Psychanalytique de Groupe* 9: 10–14.

Le Roy, J. D. (1994) Group analysis and culture, in D. G. Brown and L. M. Zinkin (eds) *The Psyche and the Social World: Developments in Group Analytic Theory*, London: Routledge.

Levine, H. B. (1987) The psychology of the nuclear threat: a bibliography, *International Review of Psycho-Analysis*, 14: 1319.

Lewin, K. (1952) *Field Theory in Social Silence*, London: Tavistock Publications.

Lichtenberg, J. D. (1975) The development of the sense of self. *Journal of the American Psychoanalytic Association* 23: 453–484.

Lintott, B. (1983) Mind and matrix in the writing of S. H. Foulkes, *Group Analysis* 16: 242–251.

Loewald, H. W. (1970) On the therapeutic action of psychoanalysis, in H. W. Loewald *Papers on Psychoanalysis*, New Haven, CT: Yale University Press.

Loewald, H. W. (1979) Reflections on the psychoanalytic process and its therapeutic potential, *Psychoanalytic Study of the Child* 34: 155–167.

Loewald, H. W. (1980) *Papers on Psychoanalysis*, New Haven, CT: Yale University Press.

Lovett Doust, J. W. (1952) Psychiatric aspects of somatic immunity: Differential incidence of physical disease in the histories of psychiatric patients, *Journal of the Royal Society of Medicine* 6: 49.

Lynch, F. W., Hinckley, R. G. and Cowan, D. W. (1945) Psychobiologic studies of patients with atopic eczema (disseminated neurodermatitis), *Arch Dermatol Syph* 51: 251.

McDougall, J. (1974) The psychosoma and the psychoanalytic process, *International Review of Psycho-Analysis* 1: 437–459.

McDougall, J. (1978) Primitive communication and the use of counter-transference, *Contemporary Psychoanalysis* 14: 173–209.

McDougall, J. (1982) Alexithymia: A psychoanalytic viewpoint, *Psychotherapy and Psychosomatics* 38: 81–90.

McDougall, J. (1989) *Theatres of the Body*, London: Free Association Books.

McLaughlin, J. T. (1975) The sleepy analyst: Some observations on states of consciousness in the analyst at work, *Journal of the American Psychoanalytic Association* 23: 363–382.

Mahler, M. S., Pine, F. and Bergman, C. (1975) *The Psychological Births of the Human Infant*, London: Hutchinson.

Main, T. F. (1967) Knowledge, learning and freedom from thought, *Australian and New Zealand Journal of Psychiatry* 1: 64–71.

Main, T. F. (1977) The concept of the therapeutic community: variations and vicissitudes. First S. H. Foulkes Annual Lecture, *Group Analysis* 10, 2: 2–16.

Malan, D. H. (1979) *Individual Psychotherapy and the Science of Psychodynamics*, London: Butterworth.

Malan, D. R., Balfour, F. H. G., Hood, V. G. and Shooter, A. M. N. (1976) Group psychotherapy: a long-term follow-up study, *Archives of General Psychiatry* 33: 1303–14.

Maratos, J. (1996) Self through attachment and attachment through self in group therapy, *Group Analysis* 29, 2: 191–198.

Marrone, M. (1994) Attachment theory and group analysis, in D. G. Brown and L. M. Zinkin (eds) *The Psyche and the Social World: Developments in Group Analytic Theory*, London: Routledge.

Marrone, M. (1998) *Attachment and Interaction*, London: Jessica Kingsley Publishers.

Marshall, L. and Zohar, D. (1997) *Who's Afraid of Schrödinger's Cat?*, London: Bloomsbury.

Marty, P. and de M'Uzan, M. (1963) La pensée operatoire, *Revue Française de Psychanalyse* 27: 1345–1356.

Matte-Blanco, J. (1975) *The Unconscious as Infinite Sets: An Essay in Bi-Logic*, London: Duckworth.

Matte-Blanco, I. (1988) *Thinking, Feeling and Being: Clinical Refleçtions on the Fundamental Antinomy of Human Beings and World*, London: Routledge.

Mead, G. H. (1934) *Mind, Self and Society*, Chicago: Chicago University Press.

Mennell, S. (1989) *Norbert Elias: An Introduction*, Oxford: Blackwell.

Menninger, K. (1958) *Theory of Psychoanalytic Technique*, London: Imago.

Menzies, I. E. P. (1960) A case-study in the functioning of social systems as a defence against anxiety, *Human Relations* 13: 95–121.

Menzies, I. E. P. (1961) *The Functioning of Social Systems as a Defence against Anxiety: A Report on the Study of the Nursing Service of a General Hospital*, London: Tavistock Publications.

Menzies Lyth, I. (1989) *The Dynamics of the Social: Selected Essays*, Vol. 2, London: Free Association Books.

Merleau-Ponty, M. (1976) *The Phenomenology of Perception*, London: Routledge and Kegan Paul.

Milgram, S. (1964) Group pressure and action against a person, *Journal of Abnormal and Social Psychology* 69: 137–143.

Miller, I. (1972) Inhibition of empathy caused by unconscious fantasy: IV, *International Journal of Psychoanalytic Psychotherapy* 1: 107–116.

Milner, M. (1952) Aspects of symbolism in comprehension of the not-self, *International Journal of Psycho-Analysis* 33: 181–195.

Milner, M. (1987) *The Suppressed Madness of Sane Men*, London: Tavistock.

Milosz, C. (1968) *Native Realm*, trans. C. S. Leech, Harmondsworth: Penguin.

Moore, R. I. (1987) *The Formation of a Persecuting Society*, Oxford: Blackwell.

Mulgan, G. (1997) *Connexity: How to Live in a Connected World*, London: Chatto and Windus.

Mullan, H. (1987) The ethical foundations of group psychotherapy, *International Journal of Group Psychotherapy* 37, 3: 403–416.

Mullan, H. (1991) Inherent moral practice in group psychotherapy, *International Journal of Group Psychotherapy* 41: 185–197.

Murphy, M. (1989) Somatisation: embodying the problem, *British Medical Journal* 298: 1331.

Napolitani, D. (1980) Beyond the individual, *Group Analysis* 13: 12–16.

Nemiah, J. C. and Sifneos, P. E. (1970) Affect and fantasy in patients with psychosomatic disorders, in O. W. Hill (ed.) *Modern Trends in Psychosomatic Medicine*, 2nd edn, London: Butterworth.

Nitsun, M. (1991) The anti-group: Destructive forces in the group and their therapeutic potential, *Group Analysis* 24: 7–20.

Nitsun, M. (1994) The primal scene in group analysis, in D. G. Brown and L. M. Zinkin (eds) *The Psyche and the Social World: Developments in Group Analytic Theory*, London: Routledge, pp. 129–145.

Nitsun, M. (1996) *The Anti-Group: Destructive Forces in the Group and their Creative Potential*, London: Routledge.

Nitsun, M. (1998a) The organizational mirror: a group-analytic approach to organizational consultancy. Part I – theory, *Group Analysis* 31, 3: 245–267.

Nitsun, M. (1998b) Part II – application, *Group Analysis* 31, 4: 505–518.
Norberg Hodge, H. (1991) *Ancient Futures: Learning from Ladakh*, London: Rider.
Obermayer, M. E., Elair, R., Fiske, C., Levitt, N., Rush, S., Storkan, M. A. and Glenn, E. (1952) Correlation of emotional status and reactivity to cutaneous stimuli in functional dermatoses, *Arch Dermatol Syph* 65: 291.
O'Donovan, W. J. (1927) *Dermatological Neuroses*, London: Kegan Paul.
Ogden, T. H. (1980) On the nature of schizophrenic conflict, *International Journal of Psycho-Analysis* 61: 513–533.
Ogden, T. H. (1994) *Subjects of Analysis*, London: Karnac.
Oppenheim, D., Emde, R. N., Hasson, M. and Warren, S. (1997) Preschoolers face moral dilemmas, *International Journal of Psycho-Analysis* 78: 943–957.
Ormont, L. R. (1984) The leader's role in dealing with aggression in groups, *International Journal of Group Psychotherapy* 34: 553–560.
Outhwaite, W. (ed.) (1996) *The Habermas Reader*, Cambridge: Polity Press.
Padel, J. (1985) Ego in current thinking, *International Review of Psycho-Analysis* 12: 273–283.
Pagels, E. (1974) *The Gnostic Gospels*, London: Weidenfeld and Nicholson.
Paparo, F. (1982) Self psychology and the group process, *Group Analysis* 17: 108–117.
Parsons, T. (1964) *Social Structure and Personality*, London: Collier-Macmillan.
Pillsbury, D. M., Shelley, W. B. and Kligman, A. M. (1956) *Dermatology*, London: Saunders.
Pines, D. (1980) Skin communication: Early skin disorders and their effect on transference and counter-transference, *International Journal of Psycho-Analysis*, 61: 315–323.
Pines, M. (1978) The contribution of S. H. Foulkes to group analytic psychotherapy, in L. R. Wolberg (ed.) *Group Therapy: An Overview*, New York: Stratton International.
Pines, M. (1981) The frame of reference of group psychotherapy, *International Journal of Group Psychotherapy* 31, 3: 275–285.
Pines, M. (1982) Reflections on mirroring, *Group Analysis* 15: 3–26.
Pines, M. (1983) Psychoanalysis and group analysis, *International Journal of Group Psychotherapy* 33: 155–170.
Pines, M. (1990) Group analysis and the corrective emotional experience: Is it relevant?, *Psychoanalytic Inquiry* 10: 389–408.
Pines, M. (1994) The group-as-a-whole, in D. G. Brown and L. Zinkin (eds) *The Psyche and the Social World: Developments in Group Analytic Theory*, London: Routledge.
Pines, M. (1997) Coherency and disruption in the sense of self, in M. Pines *Circular Reflections: Selected Papers or Group Analysis and Psychoanalysis*, London: Jessica Kingsley Publishers.
Pines, M. (1998) *Circular Reflections: Selected Papers on Group Analysis and Psychoanalysis*, London: Jessica Kingsley Publishers.
Pines, M. and Schermer, V. L. (1994) *Ring of Fire: Primitive Affects and Object Relations in Group Therapy*, London: Routledge.
Piper, W., Joyce, A., Rosie, J. and Azim, H. (1994) Psychological mindedness, work, and outcome in day treatment, *International Journal of Group Psychotherapy* 44: 291–311.

Powell, A. (1994) Towards a unifying concept of the group matrix, in D. G. Brown and L. M. Zinkin (eds) *The Psyche and the Social World: Developments in Group Analytic Theory*, London: Routledge.

Puget, J. (1991) The social context: searching for a hypothesis, *Free Associations* 21: 21–33.

Rabin, H. (1989) Peers and siblings: their neglect in analytic group psychotherapy, *International Journal of Group Psychotherapy* 39: 209–221.

Racker, H. (1957) The meaning and uses of countertransference, *Psychoanalytic Quarterly* 26: 303–357.

Racker, H. (1968) *Transference and Countertransference*, London: Hogarth Press.

Rahe, R. H. (1968) Life-change measurement as a predictor of illness, *Proceedings of the Royal Society of Medicine* 61: 1124.

Rance, C. (1998) The art of conversation: the group-analytic paradigm and organizational consultancy, *Group Analysis* 31, 4: 519–531.

Rapoport, R. N. (1997) *Families, Children and the Quest for a Global Ethic*, Aldershot: Ashgate.

Rayner, E. (1995a) Intuitions of justice and fairness in the psychoanalytic process. Unpublished.

Rayner, E. (1995b) *Unconscious Logic*, London: Routledge.

Rayner, E. H. and Rayner, H. H. (1964) Assessment for psychotherapy, *British Journal of Medical Psychology* 37: 331–342.

Read, T. (1997) Chaos, quanta and the implicate order. Can advances in mathematics and physics inform our work as psychotherapists?, *Group Analysis* 30, 1: 67–80.

Reich, A. (1951) On countertransference, *International Journal of Psycho-Analysis* 32: 26–31.

Rey, H. (1994) *Universals of Psychoanalysis in the Treatment of Psychotic and Borderline States*, London: Free Association Books.

Rice, A. K. (1965) *Learning for Leadership*, London: Tavistock Publications;

Rickman, J. (1957) The factor of number in individual- and group-dynamics, in A. Rickman *Selected Contributions to Psycho-Analysis*, London: Hogarth Press.

Ridley, M. (1996) *The Origins of Virtue*, London: Viking.

Rieff, P. (1959) *Freud: The Mind of the Moralist*, London: Gollancz.

Rifflet-Lemaire, A. (1970) Jacques Lacan, quoted by Laxenaire (1983).

Rifkind, G. (1995) Containing the containers: the staff-consultation group, *Group Analysis* 28, 2: 209–222.

Roberts, J. P. (1982) Foulkes' concept of the matrix, *Group Analysis* 16: 3–19.

Robertson, G. G. (1947) Emotional aspects of skin diseases, *Lancet* 2: 124.

Rosenthal, M. J. (1953) Neuropsychiatric aspects of infantile eczema. Special reference to the role of cutaneous pain receptors, *Archives of Neurological Psychiatry* 70: 428.

Roth, C. (1969) *A Short History of the Jewish People*, London: East and West Library.

Rothe, S. (1989) The Frankfurt School: an influence on Foulkes's group analysis?, *Group Analysis* 22, 4: 405–415.

Rouchy, J. C. (1982) Archaic processes and transference in group analysis, *Group Analysis* 15, 3: 235.

Rouchy, J. C. (1987) Identité culturelle et groupe d'appartenance, *Revue de Psychothérapie Psychanalytique de Groupe* 9: 13–19.

Rouchy, J. C. (1990) Malaise dans l'identification, *Connexions* 55: 45–56.
Rouchy, J. C. (1995) Identification and groups of belonging, *Group Analysis* 28, 2: 129–141.
Russell, P. (1982) *The Awakening Earth*, London: Routledge and Kegan Paul.
Rustin, M. (1991) *The Good Society and the Inner World*, London: Verso.
Rutan, J. S. and Alonso, A. (1982) Group therapy, individual therapy or both, *International Journal of Group Psychotherapy* 32: 267–282.
Sainsbury, P. (1960) Psychosomatic disorders and neurosis in out-patients attending a general hospital, *Journal of Psychosomatic Research* 4: 261.
Sandison, R. (1984) 500 years of group analysis, unpublished paper delivered to Group-Analytic Society, London.
Sandler, J. (1990) On internal object relations, *Journal of the American Psychoanalytic Association* 38: 859–880.
Sandler, J., Dare, C. and Holder, A. (1973) *The Patient and the Analyst*, London: Allen and Unwin.
Schafer, R. (1959) Generative empathy in the treatment situation, *Psychoanalytic Quarterly* 28: 342–373.
Schermer, V. L. and Pines, M. (eds) (1998) *Group Psychotherapy of the Psychoses*, London: Jessica Kingsley Publishers.
Schilder, P. (1935) *The Image and Appearance of the Human Body*, London: Kegan Paul.
Schlapobersky, J. (1994) The language of the group, in D. G. Brown and L. M. Zinkin (eds) *The Psyche and the Social World: Developments in Group Analytic Theory*, London: Routledge.
Schore, A. N. (1994) *Affect Regulation and the Origin of the Self: The Neurobiology of Emotional Development*, Hillsdale, NJ: Lawrence Erlbaum Associates, Inc.
Schore, A. N. (2001) Interviewed by Roz Carroll, *The Psychotherapist* 17: 25–27.
Schur, M. (1955) Comments on the metapsychology of somatization, *Psychoanalytic Study of the Child* 10: 100–164.
Schur, M. (1972) *Freud: Living and Dying*, New York: International Universities Press.
Schwartz, L., Tulipan, L. and Peck, S. M. (1947) *Occupational Diseases of the Skin*, Philadelphia: Lea and Febiger.
Scott, W. C. M (1948) Some embryological, neurological, psychiatric and psycho-analytic implications of the body scheme, *International Journal of Psycho-Analysis*: 141–152.
Segal, H. (1987) Silence is the real crime, *International Review of Psycho-Analysis*, 14: 312.
Seitz, P. F. D., Gosman, J. S. and Craton, J. (1953) Super-ego and aggression in circumscribed neurodermatitis, *Journal of Investigative Dermatology* 20: 263.
Selesnick, S. J. and Sperber, Z. (1965) The problem of the eczema-asthma complex: A developmental approach, in N. S. Greenfield and W. C. Lewis (eds) *Psychoanalysis and Current Biological Thought*, Madison: University of Wisconsin Press.
Shapiro, L. N. (1973) Confrontation with the 'real' analyst, in G. Adler and P. G. Myerson (eds) *Confrontation in Psychotherapy*, New York: Science House.
Sharp, S. A. and Rosenblatt, A. (1994) Oedipal sibling triangles, *Journal of the American Psychoanalytic Association* 42: 491–523.
Sherif, M. (1936) *The Psychology of Social Norms*, New York: Harper.
Sherwood, M. (1964) Bion's experiences in groups: a critical evaluation, *Human Relations* 17: 113–129.

Skynner, A. C. R. (1979) Reflections on the family therapist as family scapegoat, *Journal of Family Therapy* 1: 7–22.

Skynner, A. C. R. (1986) What is effective in group psychotherapy?, *Group Analysis* 19: 5–24.

Skynner, A. C. R. (1987) *Explorations with Families*, London: Methuen.

Skynner, A. C. R. (1989) *Institutes and How to Survive Them: Mental Health Training and Consultation*, London: Methuen.

Skynner, A. C. R. and Brown, D. G. (1981) Referral of patients for psychotherapy, *British Medical Journal* 282: 1952–1955.

Skynner, A. C. R. and Cleese, J. (1983) *Families and How to Survive Them*, London: Methuen.

Spero, M. (1999) Comments on the section group analysis and organizations in group analysis.

Spitz, R. A. (1951) The psychogenic diseases in infancy: An attempt at their etiologic classification, *Psychoanalytic Study of the Child.*

Spotnitz, H. (1979) Narcissistic countertransference, in L. Epstein and A. H. Feiner (eds) *Countertransference*, New York: Jason Aronson.

Stacey, R. D. (2001) *Complex Responsive Processes in Organizations*, London: Routledge.

Stein, A. and Kibel, H. (1975) Relationship of peer and therapist transference in the holistic approach: a group dynamic peer interaction. Unpublished.

Stephen, Fr. (1984) Report of R. Sandison's paper, *Bulletin of GAS* 9: 6–7.

Stern, D. (1985) *The Interpersonal World of the Infant*, New York: Basic Books.

Stokes, J. (1932) The complex of eczema. A diagnostic and etiologic analysis, *Journal of the American Medical Association* 98: 1127.

Tantam, D., Kalucy, R. and Brown, D. (1982) Sleep scratching and dreams in eczema, *Psychotherapy and Psychosomatics* 37: 26–35.

Taylor, G. (1987) *Psychomatic Medicine and Contemporary Psychoanalysis*, Madison, CT: International Universities Press.

Taylor, G. J. (1977) Alexithymia and the counter-transference, *Psychotherapy and Psychosomatics* 28, 1–4: 141–147.

Taylor, G. J. (1984) Alexithymia: Concept, measurement and implications for treatment, *American Journal of Psychiatry* 141: 725–732.

Taylor, G. J. (1987) *Psychosomatic Medicine and Contemporary Psychoanalysis*, Madison: International Universities Press.

Taylor, G. J., Bagby, R. M. and Parker, J. D. A. (1997) *Disorders of Affect Regulation: Alexithymia in Medical and Psychiatric Illness*, Cambridge: Cambridge University Press.

Thygessen, B. (1992) Diversity as a group-specific therapeutic factor in group-analytic psychotherapy, *Group Analysis* 25, 1: 75–86.

Todd, E. (1985) *The Explanation of Ideology: Family Structures and Social Systems*, trans. D Derrioch, Oxford: Blackwell.

Trevarthen, C. (1993) The self born in intersubjectivity, in U. Neisner (ed.) *Ecological and Interpersonal Knowledge of the Self*, New York: Cambridge University Press.

Turquet, P. M. (1974) Leadership: the individual in the group, in J. J. Hartman, R. D. Mann and G. S. Gibbs (eds) *Analysis of Groups*, San Francisco: Jossey-Bass.

Turquet, P. M. (1975) Threats to identity in the large group, in L. Kreeger (ed.) *The Large Group*, London: Constable.

Usandivaras, R. J. (1986) Foulkes' primordial level in clinical practice, *Group Analysis* 19: 113–124.

Van der Kleij, G. (1985) The group and its matrix, *Group Analysis* 18: 102–110.

Vidal, E. (1886) Du lichen (lichen prurigo strophilus). *Ann Dermatol Syphiligr* 17: 13.

Volkan, V. D. (2001) Transgenerational transmission and chosen trauma: an aspect of large-group identity, *Group Analysis* 34: 179–197.

Volkan, V. D., Montville, J. V. and Julius, D. A. (1991) *The Psychodynamics of International Relationships, Vol.2: Unofficial Diplomacy at Work*, Lexington, MA: Lexington Books.

Vygotsky, L. S. (1978) *Mind in Society: The Development of Higher Psychological Processes*, Cambridge, MA: Harvard University Press.

Walsh, M. N. and Kierland, R. R. (1947) Psychotherapy in the treatment of neurodermatitis, *Proceedings of the Staff Meetings of the Mayo Clinic* 22: 578.

Weldon, E. V. (1997) Let the treatment fit the crime: forensic group psychotherapy. 20th S. H. Foulkes Annual Lecture, *Group Analysis* 30, 1: 5–26.

Whitaker, D. S. and Lieberman, M. (1964) *Psychotherapy through the Group Process*, New York: Atherton.

Whiteley, J. S. (1994) Attachment and loss and the space between: personality disorder in the therapeutic community. 18th S. H. Foulkes Annual Lecture, *Group Analysis* 27, 4: 359–382.

Whiteley, J. S. and Gordon, J. (1979) *Group Approaches in Psychiatry*, London: Routledge and Kegan Paul.

Wilke, G. (1998) Oedipal and sibling dynamics in organizations, *Group Analysis* 31, 3: 269–281.

Williams, D. H. (1951) Management of atopic dermatitis in children. Control of the maternal rejection factor, *Arch Dermatol Syph* 63: 545.

Wilson, J. (1997) Matte-Blanco's theory of bi-logic and its relevance to group analysis, *Journal of Melanie Klein and Object Relations* 15, 4: 585–593.

Wilson, J. Q. (1993) *The Moral Sense*, New York: Free Press.

Wilson, W. J. E. (1842) *Diseases of the Skin*, London: Churchill.

Winnicott, D. W. (1949) Hate in the countertransference, *International Journal of Psycho-Analysis* 30: 69–74.

Winnicott, D. W. (1953) Transitional objects and transitional phenomena, In D. W. Winnicott *Collected Papers*, London: Tavistock.

Winnicott, D. W. (1960) Countertransference, *British Journal of Medical Psychology* 33: 17–21.

Winnicott, D. W. (1965a) The development of the capacity for concern, in D. W. Winnicott *The Maturational Processes and the Facilitating Environment*, London: Hogarth Press.

Winnicott, D. W. (1965b) *The Maturational Processes and the Facilitating Environment*. London: Hogarth Press.

Winnicott, D. W. (1971a) The location of cultural experience, in D. W. Winnicott *Playing and Reality*, London: Tavistock Publications.

Winnicott, D. W. (1971b) *Playing and Reality*, London: Tavistock Publications.

Winnicott, D. W. (1975) *Through Paediatrics to Psycho-Analysis*, London: Hogarth Press.

Wittkower, E. D. and Edgell, P. G. (1951) Eczema: A psychosomatic study, *Arch Dermatol Syph* 63: 207.

Wittkower, E. D. and MacKenna, R. M. B. (1947) Psychological aspects of seborrhoeic dermatitis, *British Journal of Dermatology* 59: 281.

Wolff, H. H. (1977) Contribution of the interview situation to the restriction of fantasy life and emotional experience in psychosomatic patients, *Psychotherapy and Psychosomatics* 28: 58–67.

Woodhead, B. (1955) The eczema–asthma syndrome: Psychiatric considerations. British Journal of Dermatology 67, 2: 50–52.

Wooster, G. (1983) Resistance in groups as developmental difficulty in triangulation, *Group Analysis* 16, 1: 30–40.

Yalom, I. (1985) *The Theory and Practice of Group Psychotherapy*, New York: Basic Books.

Yassky, A. D. (1973) On using the group therapist's body ego, *Group Analysis* 6: 32–35.

Zinkin, L. M. (1983) Malignant mirroring, *Group Analysis* 16, 2: 113–126.

Zinkin, L. M. (1994) Exchange as a therapeutic factor in group analysis, in D. G. Brown and L. M. Zinkin (eds) *The Psyche and the Social World: Developments in Group Analytic Theory*, London: Routledge.

INDEX

Printed in Great Britain
by Amazon

81331512R00160